RE-PRESENTING THE PAST

Aldham Robarts LRC
Liverpool John Moores University

WITHDRAWN

LIVERPOOL JMU LIBRARY

3 1111 00999 6891

Pearson
Education

We work with leading authors to develop the
strongest educational materials in history,
bringing cutting-edge thinking and best
learning practice to a global market.

Under a range of well-known imprints, including
Longman, we craft high quality print and electronic
publications which help readers to understand and
apply their content, whether studying or at work.

To find out more about the complete range of our
publishing, please visit us on the World Wide Web at:
www.pearsoneduc.com

RE-PRESENTING THE PAST

Women and History

Edited by
ANN-MARIE GALLAGHER,
CATHY LUBELSKA
and
LOUISE RYAN

An imprint of **Pearson Education**

Harlow, England · London · New York · Reading, Massachusetts · San Francisco
Toronto · Don Mills, Ontario · Sydney · Tokyo · Singapore · Hong Kong · Seoul
Taipei · Cape Town · Madrid · Mexico City · Amsterdam · Munich · Paris · Milan

Pearson Education Limited
Head Office:
Edinburgh Gate
Harlow
Essex CM20 2JE
England
Tel: +44 (0)1279 623623
Fax: +44 (0)1279 431059

London Office:
128 Long Acre
London WC2E 9AN
Tel: +44 (0)20 7447 2000
Fax: +44 (0)20 7240 5771
Website: www.history-minds.com

First published in Great Britain in 2001

© Pearson Education Limited 2001

ISBN 0 582 38219 X

British Library Cataloguing-in-Publication Data
A catalogue record for this book is available from the British Library

Library of Congress Cataloging-in-Publication Data
A catalog record for this book is available from the Library of Congress

All rights reserved; no part of this publication may be reproduced, stored
in a retrieval system, or transmitted in any form or by any means, electronic,
mechanical, photocopying, recording, or otherwise without either the prior
written permission of the Publishers or a licence permitting restricted copying
in the United Kingdom issued by the Copyright Licensing Agency Ltd,
90 Tottenham Court Road, London W1P 0LP. This book may not be lent,
resold, hired out or otherwise disposed of by way of trade in any form of
binding or cover other than that in which it is published without the prior
consent of the Publishers.

10 9 8 7 6 5 4 3 2 1
05 04 03 02 01

Typeset by 35 in 11/13pt Baskerville MT
Produced by Pearson Education Asia Pte Ltd
Printed in Malaysia, KVP

CONTENTS

LIST OF CONTRIBUTORS

Shani D'Cruze is Reader in Women's History at Manchester Metropolitan University. Her research in women's and gender history have included work on the nineteenth- and twentieth-century family, on sexual and physical violence against women, on performance, gender and leisure in the twentieth century. As well as articles, publications include *Crimes of Outrage, Sex, Violence and Victorian Working Women* (1998). She is currently co-editor of *Gender and History* journal and presently developing research on gender, crime and culture in the twentieth century.

Ann-Marie Gallagher is a Senior Lecturer in Combined Honours at the University of Central Lancashire. Her background is as Course Leader of Women's Studies, and she has a number of academic publications in the field of women, history and spirituality. As well as making contributions to academic books and journals, Ann-Marie has participated in numerous regional and national radio programmes over the last ten years. She is an active member of the Self-Education Collective and contributes to many distance-learning programmes. She also writes popular books on paganism and women's spirituality.

June Hannam is a Reader in History at the University of the West of England, Bristol. Her recent publications include contributions to *A Suffrage Reader*, eds C. Eustance *et al.* (Leicester, 2000) and *Votes for Women*, eds J. Purvis and S. Holton (2000). She has just completed a book with Karen Hunt, *Socialist Women: Britain 1880–1920s* (2001). Her current research interests are gender and labour politics after 1918 and elite women in Bristol in the nineteenth century.

Melanie Ilič is Senior Lecturer in History and Women's Studies and Women's Studies Field Chair at Cheltenham and Gloucester College of Higher Education, and Research Fellow at the Centre for Russian and East European Studies, University of Birmingham. She is author of *Women Workers in the Soviet Interwar Economy: From 'Protection' to 'Equality'* (1999). She researches in the areas of Russian women's studies and Soviet economic and social history.

Claire Langhamer is a Lecturer in History at the University of Sussex. She has recently published *Women's Leisure in England, 1920–1960* (Manchester, 2000) and is currently finishing a study of women and pubs in Second World War Britain. Her next major project will be a social and cultural history of courtship in twentieth-century Britain.

Cathy Lubelska was formerly Principal Lecturer in Social History and Women's Studies at the University of Central Lancashire. She now combines working as a director for an NHS Trust with teaching yoga and involvement in a range of freelance and voluntary projects – including work on women's health issues, past and present.

Clare Midgley is Senior Lecturer in History and Head of the Centre for Gender Studies at London Guildhall University. She is the author of *Women Against Slavery* (1992) and editor of *Gender and Imperialism* (1998) and is currently working on a new book on British feminism and empire. Clare is also active in the Women's History Network and is co-editor of the journal *Gender and History*.

Parita Mukta is a Lecturer in Sociology at the University of Warwick. Her focus is on the relationship between politics, culture and emotional structures. She has published widely on the shifts and historical transitions in women's cultural expressions, as well as on religious authoritarianism. She is studying issues of memory and narrative and her forthcoming book documents family history and specific family narratives. Parita is concerned with making historical writings and political understandings accessible to a wider readership.

Alison Oram is Reader in Women's Studies at University College Northampton where she teaches history and women's studies. Recent publications include: *Women Teachers and Feminist Politics 1900–39* (Manchester, 1996); *The Lesbian History Source Book: Love and Sex between Women from 1780 to 1970* (2001) (with Annmarie Turnbull); and chapters in *Sexology in Culture*, eds L. Bland and L. Doan (Oxford, 1998); *Votes for Women*, eds J. Purvis and S. Holton (2000). She is currently researching representations of cross-dressing women in the British popular press from 1914 to the 1950s.

Louise Ryan is Senior Lecturer in Sociology at the University of Central Lancashire. Her research on the Irish suffrage movement and Irish Republican women is published in such journals as *Gender and History*, *Feminist Review* and *Women's History Review*. Her books include *Irish Feminism and the Vote* (Dublin, 1996) and *Gender, Identity and the Irish Press, 1922–1937: Embodying the Nation* (2001). She is currently engaged in a two-year research project on Irish women's emigration to Britain in the 1930s.

Wendy Webster is Senior Lecturer in history in the Department of Historical and Critical Studies, University of Central Lancashire. Her publications include *Not a Man to Match Her: The Marketing of a Prime Minister* (1990) and *Imagining Home: Gender, 'Race' and National Identity 1945–64* (1998). She has written widely on gender and imperialism and on post-war migration to Britain, and is currently working on the impact of loss of imperial power on narratives of Britishness and Englishness. She is a Reviews Editor for *Women's History Review*, and has contributed numerous articles to *The Guardian*.

INTRODUCTION

ANN-MARIE GALLAGHER, CATHY LUBELSKA
AND LOUISE RYAN

'the writing of history is not ideologically innocent . . .'[1]

This book is about the ways in which women have been represented, mis-represented and made invisible in accounts of the past, and, as its title suggests, it looks at ways in which feminist historians are currently endeavouring to ensure that women are present and properly accounted for in future historical studies. All of the authors who feature in this volume are concerned to redress a grievous imbalance in the way that history has dealt with – or failed to deal with – women. We have all proceeded under the knowledge that until relatively recently, history as subject area, discipline and practice has been not only gender-skewed, but also largely oblivious to the extent to which its framework has been racialised and sexualised, for example; accordingly, all contributions here are characterised by the desire to avoid replicating the very oppressions our studies seek to uncover. To an extent, any history book that refocuses the practices of its discipline is, by definition, a critique of what has gone before. Yet this book offers more than a critique: this is the first phase in a process where feminist analyses of issues arising from the problems of women's representation in history both suggest and exemplify alternative, more inclusive approaches.

The central issues raised in this volume fall into four main categories. First, there is the issue of the invisibility of women in the main narratives of history. Second, where women are represented, their construction is flavoured by the particular context of the period in which the study itself is being produced, often without acknowledgement of the perspectival nature of that account. Third, there is controversy about what is, and what is not, deemed suitable as evidence, and the fact that what has often been considered unsuitable or regarded with suspicion (i.e. oral testimony and personal accounts) usually provides the best clue to the realities of past women's lived experiences. Fourth, there is the issue of which methodologies are appropriate to the creation and practice of new approaches to women's pasts. The authors in this volume engage with these issues by employing and exemplifying the innovations of feminist historical praxis. In short, this book provides not only a critique of history as it has been done, but also

1

actively puts to use new methodologies, sources and readings of the past in order to do so.

Our starting point for this book is the assumption that all of history – that is to say, various societies' versions of the past – is perspectival, and that no one escapes from this basic premise with claims of impartiality intact – including feminist historians. Feminist historians need to take on not only the task of salvaging, critiquing and rewriting stories of past women's lives and experiences, but also the responsibility to avoid carving our present-centredness into the frames of our accounts of our own, and other women's, histories. This may seem at first sight a somewhat daunting task. But the necessity for such care is writ large in the inadequacies of much of mainstream history.

Some of the earliest endeavours to write so-called histories of women, and especially of the women's movement, sought to assert the historical validity of women's lives within the parameters of existing male-dominated histories, without disrupting or questioning these. Thus, the only women who 'counted' were those whose lives, roles and actions were accorded historical significance by standards made by and appropriate to men. Predictably, the emphasis within such histories tended to be upon the public, the political and those with the power to influence the tide of what were judged to be important historical events. This often meant focusing upon the singular importance of individual women and their 'heroic' deeds. Some of the early suffrage histories were self-consciously cast within this mould in order to stress women's claims to equality on the same terms as men. This meant that within the school curriculum children only encountered women such as queens, the occasional militant suffragette (invariably a Pankhurst!) and Florence Nightingale. These characters are included not as representatives of women in history, but precisely because they were exceptional and different from the bulk of their sisters, thus reinforcing the notion that most women's roles in the past were inconsequential. In addition, as Melanie Ilic points out in her chapter in this volume, sometimes the interest in 'exceptional' women has been skewed towards prurience rather than scholarship.

It is partly because of the continued invisibility of women within mainstream historical accounts, and the ability of mainstream historians to nod in the direction of feminist critiques whilst failing to integrate the story of women, that the approaches within this volume have evolved. If traditional histories made women invisible, it was because, by pursuing what was deemed most significant and important about past, and therefore present, societies, the wrong questions were asked. Those asked within the androcentric framework that has characterised mainstream history have referred to the subject constantly within the purview of the traditionalist historian, namely males in the pursuit of masculinist roles. The questions being asked, in short, do not expect to find women in the answer, and feminists have therefore had to ask what Mary Daly has referred to as 'non-questions'. These are the questions that conventional history either has not thought to ask, or rejects as too 'subjective'. Asking such 'non-questions' entails approaches which aim to catch at some of the missing persons in various societies' versions of the past. Those missing persons are women.

An important aspect of the tenacity of those approaches which centre upon adding apparently key women to men's history has been the misrepresenting, or lack of representation, of the histories of the overwhelming majority of women. This happens in a number of ways. First, it places women within androcentric assumptions about the nature of history and, in particular, its preoccupation with 'great' (powerful) and 'good' men, which accordingly remain undisrupted. Second, even those approaches, for example within social and labour history, which have sought to challenge history's traditional focus upon the powerful and to give voice to the underprivileged have been inclined to do so with a tenaciously 'gender-blind' eye.[2] Here the working class has commonly been conceptualised within a loosely Marxist framework as male wage-earners and unemployed men, where women are considered as working class because 'their' men are. This means that such histories have been able both to acknowledge the issue of one type of power differential, in this case based upon class, while overlooking the sexualised power differential which placed men as the 'head' of households and as the prime movers in the public sphere. Thus, the male experience is seen as normative and the power dynamics of gender remain unquestioned. Such histories follow a model which sees the male worker as an actor whose domain was the world of work and whose family revolved around him, his earning power and his place in the labour market. Male workers' dependence upon the invisible workload of their wives and daughters is ignored within such a framework, and so concentration on working-class men neatly evades any necessity to look at working women's lives and their contribution to the home, family and wider society. This is but one example of a much larger difficulty with the way in which women are represented/misrepresented in many historical accounts. Rather than being represented 'in their own right' as women, they are defined in terms of their relationships to men – putting in an appearance as wives, mothers, daughters. This can be seen as a function of the unequal power relations between women and men. Third, this 'lack of an authoritative historical self', as E. Fox-Genovese puts it, incorporates the denial of women's actual historical agency, which is evinced in both conventional historical sources and historians' interpretations of these.[3] This is perhaps most obvious in the representation of women as passive, as victims, as the 'done to' rather than the

'doers'. Women are manifest, in some senses, only as a 'dependent' variable
– by implication, powerless and historically insignificant.

Assumptions about women's lack of historical agency, then, result
from and are in turn reinforced by the 'hiddenness' of women, who are
represented largely in terms of their relations with and dependence upon
men. Consequently, women are apt to be historically located separately
from the consequential worlds of men, politics and power, within the
apparently inconsequential realm of the private and domestic. The myth
of women's historical role as essentially domestic has been manifest in
writing and research which conflate the histories of women, children and
the family, veiling the distinctive and diverse histories of women *per se*.
At the extreme, an enduringly exclusive focus upon the reproductive
sphere can give rise to the essentialist assumption (too often implicit in
much historical writing) that as the timeless continuity of women's role is
biologically determined by their sex, women have no independent or
autonomous history of their own and can be, effectively, represented *out* of
history.

One of the most exciting projects of women's history concerns changes
in women's roles and conditions in society. Recovering (or re-covering)
women's history and the processes that have defined us function to overturn
both assumptions of women's biological destinies and the atrophying effects
of the apolitical belief that 'nothing will ever change'. The unavoidable
implication of change having taken place in the past is that, if things have
not always been the same, they can be changed. It is not enough, however,
for feminist historians simply to 'change the subject' if women's histories are
to be centred upon recovering the realities of women's past, lived experiences. Even though the very act of replacing men as normative historical
subjects flips traditional historical theory and methodology away from the
centre, new approaches are required to enable feminists to interpret the
past in a way which means that women are not only visibilised but that
their roles as actors and agents are more fully understood. The project of
refocusing the lens of history, then, is from the very outset one which seeks
not only to change history's existing emphasis on men as the actors and
agents of history in order to stress the role of women in past societies, but to
'do' history differently. It follows, of course, that this understanding should
seek to avoid defining women and their experiences via the categories of
oppression which informed women's lives then and now. This requires
recognition that all representations, including our own, will arise from within
a culture and a language which are marked, informed by and built upon
these oppressions. Avoiding their replication, for feminist historians, is
achieved not by positing some falsifying notion of 'objectivity' in the old
positivist sense, but by acknowledging and *including* our subjectivities to

produce a different sort of 'objectivity', the type for which 'feminist' would most accurately and happily supply a prefix.[4]

Reviewing the subjectivities of the busily constructing historian and the impact of feminist perspectives on our research directly raises a challenge to the very nature of 'history' as a discipline, a subject and a practice. This book raises important questions about the meaning, processes and methodologies of history. In focusing on the tasks facing feminist historians, we explore the new epistemologies (theories of knowledge) that have emerged, and continue to emerge, through feminist approaches to history. The word 'history' in this volume refers to the representation of the past, rather than its more commonplace meaning, which is simply to designate 'the past' as an uncontested given. Indeed, we are only too aware that there is no such thing as an unmediated, unconstructed, non-perspectival account of 'the past'. The contributors to this book all seek to challenge, analyse and critically reassess accounts of the past, and in so doing come up with some new, or competing, accounts. By focusing on history as 'versions of the past', we 'foreground the role of the narrator of past events and consequently the nature of narrative as a mode of knowing that selects, organises, orders, interprets and allegorises'.[5]

Given the problems of history in relation to women's invisibility, their misrepresentation and the wealth of sources that are treated with suspicion or simply overlooked, the task of feminist historians is manifold. First, and as already indicated above, feminist historians have to tackle the invisibility of women, and account for this curious gap in historical narratives. Second, they must look to the particular ways in which women have been represented both by historians and within historical sources themselves. In relation to this aspect of 'doing history' it is the role of feminist historians to retrace and uncover the processes through which women have been represented in narrow, particular and marginalised ways. Thirdly, it is the job of feminist historians to explore new approaches to doing history in ways which not only challenge women's invisibility but also avoid reproducing other forms of social inequality. These new approaches include the use of interdisciplinary methodologies and the use of different types of sources.

In relation to the first of these tasks, an understanding of the ways in which women have been represented or invisibilised necessitates an engagement with the power relations embedded within and informing historical accounts and records of the past. The ways in which such accounts and records have been interpreted and described by historians over time need to be explored. However, women are not only defined through inequalities of gender. The overlapping social inequalities of gender, class, ethnicity and sexuality, for example in the contexts of colonialism and nationalism, have also shaped representations of women in history.

In relation to the second of these tasks, that of acknowledging and acting upon the processes of representation, there is a clear need to tread carefully. As feminist historians our attempts to refocus attention on the exclusion and silencing of women should not lead us to prioritise some women at the expense of others in a way which reinforces social and representational inequalities. As Himani Bannerji warns: 'Without any negative intention on the historian/writer's part, her ideological knowledge frameworks, her chosen forms of re-presentation, may or may not permit certain presences or visibilities. Thus projects of recovery, of rendering visible, may continue, produce and reinforce conceptual practices of power.'[6] According to Bannerji, then, the writing of history is not an innocent or a transparent affair; at all times it includes an ideological–political dimension. The corollary of this is that researching and writing history are in themselves political acts, and there is a pressing responsibility on those feminists who consciously and actively 'make' history not to replicate the very social inequalities they set out to expose.

With reference to the third task, that of developing new approaches to doing history, the contributors to this book engage with a broad range of methodologies and pay particular attention to scrutinising the sources which are the material of our craft. In this book we not only reassess existing sources but also suggest how new sources may be used in historical re-search. This is underpinned by a critical engagement with methodology both as a tool of enquiry and in its relationship to epistemology. The types of knowledge and understanding that we now seek not only require new and innovative approaches to research methods but also demand a recon-sideration of the purpose and power of the knowledge generated.

If history is written by the winners, then part of our aim in this book is to reassess the history that has been defined by that conceptualisation and to suggest alternative readings and interpretations of historical characters and events, and new ways of doing history and representing women within it. If relations of power and inequality determine whose voice and opinions are recorded, then they also determine who has the power to speak on behalf of others, who has access to resources which aid the making of history, who is marginalised and who silenced. This book problematises the process of research and writing history and claims to 'objectivity'. We are wary, however, of creating an absolute relativism in which the hermeneutics of reflexivity become an end in and of themselves. This is counter-productive to any feminist project that seeks to understand women's past lives, experi-ences and struggles. On the contrary, mindful of the stultifying effects that this may have, we are keen to avoid arch-relativist approaches which fail to take account of the material and experiential bases of women's lived realities. As the contributors in this book aptly demonstrate, a working awareness of the perspectival and selective nature of history-making functions to acknowledge those lived realities, not to theorise them out of existence.

Once the feminist historian has situated inequalities of power as central determinants, rather than variables, in history making, there are also the difficulties and limitations inherent in all historical sources to negotiate. First, there is the issue of the survival or non-survival of sources, the former of which are often partial or fragmented. Second, the sources that do survive are based on another's interpretation of what actually happened and what was worthy of being recorded in the first place. Third, there is the historian's interpretation of the sources, an act that we have already established as political and therefore partial. The way in which some contributors to this volume have responded to the problematics of sources and interpretations has been to reassess familiar sources in the light of what we now acknowledge to be the partiality of some sources, or even to go to less familiar types of sources, developing new and innovative approaches in the process. A distinctive feature of doing history differently is the synthesis of a variety of methodologies otherwise known as 'interdisciplinarity'.

In challenging dominant and long-established historical perspectives it is necessary to push at the boundaries of what has traditionally been seen as 'history'. In attempting to include the diversities and complexities of women's lives it is necessary to consider a wide range of different sources and approaches and areas of study to ensure the greatest degree of inclusiveness. The challenge for feminist historians is to develop processes and types of representation which correspond to those of 'lives and events at the level of the everyday world'.[7] This leads to an interdisciplinarity which may well go far beyond the boundaries of what has traditionally been recognised as what Susan Stanford Friedman calls 'making' history. As Himani Bannerji has written: 'Memories, experiences, daily practices, and oral histories now jostle with conventions of disciplines, allowing for recreations never seen before. Disciplinarian purity has finally and happily yielded to hybridities such as "historical sociology".'[8]

The use of different methodologies of itself challenges traditional historical methodology to straining point, such that many history departments in universities today are still resistant to the challenges set up by initiatives such as Women's History, Black History and Gay and Lesbian History. With regard to women's history, the injection of woman-centred categories such as female sexuality, women's work, and women's art and creativity has thrown an entirely new light upon both the historical experiences of women and the failure of traditional, androcentric histories to provide an accurate picture of past human experience. But it is when feminist historians acknowledge the variety of ways in which key social determinants such as constructs of 'race' and ethnicity, class and sexuality as well as gender have impacted upon women's lived realities that we not only open up the possibility of a fuller picture, but interrogate, either directly or by natural extension, previous historical methodologies.

Interdisciplinarity, as one of the mainstays of the feminist historian's tool kit, is an approach (or, indeed, a set of approaches at any given time) which has distinguished Women's Studies from being simply 'another discipline' within the academy.[9] Reinterpreting the experiences of women in the past should take place in terms of that experience; that is to say that feminist historians accept that it is not possible to interpret lived realities with the tools or approaches offered by any one discipline alone. In order to offer an any-way accurate interpretation of that experience, we have to use something which equates most nearly to the analogical nature of the realities we seek to interpret. More than one commentator has noted the cyclical, non-linear nature of women's lives, and the multiple layers of women's experience which are shaped by the demands made upon them in patriarchal society. We know, for example, in direct contrast to the representation of women made in traditional social/labour histories, that women's lives were far more complex and were influenced by, for example, female kinship and community networks, by work both within and outside the home, and by the various means by which they maintained families. Any interpretation of women's lives must recognise the multi-dimensional nature of their lived realities. This requires not only 're-setting' the focus of historical studies to include women, but also carrying this focus through to its natural conclusion by using new, alternative methodologies with which to approach evidence of past women's experiences.

The most obvious place in which interdisciplinary approaches are applied is the (re)interpretation of sources. Approaching sources, especially written texts, entails very careful work indeed, particularly where the interpreter is an historian anxious not to make the mistakes of her predecessors in the field by applying gendered, raced, classed or heterosexist criteria around the framework of her interpretation. A prerequisite of the task of interpreting sources in this way is the act of 'seeing', which necessitates taking a consciously critical stance that invites the potential 'seer' to use the double-consciousness so often ascribed to feminists working within the academy (as insiders/outsiders) to read between the lines.[10] Only this can enable the feminist historical researcher to avoid presenting her own interpretation as another failed, flawed version of the women's experiences being described and often defined with the text under review. In order to be able to 'see', the researcher has not only to be appraised of the traps of language and of the particular lens through which the lives of the women in question are being refracted, but she has to be able to engage with a number of appropriate disciplinary approaches which she may need to synthesise – the better to understand the complex realities of the evidence with which she is presented.

The authors in this volume, accordingly, engage not only with feminist praxis but also with a range of methodologies and theories borrowed from disciplines outside of history. For example, Shani D'Cruze's use of cultural and linguistic theories enables her not only to critique the immediately available representation of women in newspaper and court records, but also to join these together, examine the 'silences' and reinterpret them from a feminist perspective – one in which issues of gender, class and sexuality are taken into account to provide access to the voices hidden in the text. Parita Mukta employs her skills as an historian while building a picture of the complex political context of the production of widow's voices in their auto-biographical writings and laments. At the same time, she looks to post-colonial feminist theory in order to uncover the layers of meaning embedded within the sources under review.

By keeping women out of the picture, mainstream histories have in fact misrepresented human history. Women's history is human history writ large, just as the Amnesty International slogan that 'women's rights are human rights' has it. It follows, then, that the approaches generated by feminist methodologies and employed therefore by feminist historians are not only suitable for the interpretation of women's lives but also those of men. But this volume is concerned to address the representation of women in history, and the ways in which women have been misrepresented or missed out altogether. Therefore, it is left to others to pick up the burden of what else the approaches of feminist history imply: a rewriting of the diverse histories of *men*.

In Part One, 'Competing representations', the authors focus on the processes of representation in order to explore the diverse and contradict-ory ways in which women have been presented/re-presented in a range of discourses. We analyse the ways in which people, events and particular social moments have been constructed in different, conflicting and compet-ing ways. Such competing representations may come about in various ways. For example, in a particular time period or context a group of women may be represented very differently in a range of sources. In such a situation, the competing representations may be informed by the conflicting beliefs, loyalties, ideologies and agendas of those writing the sources. In the case of newspapers, for instance, representations of particular women may be framed by the views of editors, journalists, newspaper owners, etc. These may contrast markedly with those found in other contemporary sources, e.g. oral testimonies, diaries, letters, autobiographies. Alternatively, representa-tions may shift over time as trends, attitudes and social expectations change:

this often necessitates gauging the extent to which representations themselves inform the nature of those changes. By analysing a range of conflicting sources either in one or several time periods, one may begin to see the processes through which individuals or groups of women have been defined, framed and constructed. Such analyses in turn reveal the implicit power dynamics that underpin the processes of constructing stories of the past, and suggest alternative readings.

In Chapter 1, 'Splendidly silent: representing Irish Republican women, 1919–23', Louise Ryan argues that women's active role in Republican militarism has been excluded from most histories of the Irish independence movement. Locating her study in the wider context of feminist analyses of militant nationalist movements in a range of post-colonial regions, Louise draws upon a growing body of interdisciplinary research. Like Alison Oram (Chapter 2) and Shani D'Cruze (Chapter 3) in this section, Louise Ryan rereads and reassesses existing sources to analyse complex and contradictory images of these controversial women. Thus, despite their apparent invisibility, autobiographies reveal a range and diversity of representations of Irish Republican women. Mainstream Irish daily newspapers tended to represent the women in particularly negative ways, as dangerous, deranged furies. This indicates not only an opposition to militant Republicanism but also to women playing non-traditional roles. Ironically, the autobiographies of Republican men reveal similar feelings of unease about women's transgression of traditional gender roles. However, these sources also reveal the complexities of men's reliance on the women and their simultaneous resentment of any perceived challenge to male authority. In the women's own autobiographical accounts of the war years one can see a more rounded series of representations of women's roles within Republicanism, but also the tensions around militarism, gender roles and soldiering. These competing representations in newspapers and men's and women's autobiographies demonstrate not only the context of women's involvement in militant Republicanism but also the conflicts and tensions which may well have led to their subsequent excision from mainstream histories of the period.

Alison Oram's chapter, 'Telling stories about the Ladies of Llangollen: the construction of lesbian and feminist histories' (Chapter 2), draws upon some of the many accounts of Ponsonby and Butler – the ladies of Llangollen – to demonstrate the change in representations of lesbians over the last two centuries. Locating her research in the context of lesbian history writing, Alison suggests that the Ladies have been constructed as the archetype of romantic love between women. In examining competing representations she begins with a discussion of contemporary accounts of the Ladies in the secret diaries of Anne Lister. Such happy domestic images are countered by the extremely negative representations in an evening newspaper of the

time. Over 100 years later, in the 1930s, the Ladies continued to be represented in a variety of ways, for example in the biography written by Mary
Gordan. In the 1970s and 1980s representations of the Ladies were
inscribed within increasingly politicised lesbian scholarship. In attempting
to challenge lesbian invisibility in history, Lillian Faderman was one of
several scholars who debated whether or not romantic friendships, such as
that of Ponsonby and Butler, should be seen as sexual or asexual. Alison
Oram argues that these competing representations located in different historical contexts reveal a great deal about changing notions of lesbianism.
These conflicting accounts probably tell us more about the shifting politics
of lesbian history writing than they do about the Ladies themselves. Lesbian
historians are not only challenging the heterosexual bias of history writing
but are opening up new ways of conceptualising the history of sexuality.

In Chapter 3, '"A little, decent-looking woman": violence against
nineteenth-century working women and the social history of crime', Shani
D'Cruze explores competing representations of women in court reports,
court minutes and newspapers. Locating her research in the context of
feminist scholarship on violence against women, Shani analyses the ways in
which late Victorian magistrates' courts represented crimes of violence in
particular ways. For example, she points out that offences were often reclas-
sified so that sexual violence was rendered invisible. Court registers are a
fascinating, if somewhat limited, research source. Registers actively engaged
in representing the defendant and complainant; naming and defining but
also classifying individuals into neat, ready-made categories. These were
usually mediated by class bias and patriarchal assumptions. In theory, court
minutes were supposed to be an accurate, word-for-word account of court
proceedings and thus appear to give voice to women's oral testimonies, i.e.
women's self-representation. However, Shani D'Cruze illustrates that the
minutes, by only recording the witnesses' answers, not the court's questions,
offer a partial and incomplete account of what went on in the courtroom.
The witnesses' responses were clearly framed and limited by the unre-
corded questions. Nevertheless, it is apparent that female witnesses and
complainants attempted to define themselves in particular ways, usually in
terms of gendered working-class respectability. Newspapers offer a third
form of representation of women's court appearances. Court proceedings
were frequently reported at great length, serving as cheap, sensational copy,
especially for local newspapers. While often reporting witness testimony
word for word like the court minutes, the journalist usually added details
about the witness's appearance, age and demeanour. As Shani suggests,
such details added a gloss to the reports which served to frame the complainants and defendants. Such representations were frequently shaped by
perceptions of the respectability or morality of the individuals. She concludes

that the historical sources discussed here illustrate the varied ways in which gender and class impacted on legal and journalistic representations of working women in cases of violence, including sexual violence. Thus Shani D'Cruze not only indicates the matrix of power relations which framed the lives and experiences of poor women in late Victorian Britain, but also suggests how an understanding of these power relations can help us analyse the processes through which these experiences have been represented in historical sources.

Part Two, 'The process of representation: visibility and invisibility', engages with a variety of aspects of women as symbol or cipher; either of nationhood or imperialism or as the repositories of honour in relation to the nation or community they come to be seen to represent. All the authors in this section demonstrate the complexity of the ways in which women, real or imaginary, receive the imprint of patriarchal judgement as a result of the gender-specified roles women are expected to inhabit. These 'roles', allotted to women in national, imperial or community life, see them as epitomising the objectives of those contexts and consequently make them the centre of contests between men. In addition, the promotion of women as 'emblematic' further serves to obscure them as active constructive agents themselves. The use of female iconography and of women as the repositories of honour and, at times, of 'progress' inevitably collapses all women into empty, malleable ciphers and denies them their status as living, acting human beings. This process effectively invisibilises women in the interests of the ideological projects which their images are conscripted to serve. But, as these studies show, the social dimension of national, sometimes imperial, enterprises can be revealed through the deconstruction of such representations.

Another feature that the contributions in this section have in common is reference to the relationship between colonial and imperial discourses and the way in which these inflected upon constructs of women as metaphors of various patriarchal and, occasionally, early feminist projects. In keeping with this volume's concentration on creating new feminist histories of women, the work in this section is characterised by the use of non-traditional sources, such as obituaries, widows' laments and colonial and colonised women's autobiographies. With reference to these 'new' sources, it is emphasised again and again that they are utilised for a multiplicity of purposes, by imperialist, nationalist and patriarchal projects, and also by some groups of women who promote their own emancipation at the expense of others.

Clare Midgley in her chapter 'Feminist historians and challenges to imperial history' (Chapter 4) looks at the ways in which feminist historians have become more aware of the misrepresentations of women inherent in gender-conscious analyses of imperialist history that nonetheless do not also take account of class, 'race' and sexuality. She looks at the challenges to traditional histories that have been produced out of feminist historical writing, and explores how feminist scholars have responded to previous exclusions practised within 'old school' imperialist history. Bringing women to the centre of histories of imperialism, she argues, is not enough: examining the privilege of race and class in relation to the real lives of white women colonisers provides a more inclusive and realistic account of colonising women's involvement in the imperial project. She points out that as research in this area has progressed, the die-hard stereotypes of white women colonisers as leisured and idle have been demolished, revealing the multifaceted and complex stories of women travellers, missionaries and other settlers. She points out the increased concern among historians with the way in which empire shaped British culture itself and suggests that gendered accounts of this aspect of imperial history have led to important and revealing insights into the formations of white English gender identities, race, sexuality, etc. and the impact on women's everyday lives in Britain. In terms of revealing and acknowledging issues of 'difference' among women, however, there is still a tendency for histories of migrants to Britain to marginalise women, and 'for histories of women to ignore the multicultural dimensions of British women's past'. Clare Midgley suggests that getting access to women's own understandings of their situations, though difficult, for example, because colonial archives often reveal more of the attitudes of colonial officials than of the lives of the women discussed within them, is not impossible. She examines the ways in which women of colour function within early feminist tracts, which traded on the position of women in non-Western societies in order to represent female subordination in the West as comparable with the 'backward' state of 'savage' societies which had been colonised by Britain. She explores how middle-class British women involved themselves in campaigns against slavery and *sati* 30 years before the commencement of petitioning for British women's own rights and asks whether and in what ways the politicisation of these women could be considered 'feminist', given the tendency of these campaigns to play up black women's 'passivity'. The emphasis here is on the ways in which representations of colonised women were manipulated by British women campaigners against slavery and to vindicate their own rights within Britain.

Parita Mukta's study, 'The stigmata of "widowhood" and Indian feminism: expanding the boundaries of international feminism' (Chapter 5), provides new insights into the lived realities behind the various representations and contestations surrounding the figure of the upper-caste widow in India. As the author points out, 'changing the past entails changing paradigms, perspectives, and the very lens of inquiry, so that the previous epochs are scrutinised with newer questions in mind, at the same time ensuring that these do not become distorted through presentist assumptions'. In this respect, the chapter engages with feminist historiography and the ways in which the feminist reclamation of the voices of women in the past have been necessary to evaluate the links between constructions of women in relation to community and nation. Parita Mukta examines the complexities of the construction and utilisation of the figure of the widow during various periods and by various groups. She points out that the reconfiguring of gender relations in the colonial period was a process which cannot be separated from the emergence of upper-caste, middle-class elites, and that feminist scholarship has been forced to refocus away from what she calls 'singular focus upon the nature of the colonial state' towards examining changes which took place in the constitution of a 'Hindu' community in the nineteenth century. The author looks at widows' writings via the example of different feminist approaches to one particular case study, that of the life and work of the activist reformer Pandita Ramabai, to offer suggestions as to how constructing the future might take its lessons from feminist historians' constructions of the past, as well as of the present.

Wendy Webster's contribution, 'Representing nation: women, obituaries and national biography' (Chapter 6), explores the ways in which death notices in *The Times* newspaper of the 1950s can be seen as part of a story of a national and imperial past, concentrating specifically upon the way that women received notices. This study appraises the function of the genre of obituary-writing in this most eminent of establishment newspapers, emphasising it as masculinised in both content and form. The author looks at how obituary notices of women often became another way of speaking about the men in their lives, thus invisibilising the very subject the notice was ostensibly there to commemorate. She notes that where notices did expand upon a woman's life, it was often to celebrate the passive role she had played in the more 'important', centralised public life of her husband or sons. Most intriguing of all, she suggests, are the tensions between public and private spheres which are negotiated through tributes to the public lives of women. In the case of feminist activists, *The Times* notices consign feminist campaigning to the past, and equality as something long-established. Here, the appropriation of the idea of equality, in a newspaper not known for its support of feminist causes, is seen as a device which defuses the politically challenging aspect of a woman's life, particularly in relation to gender conflicts. Because of the framework of the obituary genre, the 'public woman' engaged in bettering the lot of women becomes part of a story of progress; one where, in Wendy Webster's words, 'feminism is no longer necessary'. In addition to the highly gendered account of the nation-building done by men, and women's supportive though passive role in this, is the playing down of female leadership by placing women who were active in public life firmly within a femisocial sphere. Occasionally such accounts place colonised women within the sphere of the commemorated woman's care, authority or reform. Wendy points out how the dichotomies of coloniser/colonised and modern/backwards are inflected in relation to women within these obituaries. The class and 'race' dimensions of the obituaries are examined closely here, and, like Clare Midgley's study, this chapter refers us to the way in which some groups of women – notably white, middle-class women – drew upon representations of 'benighted' 'other' women (notably colonised women) in order to advance their claims to emancipation.

The chapters in Part Three, 'Re-Presenting the past: reframing women's history', all foreground the centrality of theoretical and methodological approaches in shaping women's history. Both the enduring misrepresentations and omissions of women within much traditional history, as well as the newer, feminist work detailed here, are shaped by, and in turn shape, the kind of evidence used and the methodological frameworks employed by historians. The authors here expose the inadequacies of 'mainstream' representations of women's history, as well as the reasons for these. The exclusion or distortion of women's experience is recognised as resulting from both the sources and the perspectives commonly selected. In singling out some sources as being more 'authoritative', 'objective' or valuable than others historians also privilege the voices of the powerful/influential and articulate in particular and the public worlds of men in general. A corollary of privileging some types of evidence over others is that experiential sources which are most likely to illuminate the historically unmapped features of women's lives are considered to be 'subjective' and, therefore, lacking in credibility. Importantly, too, the methodological frameworks utilised by historians are also seen to obscure and distort accounts of women's past(s). All the chapters in this section are, for example, damningly critical of constructions of the sexual division of labour, domesticity and work and the artificial separation of the spheres of production and reproduction evident in much historical analysis. The results here, in the histories of women's leisure, health and political and economic involvement with which the authors are concerned, show that the categories commonly utilised by historians either define women out or include them on men's terms. The specificity and relevance of women's experience, as well as the different meanings and contexts of their lives, thus remain hidden, unappreciated or misunderstood.

Whatever approach or mixture of approaches is employed, all the contributors in this section are agreed on the centrality of utilising feminist theoretical and methodological frameworks in the re-conceptualisation of history. The processes of 're-conceptualisation' and 're-presentation' of women in history are reciprocal, the one feeding the other. As well as providing critiques of the shortcomings of conventional categories, concepts and sources, the authors here suggest alternatives which better capture and

reflect women's history. This involves centring upon women as a fundamental category of historical analysis and consciously reframing research
paradigms so as to make more visible the 'other half of history'. Centring
upon women's actions, attitudes and contributions, such work recognises
the importance of both agency and constraint in women's lives and
foregrounds differences among women as well as between women and men.
Another shared feature of these chapters is that they all engage critically
with various constructions of gender offered by the evident. This highlights
how the varying constructions, meanings and usages of gender which colour many of the orthodox sources can be specific to particular historical
contexts, where they represent and reflect the interests of the powerful
public men who, largely speaking, produced this evidence in the first place.
The gendered focus upon women's history, the 'centring' of women as a
category of analysis, implies an inclusive analysis. This embraces interdisciplinary methodologies and an appreciation of both the diversities of women's
experiences and the wider historical processes and constructions which are
necessary in order to re-present history and change the past.

In her study 'Writing women in: new approaches to Russian and
Soviet history' (Chapter 7) Melanie Ilič argues that, historiographically,
there has traditionally been a heavy reliance upon sources which privilege
particular ethnic, masculine and elitist representations of Soviet history and
emphasise the importance of certain chronologies and events, which serve
to misrepresent or exclude much women's history. Her analysis establishes
the gendered construction of women's roles, real and imagined, including
their representation within the political iconography of the regime – as
'freedom', the 'Nation' and 'Mother Russia'. In surveying new work on
Soviet women's history Melanie demonstrates the value of identifying previously untapped, invisible or inaccessible sources to further explore representations of women's history. Her own research on women and protective
labour legislation shows how representations of women as workers and
mothers varied with changing perceptions of the economic and social needs
of the state. Her discussion of the origins and demise of menstrual leave
provision shows how this mirrored a shift in the representation of women
workers away from the need for protection to stress on equality with men,
as labour shortages increased demand for female labour.

Like Melanie, June Hannam is also concerned to redress issues of
marginalisation and misrepresentation through the gendered reading of
under-explored sources, which are used here to appraise the nature and
significance of women's role within the labour movement. In her chapter
'New histories of the labour movement' (Chapter 8) she exposes the inadequacies of models of political action, strongly influenced by Marxism,
which represent the male industrial worker as the epitome of the working

class. These approaches do not reflect the range of women's political involvement and affiliations or the complex interplay of gender and class in shaping women's political involvements and strategies. The women's pages and writings within the *Labour Leader* and other Independent Labour Party (ILP) newspapers are used as sources through which to analyse gender relations within the context of labour politics. In centring on women's voices within the movement June shifts attention from the traditional concentration upon socialism's relationship to women to focus, instead, upon women's relationship to socialism. In demonstrating the ambivalence of both socialist women and men to the challenge of feminism and suffrage this work questions established assumptions regarding the 'woman-friendly' image of the ILP and the appropriateness of existing categorisations of women's political thought and action. The tensions and complex interplay of party loyalties and gender are revealed as women contributors to the newspapers attempt to negotiate their socialist and feminist loyalties.

Cathy Lubelska's chapter, 'Chasing shadows: issues in researching feminist social histories of women's heath' (Chapter 9), is principally concerned with the construction and representation of women within conventional historical sources. Although there is a lot of material which links women to health issues, on closer examination it becomes apparent that such evidence actually tells us very little about women's own health experiences and needs. What it does show, however, are the various ways in which women were either seen to be implicated in or responsible for the health of others and of society at large. Even where women's own health is apparently the subject of discussion, a feminist reading of the sources demonstrates how this tends to become visible in particular historical contexts where it is indicative of larger concerns about women's and men's respective roles within society – for example, in relation to discussions of paid work and of motherhood. In fact, many of these sources reveal far more about the processes through which gendered concepts of 'health' and 'ill health' reflected prevailing social and political preoccupations than they do about women's health *per se*. The 'authoritative' medical and scientific sources on health articulate many biological, deterministic views of women as part of a process of gendering within which women's bodies are themselves seen as social constructions. It is argued that the frequent representations of women's 'condition' as being inherently, or potentially, pathological serves to distort or hide women's health experiences in a number of ways. The stress on the 'unhealthiness' of women legitimated increasing scrutiny and intervention in their bodies and lives and became a powerful medium through which to control women's behaviours. So influential was this male-dominated discourse that even those sources that get closest to women's experiences are coloured and in some respects corrupted by it.

In her chapter 'Towards a Feminist Framework for the History of Women's Leisure, 1920–60' (Chapter 10) Claire Langhamer argues that leisure, too, has been constituted as a gendered concept by historians. She exposes the weaknesses and inadequacies of definitions of leisure which are rooted in a specifically male wage-earning model, where leisure is seen to exist in direct opposition to paid work. This is seen to exclude or invalidate women's experiences of a blurring of distinctions between work and leisure within a context of unpaid domestic labour. She is also critical of the privileging of certain forms and representations of leisure over others, as evidenced in the 'topic' approach which foregrounds formal, public sporting and commercial activities, where women's participation is exceptional rather than representative. In seeking to understand the complex relationship between women and leisure Claire proposes a new, interdisciplinary feminist model which draws upon contemporary research in the field of leisure studies to create a 'fluid theoretical framework in which meaning and context assume central importance'. Within this framework her oral history research on women's leisure in Manchester provides additional source material with which to access women's hitherto hidden experiences. It also becomes a means of reconceptualising and, thus, re-presenting women's relationship to leisure, where women's own understandings and accounts of their leisure experiences can be interrogated. Her analysis reveals the many ambiguities of women's attitudes to leisure and the role of changing contexts – especially in the female life cycle and marital status – in shaping the experiences and meanings of leisure which women described. The examination of features on women and leisure in the *Manchester Evening News* corroborate some of these ambiguities, as well as the influence of changing historical contexts upon women's leisure.

Notes

Throughout, place of publication of cited sources is London unless otherwise stated.

1. Ruth Roach Pierson and Nupur Chaudhuri, eds, *Nation, Empire, Colony: Historicizing Gender and Race* (Bloomington, Ind., 1998), p. 15.

2. Cathy Lubelska, 'Gender in the curriculum', in A. Booth and P. Hyland, eds, *History in Higher Education: New Directions in Teaching and Learning* (1996).

3. E. Fox-Genovese, 'Placing women's history in History', *New Left Review* (1983), pp. 5–29.

4. Kum-Kum Bhavnani, 'Tracing the contours: feminist research and feminist objectivity', *Women's Studies International Forum* 16/2 (1993), pp. 95–104.

5. Susan Stanford Friedman, *Feminism and the Cultural Geographies of Encounter* (Princeton, NJ, 1998), pp. 200–1.

6. Himani Bannerji, 'Politics and the writing of history', in Roach Pierson and Chaudhuri, eds, *Nation, Empire, Colony*.

7. Ibid., p. 288.

8. Ibid., p. 296.

9. Ann-Marie Gallagher and Cathy Lubelska, 'Transferable skills, "graduateness" and the learning process in Women's Studies', in Margaret Archibald and Nimal Jayaratna, eds, *Proceedings of the National Conference on Outcomes and the New Quality Agency* (1997).

10. Liz Stanley, 'My mother's voice? On being a native in academia', in Louise Morley and Val Walsh, eds, *Feminist Academics: Creative Agents for Change* (1995), p. 185.

PART ONE

Competing representations

CHAPTER ONE

Splendidly silent: representing Irish Republican women, 1919–23

LOUISE RYAN

Women haven't had an easy relationship with nationalism . . . they have often been treated more as symbols than as active participants by nationalist movements organised to end colonialism and racism.[1]

Nationalism is a gendered project which depends on powerful constructions of gender differences.[2] Anne McClintock argues that all too often gender difference between women and men 'serves to symbolically define the limits of national difference and power between men'.[3] Within nationalist rhetoric, women may become circumscribed by images of weakness, passivity, innocence and virtue. However, it would be simplistic to perceive women only within such narrow constructions. While the national soldier/hero is almost exclusively represented as male, embodying the idealised characteristics of national manhood, women have frequently participated in nationalist conflicts and military encounters.[4] But although militant nationalist movements have often encouraged women's active involvement in times of 'national crisis', especially in anti-colonial struggles, it is apparent that women's role in armed conflict raises many uncomfortable questions, not least in relation to the maintenance of gender hierarchies and women's traditional mothering roles.[5]

Nationalisms emphasise women's biological reproduction of the nation: women are the givers and nurturers of life. Armed combat, fighting for one's nation, is central to constructions of manhood: thus women soldiers, takers of life, are not only perceived as threatening to masculine order and authority but have a potentially destabilising effect on the nation.[6] 'To allow women entrance into the central core of the military would throw into confusion all men's certainty about their male identity.'[7] This leaves the difficulty of how to make use of women's contribution to militant nationalist movements 'without violating popular notions of femininity, masculinity and the social order itself'.[8] According to Nira Yuval-Davis, this can be achieved through 'ideological constructions of manhood and womanhood' which frame women's position in the military around 'dichotomies of combat/non-combat and front and rear'.[9]

These 'ideological constructions' of gender are clearly discernible in the particular representations of militant women. By analysing a variety of competing representations this chapter explores some of the tensions and contradictions underpinning women's active participation in the Irish militant nationalist campaign (1919–23). Women have been largely excluded from mainstream histories of the campaign for Irish self-determination.[10] Despite a growing body of feminist research, the history of nationalist struggle remains largely a masculine story in which brave heroes fought to protect the 'motherland'.[11] Although the emblematic woman, the female symbol of Ireland, the embodiment of the nation, is well represented in poetry, legends and visual art, the complexities of women's active involvement in the armed military campaign are simplified or ignored.[12] The usual representation of Republican women is invisibility (or non-representation).

Himani Bannerji argues that 'as an integral part of the project of writing history, "representation" presents us with a great deal of complexity'.[13] Being the researcher and writer of this chapter, actively engaging with competing representations of Republican women, I am aware that my account may also be framed as a particular representation. It is appropriate, therefore, to locate myself in relation to this research. As an Irish woman who grew up in Cork steeped in the images, stories and songs of masculine Republicanism, I have my own personal store of representations of the past. However, I do not wish to present a narrative of the Republican movement. In addition, this chapter is not attempting simply to locate and reinstate women who have been written out of history. Neither am I proposing a revisionist critique of the Republican agenda. Instead, drawing on wider feminist analyses, I examine how women who engaged in military conflict and transgressed gender roles have been depicted in a variety of primary sources. In so doing I explore how representations of warfare are underpinned by the complex intersections and competing constructions of masculinities and femininities.

Analysing a range of primary sources, my research has uncovered a variety of competing representations. The chapter is divided into four sections, each of which analyses a different set of sources and assesses the ways in which Republican women have been depicted. Sources such as newspapers, propaganda publications and autobiographies offer distinct forms of representations, and clearly the images and stories which appear in a daily newspaper will differ significantly from the more personal accounts given in autobiographies. To some degree, therefore, the medium helps to shape the nature of the representation. In offering competing representations of Republican women, these primary sources indicate the various ways in which women's active participation in armed conflict has been described, explained and justified.

I begin with the mainstream daily newspapers. Not only do they offer many stories of women's varied involvement in the conflict, but they also map the changing perceptions of Republican women in the transition from the War of Independence to the Civil War. The image of 'neurotic girls' – violent, bitter, irrational Republican women – was widely used during the Civil War and suggests the particular gender dynamics of that conflict. In supporting the Free State administration against the Republicans, the mainstream newspapers also indicate official state attitudes to women's role within militarism.

Second, the Republican propaganda press reflects the complexities and negotiations around women's very active involvement in militarism. There is a strong tendency to contain representations of women within traditional roles; as 'victims of villainy' the women are used to represent the brutality of the Free State authorities. In giving voice to the leadership of the Republican movement, sources such as *Poblacht na hEireann* provide a valuable insight into the tensions around women's demands to participate in guerrilla warfare. These tensions are even more apparent in my third source, the autobiographies of male Republicans. While indicating the important tasks undertaken by 'splendidly silent' 'Cumann na mBan girls', these very personal accounts reveal the unease which many of the men felt about the transgression of gender roles.

In each of these three types of primary sources representations are clearly underpinned by gender discourses which situate the women in relation to competing masculinities, as both Free State men and Republican men attempt to undermine the chivalry, authority and morale of their opponents. In attempting to get a very different picture of Republican women, I draw upon four autobiographical accounts written by women who actively participated in Cumann na mBan, the women's wing of the Irish Republican Army (IRA). These sources offer unique, multifaceted representations of women's involvement in war indicating the complex negotiations around militarism and gender. In several cases the women reject traditional feminine passivity. They were no 'fragile damsels' but 'soldiers' ready to die for the Republic. While these sources offer a more rounded picture of women's courage and determination, as autobiographies they are self-conscious forms of self-representation. All four books were written many years after the armed conflict and were obviously motivated by an attempt to counter the prevailing negative representations and the non-representations of Republican women.

While all of these various sources illustrate the range of competing representations of Republican women, they also focus attention on the transcendence/transgression of gender roles in the context of nationalist conflict. The subsequent exclusion of these women from historical accounts of the period suggests the particularly gendered processes of selectivity informing social constructions of history.

'Neurotic girls': Republican women in the mainstream daily newspapers

The War of Independence (1919–21) was a watershed in Irish–British relations. Despite having little ammunition or weaponry at their disposal the IRA carried out a successful guerrilla war against the occupying British army. The nationalist women's organisation, Cumann na mBan, was originally set up in 1914 and became affiliated to the IRA during the War of Independence; by 1921 it had grown to include over 800 branches.[14] Margaret Ward has described this group as being, in effect, an army of women.[15] Cumann na mBan carried out a range of tasks including intelligence work, carrying despatches and gun smuggling. However, they also undertook more traditional tasks like nursing and cooking. Thus these women played both conventional and highly unconventional roles.

As the most intense fighting of the War of Independence took place in Dublin and in the southern counties around Cork, I have focused on the largest circulating newspapers from those regions: the mainstream national daily, the *Irish Independent*, based in Dublin city, and the southern provincial daily, the *Cork Examiner*. From reading these papers it appears that the press tended to depict women as victims of the conflict rather than as active participants. As the armed conflict intensified, especially between late 1920 and early 1921, the *Irish Independent* and the *Cork Examiner* paid increasing attention to British reprisals on civilians, particularly women. Female activists such as Mary Bowles, arrested in possession of a pistol, revolver and Lewis machine gun, tended to be represented as 'sensational' exceptions rather than serious threats to public safety and social order.[16] This paucity of representations of women as activists may reflect the relatively low numbers of women who were arrested and imprisoned during that period.[17] This is not to imply that women did not participate in the War of Independence, but the perception and representation of their participation differs markedly from that of the Civil War. In comparison to their higher profile during the later conflict, women's active involvement in the period 1919–21 was more secret, hidden and underground.

In the summer of 1921 a truce was declared between the British government and the Irish Republicans. However, the subsequently negotiated
Anglo-Irish treaty which reinforced the partition of Ireland and established
the southern Free State proved extremely divisive, splitting the Republican
movement and leading eventually to civil war.[18] As the newly established Free
State authorities fought their former comrades in the Republican movement,
public opinion was generally opposed to the war. The IRA, significantly
reduced in number following the split over the treaty, and lacking the widespread popular support it had enjoyed during the War of Independence,
was now increasingly reliant on women activists. Cumann na mBan was, in
fact, the first organisation officially to reject the Anglo-Irish treaty, and in
addition, all six of the women elected to the Irish parliament vociferously
opposed the treaty. Thus, from the outset, women were very publicly and
visibly associated with the Republican campaign.

Between 1922 and 1923 the *Cork Examiner* and the *Irish Independent* repeatedly highlighted women's complicity in the armed conflict. Questions
need to be raised not only about how these women were represented but
also about why the press now began to pay them so much attention. In
some ways, of course, the mainstream press was merely echoing the views
of the Free State government and the Catholic Church. The Catholic hierarchy was very hostile towards the Republicans generally and to women's
role in the conflict in particular. For example, Cardinal Logue in his Lenten
pastoral 'deplored that a number of women and girls had become involved
in this wild orgy of violence'.[19] In October 1922 the hierarchy issued an
excommunication order against all Republicans who persisted in opposing
the state.[20] The particular impact of this on Republican women will be
discussed later.

In addition, newspaper images of Republicans must be understood within
the context of strict press censorship. By order of the Free State government
newspapers were instructed on the acceptable language of the conflict:
Republicans were to be called 'irregulars' and never described as an army
or as troops but instead as 'bands'.[21] However, it was not merely censorship
which shaped press reporting during the Civil War. Many newspapers,
especially the national press, demonstrated a 'rabid anti-republicanism'[22]
and 'were quite willing to follow the official line'.[23] Thus newspaper reports
are very valuable in providing an insight into official representations of
'violent and irrational' Republican women.

Under the heading 'Young Girls Throw Bombs' the *Cork Examiner* reported that:

> Throughout last night, as well as during the early hours of this morning, a
> number of attacks were made on National troops in different parts of the

city . . . An attack was made on a Crossley tender . . . The principal attackers were some young girls, who threw bombs at the vehicle – a new feature in street attacks.[24]

The report stressed that casualties were mainly civilian. It is noteworthy that the Republican newsletter, *Poblacht na hEireann*, flatly denied that 'girls had thrown bombs at Free State soldiers', describing the story as 'an absolute fabrication'.[25] Possible reasons for this denial will be discussed later. Such discrepancies in reporting suggest the disputed nature of women's involvement in the armed conflict.

At a time when most of the men were either in prison or 'on the run', official demonstrations of Republicanism were frequently undertaken by women. The press highlighted several processions involving contingents of Cumann na mBan dressed in military uniform.[26] By participating in displays such as these, women were locating themselves very visibly in the public sphere; by wearing uniforms they were representing themselves as an organised military force. This could be interpreted as a challenge to traditional gender roles and may explain some of the anxieties around the women's unnatural and unfeminine behaviour. However, while parading in military uniform was important for Republican women, the use of disguise to avoid attention was of equal importance. The headline 'Girls with Machine Guns'[27] relates to the arrest of three 'irregulars' in Kerry. An eyewitness reported that two young women had escaped from the scene, concealing machine-guns under their shawls. 'The soldiers had no suspicion of the innocent-looking peasant girls, who were apparently on their way home from market.' The article evokes an image of humble, rural 'peasant girls' wearing the traditional shawl. The apparent innocence and naturalness of this image contrasts sharply with the brutal reality of women 'irregulars' as enemies of the state, concealing dangerous weapons beneath their clothes. But the article also suggests some of the complexities around the roles of women Republicans who played with their femininity and donned traditional female attire when engaged in activity which was very far removed from acceptable feminine behaviour.

Such was the growing concern about women's active militarism that the Free State president, William Cosgrave, issued the following statement:

In England, fortunately for her, the 'Die-hards' are men with whom the pen dipped in gall is mightier than the sword; but unhappily in Ireland the 'Die-hards' are women, whose ecstasies at their extremest can find no outlet so satisfying as destruction – sheer destruction. Weak men in their atmosphere seek peace in concurrence with their frenzy, and even children are exalted by having their revolvers thrust into their little hands.[28]

In this statement, Republican women are depicted as irresponsible mothers thrusting revolvers into the hands of innocent children. Their immorality is represented by the sexualised image of women experiencing ecstasy through violence and destruction. As argued earlier, women's contribution to the nation is primarily measured in terms of traditional tasks such as reproduction and mothering.[29] The deviance and dangerousness of Republican women is emphasised by their bad mothering. This sentiment was also expressed by a leading supporter of the Free State government and an avid anti-Republican, P. S. O'Hegarty. He called the women 'furies' and held them largely responsible for the ferocity of the civil war: 'They became practically unsexed, their mothers' milk blackened to make gunpowder, their minds working on nothing save hate and blood.'[30]

This quotation neatly summarises the transgression of gender roles. Instead of being mothers, the givers of life, Republican women are not only 'unsexed' but their milk, the symbol of life, is transposed to black gunpowder, the symbol of death and destruction. The notion of dangerous, irrational women is reinforced in a Free State government report published in the *Irish Independent* under the headline 'Neurotic Girls': 'Neurotic girls are amongst the most active adherents to the irregular cause, because hitherto it has been safe to be so. Many of them have been known to accompany men on expeditions of murder, concealing arms in their clothes until required, and taking them back when used, relying for safety on the chivalry of those whose deaths they were out to encompass.'[31]

The construction of Republican women as not merely dangerous but immoral and neurotic significantly impacted on the related images of Republican men. Sarah Benton has argued that militant Republican men sought to emphasise such manly values as courage, loyalty and strength.[32] However, from both of these newspaper reports it is apparent that the obvious presence of women among the Republican ranks was used by their political opponents to undermine those manly virtues. The participation of women was used to represent male Republicans as the very opposite of manly. In Cosgrave's statement, Republicans are depicted as weak men who cannot control their frenzied women. In the quote above they are constructed not as authentic soldiers but as cowardly assassins shielding behind women's underskirts.

There were several newspaper reports of armed women actually threatening violence. For example, on both 22 January and 1 February the *Cork Examiner* reported incidents in which armed women surrounded and threatened members of the Dublin Metropolitan Police. In both incidents the women had been painting Republican slogans on city walls and buildings. Under the strict censorship laws this was one of the few means of communication available to Republicans. Under the headline 'Girls with Webleys'

29

LIVERPOOL
JOHN MOORES UNIVERSITY
AVRIL ROBARTS LRC
TEL. 0151 231 4022

the *Examiner* recounted how a constable observed a young woman 'defacing' a wall of Trinity College in the centre of Dublin city. 'He proceeded to take her into custody when two other young women brandishing Webley revolvers approached him, and ordered him to clear away and cease interference with the young lady he was about to take into custody.'[33]

Such newspaper reports constructed images of Republican women as threatening, dangerous and unconventional, displaying blatant disregard for the police, the military and the Free State government. They transgressed acceptable gender boundaries, wore uniforms, occupied public, militarised zones, carried guns and ammunition. By labelling them 'diehards' and 'neurotic girls' and by emphasising their unconventionality, the press sought to deny them any legitimacy as political or military actors. Their femininity, indeed their womanliness, was called into question. They were unsexed by participating in warfare. Clearly in the eyes of the mainstream daily press, the Free State authorities and the Catholic hierarchy women had no place in militarised arenas. In addition, by condemning Republican women these representations defined, by contrast, the acceptable roles for Irish women. Women should be good mothers, remaining in the domestic sphere and respecting the authority of their husbands, the Church and the state. Thus passive and obedient feminine roles were defined in relation to masculine power and authority. Republican masculinity was represented as weak and ineffectual because it was unable to control frenzied Republican women. It is important, therefore, to assess how official Republican sources represented Republican women and negotiated their obvious transcendence of traditional gender roles.

'Victims of villainy': representations of women in the Republican press

Published between January 1922 and March 1923, the underground newspaper *Poblacht na hEireann* provides a useful insight into Republican propaganda and offers alternative representations of Republican women. Initially women were depicted in very particular ways: as the mourning mothers of Republican martyrs, as the brave guardians of Republican homes and families, as the caring sisters and nurses of wounded heroes. Republican mothers and wives were usually depicted as strong, silent and suffering, stoically bearing the burdens of hardship and state 'terrorism', maintaining family life in the face of adversity, their loyalty to the cause and devotion to their menfolk unquestioned. However, as the Civil War progressed and the number of arrested and imprisoned women rose dramatically, *Poblacht na hEireann* devoted increasing space to reporting the arrests of women. For example, on just one day in February 1923, 29 women were arrested in Cork and taken by lorry to the 'Female Gaol'. The paper reported the ill-treatment and harsh conditions endured by the women: 'The cells were very dirty – cigarette ends and other remnants strewn on the floor . . . there was no suggestion that any of the girls should wash and no water was provided for them. The majority got no dinner.' Nineteen of the women were then taken by ship to Dublin; they 'were shockingly treated on board ship'.[34]

Stories such as these suggest the depravity of the Free State forces. On 11 November 1922 the paper carried the headline 'War on Women', listing the arrests of several Republican women, including Honor Murphy, who worked at the *Poblacht* offices, and Bridie O'Mullane, publicity director of Cumann na mBan. The article argued that the Free State authorities were deliberately 'embarking on the wholesale imprisonment of Republican women in Ireland'. Unable to defeat the Republican forces by fair means, the Free State leaders decided to 'attack them through their women'. This was seen as proof of their 'cowardly villainy'. The report does not suggest that the women were arrested and imprisoned because they were important Republicans; active participants in the war. Instead, the women are represented as mere pawns in the deadly games of the unscrupulous 'Free Staters'. This is interesting because it uses women to highlight the cruelty of the Free State men, in much the same way that the mainstream press used women to highlight the weakness of Republican men. In both cases the women are not represented as important actors in their own right but as a testing ground for masculine authority, power and chivalry. *Poblacht* appears to suggest that the women are being imprisoned purely in an attempt to weaken the morale of Republican men. Tensions underlying women's imprisonment are particularly apparent in reports of women's hunger strike.

On 10 November 1922 *Poblacht* reported that five women were on hunger strike in Mountjoy. On 15 November 1922, under the headline 'Twelve Days', it reported Mary MacSwiney's ongoing hunger strike, adding: 'She is not physically capable of enduring so long under the torture as her great brother. The sands are running out. A few days, another day may bring an indelible disgrace on this Nation.' Miss MacSwiney could not repeat the sacrifice of her 'great brother', the Lord Mayor of Cork, Terence MacSwiney, who died in Brixton Prison, London, on the 75th day of his hunger strike. She could not repeat his feat for many reasons, but primarily because she was a woman. It was unthinkable that women should be permitted to endure this suffering, or perhaps more unthinkable that they should be permitted to become martyrs.

On 1 February 1923 *Poblacht* reported that there were 58 Republican women prisoners in Mountjoy in terribly overcrowded conditions, and that two of them were being punished in solitary confinement. On 21 February the paper again questioned why so many women were in prison and illustrated that these women were primarily wives and mothers. Mrs Doody, whose husband was also in prison, left three young children in the care of their grandmother, and Mrs Cogley, whose husband was imprisoned as well, had to leave 'two children at the mercy of the world'. Jenny Coyle, one of the youngest prisoners, was only a 'school girl'. While such reports may be seen as valuable propaganda illustrating the cruelty of the Free State administration, they may also be seen as attempts to undermine the seriousness of Republican women. Within a Republicanism which glorified the sacrifices of heroic young men like Terence MacSwiney, the notion that elderly women, mothers and young schoolgirls were in prison, on hunger strike, demanding political status, may well have seemed an anathema.

There are thus some interesting similarities in the competing representations of Republican women in the mainstream and Republican press. Both sources share a sense of unease about women's active involvement in armed conflict and both sources undermine the women in particular ways. While newspapers like the *Irish Independent* and the *Cork Examiner* ridicule the women as 'neurotic die-hards', *Poblacht* portrays them as victims of war. Clearly the Republican press could not simply ignore the widespread arrests and imprisonment of female activists, but instead it tried to play down their activism by emphasising their suffering at the hands of the 'brutal' Free Staters. However, it is important not to oversimplify *Poblacht*, as there is some evidence of tensions between its male and female contributors. The women who contributed to its pages offered a contrasting view of women's motives and contributions to the armed struggle. A letter from Cumann na mBan published in November 1922 read:

> We offer our admiration and pledge our whole-hearted support to the women prisoners in the fight they are putting up in defence of the civil rights of Republicans. They are giving us an example of how the fight may be maintained even within prison walls, and should death claim them, they will die happy, knowing that their Sacrifice will not be in vain.[35]

In December 1922 Mary MacSwiney wrote a letter outlining Republican women's commitment to the military struggle: 'We promise that we shall uphold the banner of truth, of honour, of true freedom and of the Republic in the face of all tyranny and falsehood; did they massacre every man in Ireland.'[36]

Clearly these women did not see themselves as mere pawns whose imprisonment simply demonstrated Free Staters' lack of chivalry. They presented themselves as active Republicans who were prepared to make the ultimate sacrifice of dying for their cause. In the quotation above MacSwiney suggests that women would continue the fight even without the men. However, such confident assertions may be interpreted as indications of the 'hysteria', 'intransigence' and 'bitterness' of which Republican women were so widely accused.[37] *Poblacht na hEireann* reveals several complex and even contradictory images of women and begins to illustrate not just the range of competing representations of Republican women but the underlying dynamics between men and women within the Republican camp.

'Splendidly silent': Republican men and 'Cumann na mBan girls'

The women rendered heroic service. Even outside the ranks of the young and active girls organised in Cumann na mBan, who carried despatches, nursed the sick and wounded, providing clothing, first-aid equipment, funds, and risked their lives as freely as the men, there were women and girls who kept many a long vigil, who cooked and washed and provided shelter, and who were, when the tests came, splendidly silent, immune alike to threats and brandishments.[38]

In his biography of IRA leader Liam Lynch, fellow IRA man Florence O'Donoghue provides some fascinating snippets of information about the role of Republican women in both the War of Independence and the Civil War. It is noteworthy that O'Donoghue emphasises the women's silence – 'splendidly silent': their loyalty was demonstrated by their ability to keep their mouths shut. Their silence and invisibility enabled them to be effective couriers and trustworthy secretaries. But such qualities did not help them to achieve recognition or fame and may well have contributed to their exclusion from historical accounts of the wars. In the social construction of history, silent and invisible women are unlikely to receive any significant attention.

While O'Donoghue acknowledges the courage and determination of women and the risks they took, he does not explicitly address their particular contributions but simply mentions them in passing. The women appear as shadowy figures in the background, not as central characters in their own right. In the quote above, he divides Republican women into two categories. These are very revealing and suggest some of the ways in which women's activism may have been negotiated, accommodated and contained. First, there are the 'girls' of Cumann na mBan; young and active, risking their lives for the cause. This is a recurring image in the autobiographies of male Republicans.[39] While acknowledging the bravery of these women, this image reduces them to a homogeneous group of nameless 'girls'. Second, O'Donoghue refers to civilian women and girls who provided food and shelter. Although these women were of crucial importance to a guerrilla army and are acknowledged by all the Republican autobiographies, they are narrowly contained within the domestic sphere doing traditional, 'womanly' tasks.

According to Cynthia Enloe, nationalist warfare frequently involves a split between older, married women who 'perform support or homefront roles, while unmarried women are channelled into more military roles'.[40] While there was an obvious tendency to represent Irish Republican women in this way, I believe that this is an unhelpful dichotomy which underestimates the blurring of boundaries between 'home front' and 'battle front'. Such a dichotomy also simplifies the complex constructions around militarism and domesticity. As discussed earlier, there were some concerns within the Republican movement about women's transgression of traditional gender boundaries. Nira Yuval-Davis writes that women soldiers have usually been perceived as threatening 'unless controlled and distinguished from male soldiers by emphasizing their femininity'.[41] From reading the autobiographies of Republican men it is obvious that Cumann na mBan women are repeatedly portrayed in very gender-specific ways. Even though the women are often depicted as active and courageous, they are also clearly distinguished from Republican men by their feminine qualities. Describing an IRA training camp in 1921, Ernie O'Malley emphasises the particular role of Republican women:

> The Cumann na mBan girls in their turns came to cook and wash. Fresh flowers in empty tin cans would appear on tables; sweet pea, wild roses, bunches of heather, and carnations. The girls came on foot, on bicycles, in ponies and traps, some of them in uniform. They always brought presents: honey, homemade jam, freshly churned butter . . . packages of cigarettes.[42]

Thus even independent, confident young women cycling around the countryside wearing military uniform were safely contained within the parameters of femininity. But O'Malley's books also testify to the courage and determination of women. Describing their involvement in the Civil War, he says: 'they were our comrades, loyal, willing and incorruptible'.[43] In my view, the writings of IRA men such as O'Donoghue and O'Malley, as well as the many other similar autobiographical accounts of the war years, indicate the attempts to negotiate gender roles. Women's roles are represented as militarised and simultaneously feminised. The emphasis on clear-cut gender roles and hierarchies helps to frame the relationship between Republican men and women.

'No fragile damsels':
women's self-representations

In the introduction to her memoirs written almost 50 years after the War of Independence, Cork-based Cumann na mBan activist Lil Conlon explains that she has written her personal account because, to her disappointment, nobody else has chronicled women's participation in that period of history. She adds that there has been 'little or no mention' of those women who did such 'gallant and heroic' work for the cause of Ireland.[44] Conlon represents Cumann na mBan activists not merely as loyal and selfless but as fearless and determined:

> here was no fragile damsel – but a cailín [girl] set in a more durable mould, attuned to the exigency of the period and eager to throw in her lot with her male companions. All were scions of a warlike race, vibrant living creatures, imbibed with a national spirit, consorting daily with danger and ready for the supreme sacrifice should it be demanded of them.[45]

In this quote Conlon represents the Republican woman in contrast to traditional femininity: she is not a fragile damsel. Instead she is warlike, active and strong. Conlon locates the woman in a position of equality with her 'male companions'. The ultimate test of that equality is her preparedness to make the supreme sacrifice: to die for the cause. Throughout the Republican movement there was a great reluctance on the part of men to allow women to become martyrs: all martyrs were men, women were their mourners, keepers of their memory.[46] Yet in Conlon's quotation and in the quotation from *Poblacht* cited earlier it is apparent that some Republican women were prepared to contemplate martyrdom.

Conlon acknowledges the suffering of women but without constructing them as passive or helpless victims. With many IRA men 'on the run' for the duration of the war, the British military frequently enacted their 'reprisals' on civilian targets, and many homes and businesses were destroyed. Women suspected of Republican sympathies were especially vulnerable to attack. Conlon recounts numerous attacks on women. The following quotation describes the experience of Cumann na mBan activist Bab Hogan: 'At 1 a.m. her home was entered by some masked men who cut off her hair. She rushed out the back door, over the wall and into a neighbour's backyard where she stayed for the remainder of the night.'[47] Conlon states that constant military raids on homes illustrated the perceived importance of the domestic sphere as a site of resistance during the guerilla war. The British military was aware that 'the civil population were ardent supporters of the

Volunteers [IRA] – feeding and housing them . . . all of which were invaluable to men "on the run" '.[48]

The blurring of the boundaries between the 'home front' and the 'battle front' framed domestic activities within a militarist context. Thus women who contributed to the war effort within the 'home front' took grave risks and should be seen as active participants in war. Providing shelter for IRA men 'on the run' was frequently taken for granted by the men themselves, but for the women it was a demanding, risk-filled and often thankless task. By comparing male and female accounts of the same incident one can see how different stories and self-representations emerge. In his personal account of the War of Independence, *The War in Clare*, IRA guerrilla leader Michael Brennan tells the story of his escape from Bandon town, a heavily policed, Unionist stronghold in West Cork. His brief account is quoted here to illustrate the comparison with a conflicting account of the same event:

> I stayed a few days at Healy's of Bandon and, after long discussion as to the ways and means of getting to Dublin I decided to travel on the ordinary train wearing the very simple disguise of a British officer's cap . . . As an additional precaution somebody provided me with glasses. The Healys drove me to Cork station.[49]

In line with much of Brennan's book this account presents the picture of a cool, capable and courageous young IRA man. The same incident is described very differently by the Healy family. Kathleen Keyes McDonnell (*née* Healy), an active member of Cumann na mBan, provided an IRA safe house in the Bandon area. In her autobiographical account, *There Is a Bridge at Bandon*, she gives an alternative version of Brennan's escape from the town. On the run from the authorities, Brennan was hidden in the Healy home for two weeks. The Healys were well-known Republicans and risked their lives by sheltering a wanted man. McDonnell describes how her sister Peg acted as a courier, ensuring that Brennan was kept in contact with headquarters in Dublin. After two weeks his orders came to travel to Dublin. Peg managed to secure various items of clothing to disguise Brennan's appearance. Cork was the most militarised county in Ireland, with over 10,000 heavily armed British troops patrolling urban and rural areas. Peg drove Brennan to the city, encountering several military checkpoints en route.

According to Kathleen McDonnell, Brennan was very aware that he owed his life to her sister: 'Miss Healy's prompt action saved me from capture in Cork; her initiative and quick wit enabled me to reach Dublin safely. As I was armed and had every intention of fighting she took very grave risks.'[50] Although this quote is attributed to Brennan, it does not appear in his book; in fact, he makes no mention of Peg Healy. These conflicting accounts demonstrate the extent of Republican women's excision from history, and also demonstrate the importance of comparing different sources; in particular, sources in which women represent themselves. As a known Republican, Kathleen McDonnell was kept under surveillance by the military. Her home and business were regularly raided. She describes one 'tyrannical raid . . . during which the officer held a revolver close to my face, threatening me with the contents if I did not tell where my husband was'.[51]

Kathleen Clarke, member of the Irish parliament (Dail), Sinn Fein local councillor and first female Lord Mayor of Dublin, was one of the most outspoken Republican women of her time. Her memoirs were edited by Helen Litton and posthumously published as *Revolutionary Woman*. Clarke also offers vivid descriptions of British military raids on her home during the War of Independence. On one occasion her sister Agnes was dragged from the house in the middle of the night and her hair cut off with a razor. But the family continued to provide shelter for the IRA. For example, Clarke recounts how a man was hidden in bed beside her elderly mother while British soldiers searched the house and interrogated the women for hours.[52] Like Conlon and McDonnell, Clarke represents Republican women as loyal, dedicated and courageous:

> We learned to take chances without turning a hair; we never knew when walking along the street but that we might run into an ambush, or be held up by British military . . . They were trying and stirring times, but the spirit of the people was so wonderful, one felt so proud.[53]

Clarke, along with the other women members of the Irish parliament, voted against the Anglo-Irish treaty which she described as 'a surrender of all our national ideals'.[54] She wrote: 'I hate war, particularly civil war, though I realise one must fight for what one wants in this world.'[55] During the Civil War, Clarke, like many other Republican women, experienced the ignominy and irony of having her home searched by Irish troops wearing the uniform of the Irish Free State army. Towards the end of the war she was arrested along with fellow politician Mary MacSwiney and taken to Kilmainham prison.

While Kathleen Clarke only spent a short time in prison during the Civil War, this period was marked by the widespread arrest and imprisonment of Republican women. Kilmainham Gaol and the North Dublin Union were turned into women's prisons during the war to accommodate the large number of female political prisoners.[56] Margaret Buckley's *The Jangle of the Keys* is an insightful autobiographical account of imprisonment during the Civil War. Writing in the preface to the book in 1938, Mary MacSwiney emphasised its value as a historical record: 'These gaol chronicles are useful records, and there are far too few reliable records of the history of the past twenty years in Ireland.'[57]

Buckley, a prisoner between January and October 1923, constructs representations of Republican women which contrast markedly with the negative stereotypes propounded by the dominant discourses in the Irish Free State. She describes the women as political prisoners, as distinct from ordinary convicted prisoners. They insisted on being treated like 'politicals', using the hunger strike as their main weapon. 'The hunger strike was the only weapon we could wield, and we felt justified in using it. We were Irishwomen of good character, accused of no criminal intent.'[58] The women represented many contradictions: on the one hand they were dedicated to armed conflict, but, on the other hand, they were extremely religious, they built altars and prayed the rosary together on their knees. In fact, the women's attitude to religion is interesting. Most were very devout: they prayed daily and attended mass. However, they refused to give in to the pressures of the Catholic hierarchy and remained philosophical about the mass excommunication which had taken place in 1922: 'We never confused the Creator with His creatures.'[59]

Like Republican men, the women used military titles in prison and on occasion wore their military uniforms. Buckley was appointed quartermaster, while Lily McClean drilled the 'troops'. 'I have never seen any woman call out orders and enforce them like Captain McClean. Drill over, the "troops" marched round and round the compound, singing . . . over looked by soldiers.'[60] While describing the terrible conditions in which the women were held, Buckley does not present the women as helpless victims. There were frequent attempts to break out from prison and several women did manage to escape. Buckley imposed military order on the women. She referred to the women's 'regime of self-discipline'.[61] When one of the younger women became upset and started to cry, Buckley reminded her that 'she was a soldier'.[62] Buckley's representation of the women as disciplined soldiers contrasts markedly with the prevailing negative representations of 'neurotic girls' or 'victims of villainy'.

The recurring image which emerges from all four of these autobiographical accounts is that of strong, courageous, steadfast and patriotic women. Writing several decades after the armed conflict, these women would have been very familiar with the prevailing negative views about their wartime work. Their self-representations were thus, in my opinion, consciously framed in opposition to stereotypes of neurotic die-hards. However, while it was relatively straightforward to challenge the derogatory images that had filled the pages of the mainstream press, it was a different matter to challenge the more complex images constructed in the writings of male Republicans. These four women avoid any criticism of IRA men and do not attempt to undermine their masculinity. But they do emphasise women's important contributions to the war years and the varied ways in which the men relied on their support and resourcefulness. With most IRA men in prison or on the run for the duration of the conflict, the women represent themselves as strong, self-reliant and capable. For these women there appears to have been no contradiction between their femaleness and their Republicanism. Although acknowledging the suffering and sacrifices, they do not portray themselves as weak, vulnerable victims. Whether on the militarised home front or in the prison cell, they represent a transcendence of traditional gender roles, rejecting feminine passivity and instead framing their wartime experiences in terms of active agency.

Conclusion

Himani Bannerji claims that writing history is not an innocent affair.[63] In the social construction of Irish history it is apparent that assertive and unconventional Republican women have been selected out of representations of the past. Historical versions of Ireland's campaign for independence have been defined by the conflicting agendas of the 'Free Staters' and militant Republicanism. Women activists have been circumscribed within these competing discourses of masculine bravery, heroism and cowardice. Depending on one's political sympathies, women have been contained within dichotomies of the silent, vulnerable woman in the home or the demonised 'fury' in the battle zone. Instead of assessing women's complex negotiations across gender boundaries, both images deny the diversity of women's roles and present simple gendered stereotypes. Silent, invisible women and frenzied women have had no place in glorious national histories.

A clear example of the non-representation of Republican women can be seen in *Green against Green*, Michael Hopkinson's 'fresh approach to the Civil War' which claims to be 'based on detailed scholarship'.[64] Women who featured prominently in earlier accounts of the war are here either completely absent or reduced to footnotes. There are only six references to Cumann na mBan and even then the women are described as 'irate'[65] and 'hardline'.[66] But even this is somewhat better than Joost Augusteijn's 1996 publication *From Public Defiance to Guerrilla War*, which focuses exclusively on male Republicans and neglects Cumann na mBan altogether.[67]

Only in the autobiographies of Republican women does one find a more rounded picture of their activism and commitment. However, I suggest that in these writings one also begins to see the processes which led to their excision from history. The women were engaged in secret and virtually invisible work which has been easily ignored or simplified as insignificant. As early as Buckley's book in 1938 and as late as Conlon's book in 1969 there was the dawning realisation that their histories were not being written and they were being sidelined in accounts of masculine warfare and heroism. Their exclusion from historical accounts not only renders invisible but also simplifies women's complex relationship with violence, militarism and propaganda. Although some feminists have begun to interrogate women's involvement in warfare,[68] the representation of men as 'naturally linked to war' and women as 'naturally linked to peace' continues to be very prevalent.[69] Women's active participation in nationalist campaigns remains highly controversial and reveals the ongoing negotiations of gender roles within militarised contexts.[70] In challenging past representations of militant women, such as the members of Cumann na mBan, perhaps it is possible to influence representations of future generations of militant women.

Further reading

Sarah Benton, 'Women Disarmed: The Militarisation of Politics in Ireland', *Feminist Review* 50 (1995), pp. 148–72.

Frances Blake, *The Irish Civil War* (London, 1986).

Margaret Buckley, *The Jangle of the Keys* (Dublin, 1938).

Kathleen Clarke, *Revolutionary Woman* (Dublin, 1991).

Lil Conlon, *Cumann na mBan and the Women of Ireland* (Kilkenny, 1969).

Charlotte Fallon, *Soul of Fire: A Biography of Mary MacSwiney* (Cork, 1986).

Anne Haverty, *Constance Markievicz: An Independent Life* (London, 1988).

C. L. Innes, *Woman and Nation* (Hemel Hempstead, 1993).

Helen Litton, *The Irish Civil War: An Illustrated History* (Dublin, 1997).

Sinead McCoole, *Guns and Chiffon: Women Revolutionaries and Kilmainham Gaol* (Dublin, 1997).

Kathleen Keyes McDonnell, *There Is a Bridge at Bandon* (Cork, 1972).

Diana Norman, *Terrible Beauty: A Life of Countess Markievicz* (London, 1987).

Louise Ryan, 'Furies and Diehards: Women and Irish Republicanism in the Early Twentieth Century', *Gender and History* 11/2 (1999), pp. 256–75.

Ruth Taillon, *When History Was Made: The Women of 1916* (Belfast, 1996).

Margaret Ward, *Unmanageable Revolutionaries: Women and Irish Nationalism* (London, 1989).

Margaret Ward, *Maud Gonne: A Life* (London, 1990).

Margaret Ward, *In Their Own Voice: Women and Irish Nationalism* (Dublin, 1995).

Notes

1. Cynthia Enloe, *Bananas, Beaches and Bases: Making Feminist Sense of International Politics* (London, 1989), p. 42.

2. Anne McClintock, 'Family feuds: gender, nationalism and the family', *Feminist Review* 44 (1993), pp. 61–80.

3. Ibid., p. 62.

4. See, for example, Enloe, *Bananas, Beaches and Bases*; Mary Layoun, 'Telling spaces: Palestinian women and the engendering of national narratives', in Andrew Parker et al., eds, *Nationalisms and Sexualities* (New York, 1992); Nira Yuval-Davis, *Gender and Nation* (London, 1997).

5. Ketu Katrak, 'Indian nationalism, Gandhian "Satyagraha" and representations of female sexuality', in Parker et al., eds, *Nationalisms and Sexualities*.

6. Louise Ryan, 'Furies and die-hards: women and Irish Republicanism in the early twentieth century', *Gender and History* 11/2 (1999), pp. 256–75; Cynthia Enloe, *Does Khaki Become You?* (London, 1983); Yuval-Davis, *Gender and Nation*.

7. Enloe, *Does Khaki Become You?*, p. 15.

8. Ibid., p. 7.

9. Yuval-Davis, *Gender and Nation*, p. 103.

10. Margaret Ward, *Unmanageable Revolutionaries: Women and Irish Nationalism* (London, 1989).

11. C. L. Innes, *Woman and Nation* (Hemel Hempstead, 1993).

12. Breda Gray and Louise Ryan, '(Dis)locating "woman" and women in representations of Irish nationality', in Anne Byrne and Madeleine Leonard, eds, *Women and Irish Society* (Belfast, 1997); Breda Gray and Louise Ryan, 'The politics of Irish identity and the interconnections between feminism, nationhood and colonialism', in Ruth Roach Pierson and Nupur Chaudhuri, eds, *Nation, Empire, Colony: Historicizing Gender and Race* (Bloomington, Ind., 1998).

13. Himani Bannerji, 'Politics and the writing of history', in Roach Pierson and Chaudhuri, eds, *Nation, Empire, Colony*, p. 287.

14. Lil Conlon, *Cumann na mBan and the Women of Ireland* (Kilkenny, 1969).

15. Ward, *Unmanageable Revolutionaries*.

16. *Cork Examiner*, 17 January and 25 February 1921. For a fuller discussion of newspaper reporting on Republican women, see Ryan, 'Furies and die-hards: women and Irish Republicanism'.

17. Sinead McCoole, *Guns and Chiffon: Women Revolutionaries and Kilmainham Gaol* (Dublin, 1997).

18. Helen Litton, *The Irish Civil War: An Illustrated History* (Dublin, 1997).

19. Charlotte Fallon, *Soul of Fire: A Biography of Mary MacSwiney* (Cork, 1986), p. 98.

20. Ibid., p. 88.

21. Ernie O'Malley, *The Singing Flame* (Dublin, 1992), pp. 176–7.

22. Frances Blake, *The Irish Civil War* (London, 1986), p. 34.

23. Ibid., p. 35.

24. *Cork Examiner*, 16 October 1922.

25. *Poblacht na hEireann*, 21 October 1922.

26. *Cork Examiner*, 4 December 1922.

27. *Cork Examiner*, 23 September 1922.

28. *Irish Times*, 1 January 1923.

29. Yuval-Davis, *Gender and Nation*, and Enloe, *Does Khaki Become You?*

30. Cited in Liam O'Dowd, 'Church, state and women', in Chris Curtin, Pauline Jackson and Barbara O'Connor, eds, *Gender in Irish Society* (Galway, 1987), p. 10.

31. *Irish Independent*, 1 January 1923.

32. Sarah Benton, 'Women disarmed: the militarisation of politics in Ireland', *Feminist Review* 50 (1995), pp. 148–72.

33. *Cork Examiner*, 22 January 1923.

34. *Poblacht na hEireann*, 23 February 1923.

35. Ibid., 10 November 1922.

36. Ibid., 18 December 1922.

37. O'Dowd, 'Church, state and women'.

38. Florence O'Donoghue, *No Other Law* (Dublin, 1954), p. 107.

39. Tom Barry, *Guerrilla Days in Ireland* (Dublin, 1997); Dan Breen, *My Fight for Ireland's Freedom* (Dublin, 1997); Ernie O'Malley, *On An Other Man's Wound* (Dublin, 1994).

40. Enloe, *Does Khaki Become You?*, p. 164.

41. Yuval-Davis, *Gender and Nation*, p. 101.

42. O'Malley, *The Singing Flame*, p. 21.

43. Ibid., p. 148.

44. Conlon, *Cumann na mBan*, p. 1.

45. Ibid., p. 168.

46. Ward, *Unmanageable Revolutionaries*.

47. Conlon, *Cumann na mBan*, p. 123.

48. Ibid., p. 145.

49. Michael Brennan, *The War in Clare* (Dublin, 1980), p. 40.

50. Brennan, cited in Kathleen Keyes McDonnell, *There Is a Bridge at Bandon* (Cork, 1972), p. 128.

51. Ibid., p. 117.

52. Kathleen Clarke, *Revolutionary Woman* (Dublin, 1991), pp. 180–1.

53. Ibid., p. 176.

54. Ibid., p. 191.

55. Ibid., p. 199.

56. McCoole, *Guns and Chiffon*.

57. MacSwiney in Margaret Buckley, *The Jangle of the Keys* (Dublin, 1938), p. vii.

58. Ibid., p. 31.

59. Ibid., p. 30.

60. Ibid., p. 59.

61. Ibid., p. 113.

62. Ibid., p. 115.

63. Bannerji, 'Politics and the writing of history', p. 290.

64. Cited in sleeve notes, Michael Hopkinson, *Green Against Green* (London, 1988).

65. Ibid., p. 254.

66. Ibid., p. 5.

67. Joost Augusteijn, *From Public Defiance to Guerrilla Warfare* (Dublin, 1996).

68. Floya Anthias and Nira Yuval-Davis, eds, *Woman – Nation – State* (London, 1989); see also Enloe, *Does Khaki Become You?* and *Bananas, Beaches and Bases*.

69. Yuval-Davis, *Gender and Nation*, p. 94.

70. Julie Peteet, 'Icons and militants: mothering in the danger zone', in *Signs* 23 (1997), pp. 103–29.

CHAPTER TWO

Telling stories about the Ladies of Llangollen: the construction of lesbian and feminist histories

ALISON ORAM

In 1778, two women caused a scandal in their families by eloping from their native Ireland to live together in Wales. Both were from branches of the Irish aristocracy and had received a genteel upbringing, though both were younger daughters without much expectation of inheritance. They had first met ten years previously. At that time the younger, thirteen-year-old orphan Sarah Ponsonby, was boarding at a school near Kilkenny Castle, the family seat of the Butlers. Eleanor Butler was 29, but despite the age gap between them they formed a deep and affectionate friendship, cemented by their love of books. Over the years they developed a mutual desire to spend their lives together. In 1778, aged 23 and 39, they each climbed out of the window of their respective family homes dressed in men's clothes and, with the help of trusted servants, set off for the ferry at Waterford. Before they were able to take the next boat, however, their families set off in hot pursuit and ran them to ground in a barn. Eleanor's parents threatened to send her to a convent for the rest of her life, but she ran away again to join Sarah at her aunt's home, and both families eventually agreed to let them go, accompanied by a maid. After touring Wales for some months and spending most of their accumulated funds, they found a cottage near the town of Llangollen in the Welsh borders, and settled down to live a fairly poverty-stricken (by gentry standards) but blissfully happy existence for the next 50 years. The Ladies' decision to reject frivolous and worldly society and retire to live in a simple and quiet manner in the countryside resonated strongly with contemporary ideas of Romanticism, and over the years they became celebrated in literary circles and among European and English royalty. Acclaimed by greater and lesser poets, they were not writers themselves – except of letters and journals – but were very well read and informed conversationalists.[1]

The aims of lesbian history

This chapter is not going to be about the lives of the Ladies of Llangollen, but about how they have been represented and mythologised by others in their own time and since, especially by lesbians and feminists seeking to construct identities and a history. Having a sense of our past is vital to lesbians as individuals and as a group. This need parallels that of other marginalised groups: lesbian history in the past twenty years has been written alongside the new histories by gay men, black people and women. Feminists have had to rescue women's history from obscurity, but at least women are deemed to have existed. Lesbian history has had the added task of asserting lesbian lives against the attempted (and largely successful) erasure and denial by a mainstream heterosexist view of past societies.[2]

Without family histories which include gay sexuality, lesbians have sought other forebears to justify their desires and aspirations as individuals.[3] Constructing lists of lesbians from the recent or ancient past – some elite, some infamous, some as role models – has been commonplace in twentieth-century gay writing.[4] In 1906 Edward Carpenter cited Queen Christine of Sweden and Sappho among the great leaders and artists of the 'intermediate sex'.[5] The attribution of lesbianism to disparate women from the past, often read against the grain, legitimates a stronger sense of personal and sexual identity in a heterosexual society which suppresses expressions of lesbian desire.

Naming lesbians in the past also creates a sense of a historical community, and another function of lesbian history is building a contemporary *group* identity, indicated in the titles of recent books such as *Not a Passing Phase* or *Inventing Ourselves*.[6] All kinds of groups may create bonds through their awareness of a common history – nations, ethnicities, groups based on political or class identities as well as on gender and sexuality.[7] Group identity validated (at least in part) by recourse to the past suggests continuities and similarities between past and present – a living past intimately connected with current identities. For lesbians, this process implies questions about the definition of sexual desires and communities. Who is included, and who not, as being like ourselves today?[8]

History-writing has political functions for any of its authors and subjects. For feminists, lesbians, black people and other oppositional groups in the last decades of the twentieth century it encouraged and informed contemporary political campaigns. Historical research was an important part of the early Women's Liberation Movement's activities, for example, revealing a tradition of powerful women and of feminist politics.[9] Early lesbian history not only named important lesbians from the past but also identified political networks powered by love between women, for example within the late nineteenth- and early twentieth-century women's movement.[10] This historiography aimed to bolster political consciousness and confidence, to challenge mainstream patriarchal, heterosexist discourses about the past and the present, and to analyse the causes of present-day inequality and discrimination.[11]

Writing lesbian history thus serves many purposes. As with other historiographies, it reflects the individuals, groups and time periods that produce it.[12]

> [T]he purpose of our continual engagement with history . . . is not to get at its essential underlying truth, but to use it to make sense of our own situation. As the present changes, the relationship between past and present changes also, and with it the meaning the past . . . has for us. The process of making and remaking the past is therefore not so much cognitive as creative: less about 'finding out', and more about attributing meanings.[13]

As lesbian culture and politics change, so do the meanings which are made from the past,[14] as this chapter will demonstrate using the Ladies of Llangollen as a case study.

Like the majority of 'famous lesbians' from the past, the Ladies' memory and the material legacy of their house and diaries has been preserved only because of their class status and contemporary importance. Nevertheless, for very many individual women, the story of the Ladies rapidly became an archetype of lesbian existence – the romantic ideal of the devoted female partnership that endures unto death. This has been appropriated by different generations of lesbian writers to fit their own conceptions of the perfect kind of passionate relationship between women. What these reinterpretations show is the complexity and variety of lesbian identity, and the lively debates between different understandings of it. One perennial issue has been the *kind* of love between women that the Ladies stood for. Was theirs a romantic friendship, a domestic partnership, or could their love be read as also including sexual desire and expression? Another important element for some writers has been the link between lesbianism and feminist politics, which has also been projected onto the Ladies in a number of ways.

I shall be discussing the contrasting use of history to construct lesbian identity by focusing on a number of published and unpublished representations of the Ladies of Llangollen in different historical periods. In their own lifetimes they quickly became the carriers of other women's dreams and desires, as the contrasting early nineteenth-century perspectives of the poet Anna Seward and the diarist Anne Lister illustrate. In the twentieth century the Ladies of Llangollen were celebrated as key figures in a specifically

British lesbian heritage and popular history. (Indeed, they were *mis*repres-ented as British despite their proudly reiterated Irish national identity which was gradually obliterated.) The first account to represent the Ladies as part of a historical tradition of love between women was the biography pub-lished by Mary Gordon, written from the perspective of suffrage femin-ism.[15] From the turn of the century the scientific categorisation of sexual practice by sexologists including Havelock Ellis made contemporaries in-creasingly aware of the possibility of sexual relationships between women, and in the inter-war years we see the Ladies referred to more explicitly as signifiers of lesbian sexuality. The final section of this chapter will show how these concerns about the importance of sexual desire and the relevance of feminist politics to lesbian identity were played out vigorously in 1980s' and 1990s' readings of the Ladies of Llangollen by lesbian historians.

The Ladies in their own lifetimes

After settling in Llangollen in 1780, Eleanor Butler and Sarah Ponsonby meticulously tried to carry out their ideal way of life of quiet retirement from the world: gardening, and self-improvement through books and journal-keeping. Since this was a fashionable ideal of the time, their lifestyle aroused much interest from their peers, they soon acquired a public profile, and, ironically, their 'sweet retirement' was increasingly broken by the many visitors they received from the late 1780s onwards. Those who celebrated their perfect friendship, charming cottage and garden and intelligent con-versation included the local gentry, their relatives passing on the road between London and Holyhead, where the ferry left for Ireland, poets and writers, royalty and statesmen; indeed almost everyone of note in their lifetimes. Among these visitors and correspondents they maintained a fairly close circle of women friends (several themselves noted diarists and writers), some of whom were particularly fascinated by their partnership.[16]

A few acquaintances ridiculed their pretensions, and there were some comments on their odd and masculine appearance, since from the 1790s both women wore cropped hair, beaver hats and old-fashioned riding habits.[17] The worst public smear came in 1790, when the *General Evening Post* published an article about them entitled 'Extraordinary Female Affection' which described them as having resisted marriage and as taking masculine and feminine roles in their household. It portrayed Eleanor Butler (in real-ity 51 years old, short and stout) as: 'tall and masculine, she wears always a riding habit, hangs her hat with the air of a sportsman in the hall, and appears in all respects as a young man, if we except the petticoats which she still retains'. The Ladies found this imputation of gender (and possibly also sexual) transgression intolerable and threatened to sue for libel. On the whole, though, their close and loving relationship was seen as perfectly proper and indeed commendable, and, since they were respectable aristocratic women, such an attack was easily brushed off.[18]

Even during their own lifetimes, the Butler–Ponsonby partnership was perceived in very different ways by other women who themselves loved women. One contemporary who wrote at length about the Ladies was the author and poet Anna Seward, who saw them as enviable role models for the life she longed to live, but could not. Anna Seward had an intense and passionate attachment to her friend Honora Sneyd, whom she had known and been close to since their girlhood. Unhappily for Anna, Honora married, and Anna wrote many angry and anguished poems about this betrayal. Anna Seward met the Ladies of Llangollen in 1795 and became part of their close circle of women friends. Lillian Faderman argues that she strongly identified with them – writing the equivalent of a whole volume of poetry about them praising their love – since they were able to do what she could not: live with their beloved partner. Indeed the Ladies exemplified the ultimate fantasy of romantic friendship, to set up home together, which few women had the means to live out in this period.[19] Anna Seward wrote enthusiastically to her other friends about the Ladies' Edenic domestic life and their devotion to each other. Llangollen Vale, she wrote in 1796, was consecrated three times, 'by valour, by love, and by friendship'.[20]

Further support for the proposition that the Ladies were important for lesbian identity in their own time can be found in Anne Lister's speculations in her journal for 1822. Anne Lister, an upwardly mobile member of the Yorkshire landed gentry, lived at Shibden Hall near Halifax, never married and had a series of sexual relationships with women which she wrote about frankly, though in code, in her extensive diaries, parts of which have now been published.[21] On a holiday tour with her aunt to Wales in 1822, the 31-year-old Anne made great efforts to secure an introduction to the Ladies, whom she had first read about in a magazine article some twelve years previously. At the start of the trip, Anne Lister met up briefly with her married lover Marianne, when she and her aunt stopped overnight in Chester. At this time Anne felt particularly pessimistic about ever realising her dream of living with Marianne. The two women had hoped that Marianne's elderly husband, and thus the marriage, would not last for more than a few years. On reaching Llangollen, Anne found that the very elderly Lady Eleanor Butler was ill and so she could not meet the Ladies, but she and her aunt were shown round the gardens of their house. She wrote that evening in her diary: 'My expectations were more than realised & it excited in me, for a variety of circumstances, a sort of peculiar interest tinged with melancholy. I could have mused for hours, dreampt dreams of happiness, conjured up many a vision of . . . hope.'[22]

On her return to Llangollen ten days later, Anne was invited to meet Sarah Ponsonby for an hour. After discussing her friend's continuing illness, and their reading of the classics, Sarah Ponsonby described how they had lived in Llangollen for 42 years. That evening Anne reflected: 'I envied their place & the happiness they had had there. Asked if, dared say, they had never quarrelled. "No!" They had never had a quarrel. Little differences of opinion sometimes. Life could not go on without it, but only about the planting of a tree, and, when they differed in opinion, they took care to let no one see it. At parting, shook hands with her and she gave me a rose. I said I should keep it for the sake of the place where it grew.'[23] The contrast between their happy achievement of a domestic marriage and the uncertain future she had with Marianne made Anne depressed.

A week after returning to Halifax, Anne Lister recorded in her diary part of a letter she had received from Marianne who had written: 'The account of your visit is the prettiest narrative I have read. You have at once excited & gratified my curiosity. Tell me if you think their regard has always been platonic & if you ever believed pure friendship could be so exalted. If you do, I shall think there are brighter amongst mortals than I ever believed there were.' Anne added, 'I cannot help thinking that surely it was not platonic. Heaven forgive me, but I look within myself & doubt. I feel the infirmity of our nature & hesitate to pronounce such attachments uncemented by something more tender still than friendship.'[24] Here we see Anne Lister and her lover speculating about whether the Ladies of Llangollen were like themselves, that is, did they have a relationship which was expressed sexually? Anna Clark has argued that Anne Lister sought to develop a sexual identity for herself using whatever ideas and models were available in her contemporary culture.[25] The Ladies had formed the kind of life partnership she dreamed of, but in contrast to Anna Seward she was keen to project her own desire for sexual expression as being part of their great love.

Mary Gordon: representing the Ladies as part of a lesbian history

The Ladies remained important as a public representation of love between women. After their deaths, their house was sold to another female couple who lived there in the 1830s and 1840s.[26] In the twentieth century a pioneer woman doctor, Mary Gordon, was the first writer to place the Ladies in a history and tradition of love between women. Although Mary Gordon's full-length biography, *Chase of the Wild Goose*, was published in 1936, its approach and sensibility belong in the late nineteenth century: the time of her own young womanhood. Gordon (1862–1941), who became the first woman inspector of prisons, trained as a doctor during the 'New Woman' era, and was a strong supporter of the suffrage cause. Her account of the Ladies of Llangollen reflects, I suggest, a turn-of-the-century feminist culture which valued female friendship, supported marriage refusal in favour of an economically independent life, and sought the emancipation of women.

Mary Gordon became interested in the Ladies in her 70s when, while studying with the psychoanalyst Carl Jung, she had a dream which led her to revisit Llangollen where she was inspired to write their biography. In the Foreword to her book, Gordon writes that she is recreating a true history from the facts: 'I have taken every pains to ground my tale on the things nearest to reality . . . .'[27] Like a good historian she discusses the reliability of her sources which included the journal kept by the Ladies, and letters and diaries of their friends and relatives, all recently published (in 1930) as *The Hamwood Papers*. As well as these conventional sources, she says she has also made use of 'the house and locality in which they lived so long, the colours with which they imbued their thinking, feeling and whole atmosphere . . .'.[28] What she actually does in the book is create a very personal interpretation of their lives, based partly on the historical facts, but which also includes a number of completely fictionalised events and conversations.

Mary Gordon's reframing of the Ladies in the context of her own identity is evident in her account of the first meeting between Eleanor Butler and the schoolgirl Sarah Ponsonby, where she introduces the key elements which define their relationship: intellectual companionship, marriage refusal, and the power of their love for each other. Eleanor Butler invites Sarah up to her sitting room in Kilkenny Castle for an informal supper, creating a scene reminiscent of the coffee parties enjoyed by late nineteenth-century women university students in their studies. There is a cosy fire, there are tables covered with books and papers, and comfortable armchairs. The two women quickly find a meeting of minds, common interests and sympathies. Their emotional interest in each other begins to be expressed during a conversation about marriage refusal, when Sarah asks Eleanor:

> 'Do you mean you intend not to marry? [. . .] I have never heard anyone say that before.' 'One doesn't say it, of course. [. . .] [I]t wouldn't suit me to marry. I must own my own life. I might want to do a great many things which marriage would prevent. One has to choose.' 'But . . . people may fall in love.' 'Well . . . yes . . . they may. I am realizing that they could.'[29]

But Mary Gordon was not entirely sure how to represent the women's relationship with each other. She stresses the depth of their love and the seriousness of their commitment. When negotiating with their families for their freedom to leave Ireland and live together, she has Eleanor use the words of the marriage ceremony. She emphasises that their feelings were mutual, quoting Sarah Ponsonby as saying '"I will live and die with Miss Butler"'.[30] While she suggests that one or two people in their circle believed their relationship was improper in its intensity and hinted at lesbianism,[31] she is particularly concerned to defend them against twentieth-century readings of homosexuality:

> She [Miss Goddard, a family friend] forgot that Miss Butler had a 'debauched mind' and defended her by maintaining the romantic friendship theory, which ruled out any involvement with male persons. What, in the eighteenth century, a romantic friendship was supposed to imply, that she helped their relations to uphold. And since no terrible scientific names were in existence to describe phenomena of the kind, the escapade remained romantic, to the entire peace of the subjects themselves.[32]

Mary Gordon wanted to protect the Ladies' reputation against later sexological redefinitions of them as lesbians. But she was also aware that they did not really fit very well into the model of romantic friendship, as she went on to note that a friendship 'pursued in this extreme manner', abandoning friends, family, luxury and social position for elopement, had no parallels in late eighteenth-century society.[33] Suffrage feminism gave Gordon no alternative interpretations to frame the Ladies as sexual subjects, but she still sought to emphasise their passion for each other.

In her book, Mary Gordon creates a strong connection between the Ladies and the present day, by portraying them as spiritual forerunners of later feminists and her own generation of loving women friends.[34] She does this in the final section of the book, entitled 'The Ladies Meet Me', in which she thoroughly reinvents the Ladies. Gordon describes how the Ladies appeared to her as ghosts, first on an early morning walk near Llangollen and then, by arrangement, the following night for an extended conversation at their old home.[35] In this way Mary Gordon herself enters the Ladies' story. Believing that Eleanor Butler and Sarah Ponsonby, like herself, are mainly interested in the changes in women's position since their lifetimes, she proceeds to dominate the conversation, discussing the difficulties of marriage resistance in the eighteenth century and telling them about women's increased freedoms since. She describes the rebellion of mid-nineteenth-century women, the suffrage movement and the achievement of women's political equality, recounting her own part in this. During her own lifetime, she has seen equality in divorce, married women's property rights and the use of birth control. Now recast as feminists, the Ladies respond with enthusiasm to this information. 'Lady Eleanor's large serious eyes rested on my face. She took her friend's hand and held it. "Miss Ponsonby and I are finding all you say incredibly good news." '[36]

Intertwined with this strand of the conversation are references to their precedent as a female couple. Gordon asserts that there is now an easier climate for single women and women couples: 'No one thinks it remarkable now if two friends prefer to live together. They do so all over the country. You two friends would be no exception nowadays.'[37] Gordon makes it absolutely clear that the Ladies were pioneers and role models for later women like herself who loved women:

> Is it nothing to have shown the world a perfect love . . . That was indeed doing your bit. Had you any idea how many women have been on a pilgrimage to this little old house of yours? Silently, saying nothing to anybody – but they came. [. . .] You made the way straight for the time that we inherited. You meditated among your books and dreamed us into existence. You handed on to us your passionate love of freedom plus honour.[38]

As the sun is about to rise, Mary Gordon takes her leave of the ghostly Ladies in a poignant and sentimental ending to the book:

> Sarah Ponsonby stepped up to me and looked at me with a deep solicitude. [. . .] 'And you . . .' she said. 'Have you no one . . . .' 'To call me Beloved . . . and go with me? No one. I thank you for your sweet concern. But one must not quarrel with one's own share of the price of our freedom. Good-bye.'[39]

In fact Mary Gordon had earlier in her life been involved in a close relationship with another woman whom she referred to as 'Frank'. It appears from her letters that this relationship broke down in 1922 when Mary Gordon had recently retired.[40] In so strongly identifying with the Ladies of Llangollen towards the end of her life, Mary Gordon was publicly asserting her feminist past and also establishing her own identity as a woman who loved women.[41]

Mary Gordon uses very powerful devices at the end of her biography to emphasise the significance of the Ladies' love. She takes seriously the dream which leads her to return to Llangollen, as if there was a fate or purpose leading her to connect with the Ladies, and applies a Jungian interpretation to the Ladies' role as spiritual forerunners of twentieth-century women lovers. The meetings with the ghostly Ladies ironically enable them to become live characters, not dead subjects. Terry Castle argues that lesbian sexual desire has haunted Western literature since the eighteenth century in the form of a ghostly presence. This desire has to be repressed by patriarchal culture because it threatens it so fundamentally, but even though disavowed, the phantom lesbian pops up all over the place.[42] The Ladies' ghosts signify lesbian desire, and their appearance legitimates Mary Gordon's vision of a historical tradition of love between women.

Lesbianism and the Ladies between the wars

In the inter-war years others shared Mary Gordon's uneasiness with the new sexual definitions of love between women put forward by sexologists and psychologists. The privately published journal *Urania* similarly looked back to a pre-First World War feminist politics while also developing a radical new theory proposing the abolition of sex and gender boundaries. It enthused about passions between women, however, and had a strong if veiled lesbian sub-text, printing articles on Sappho, *The Well of Loneliness* and women cross-dressers.[43] In 1937 it reprinted an *Observer* review of Mary Gordon's book which favourably described the love of the Ladies and quoted from their journal. 'The ultimate charm of the book, of course, is that it is a rhapsody in praise of friendship by one who understands how love endures.'[44]

Such a restrained perspective on love between women did not suit everyone, however. In the 1920s and 1930s, a strong sense of lesbian identity was developing among some women, and lesbian sub-cultures were beginning to develop in Britain, at least among metropolitan artists and writers. With this growing awareness of the possibilities of sex between women, the Ladies of Llangollen became more sexualised reference points. Virginia Woolf, when first seized by inspiration to write the book which later became *Orlando*, used the Ladies to signify lesbianism. On 14 March 1927 she wrote in her diary:

Suddenly between twelve & one I conceived a whole fantasy to be called 'The Jessamy Brides' – why, I wonder? I have rayed round it several scenes. Two women, poor, solitary at the top of a house. One can see anything (for this is all fantasy) the Tower Bridge, clouds, aeroplanes. [...] It is to be written as I write letters at the top of my speed: on the ladies of Llangollen; on Mrs Fladgate; on people passing. No attempt is to be made to realise the character. Sapphism is to be suggested. Satire is to be the main note – satire and wildness. The Ladies are to have Constantinople in view. Dreams of golden domes.[45]

Orlando, described as the 'longest and most charming love-letter in literature', was conceived, of course, after her love affair with Vita Sackville-West.[46] The main character, Orlando, based on Vita, moved through time, changed sex and fell in love with both men and women. Unfortunately the Ladies did not survive to the final version, but it is significant that in her first rush of ideas Woolf used them as a touchstone to suggest love between women.

The Ladies of Llangollen were also referred to – ironically or otherwise – by the novelist Sylvia Townsend Warner and her lover, the young poet Valentine Ackland, to mark the nature of their love. In March 1931, soon after the start of their relationship, Valentine gave Sylvia a toothpick box with a plait of blonde hair in the lid: 'we decided on no evidence that Sarah Ponsonby gave it to Eleanor Butler'.[47] On another occasion, Sylvia's mother gave her a small china pomade pot which had a picture of the Ladies of Llangollen on it. Sylvia wrote to Valentine: 'isn't it pleasing to think that the Ladies had so lasting a renown as to get on to memorial pomade pots? And what do you make of my mamma? Personally I am much pleased with her for this spirited and affable little dig in our ribs.'[48] These references to the Ladies of Llangollen in jokes and banter show how personal sexual identity – perhaps especially if it goes against the grain of social approval – can be validated by a sense of historical precedent.

These varied representations of the Ladies of Llangollen indicate the fluidity of the conceptualisation of lesbianism in the 1930s.[49] It was now a definite sexual identity for many, following the medical and scientific definitions established from the beginning of the century, but there also remained a more equivocal version of love between women that was less explicit about sexual feeling.

Writing lesbian history since the 1970s

As I suggested at the beginning of this chapter, lesbian history since the 1970s has been very concerned with issues of identity: of building a contemporary lesbian and feminist politics. Lesbian-feminist writers sought to widen definitions of lesbianism away from the purely sexual. Following Adrienne Rich (and other theorists) they aimed to highlight women's independence from men, bonding between women and feminist resistance to patriarchy, as well as sexual desire and sexual practice, in defining lesbianism. As a means of looking for a lesbian past this was particularly useful, since we usually only have snippets of evidence about the depth and nature of women's relationships with each other.[50]

We can see this establishment of a new concept of lesbianism, as a political as well as a sexual identity, in the pioneering work of Lillian Faderman, an American literary historian who wrote *Surpassing the Love of Men* in 1981. In her book, Faderman presented eighteenth- and nineteenth-century romantic friendship as the ideal model of lesbianism, and, for her, the Ladies of Llangollen were the most successful early example. Indeed, Faderman elided romantic friendship completely with 1970s lesbian-feminism. In the Introduction to her book she wrote:

> 'Lesbian' describes a relationship in which two women's strongest emotions and affections are directed toward each other. Sexual contact may be a part of the relationship to a greater or lesser degree, or it may be entirely absent. By preference the two women spend most of their time together and share most aspects of their lives with each other. 'Romantic friendship' described a similar relationship.[51]

Faderman stressed the power of romantic friendship as a love relationship and represented it as a natural passion which might develop from respect, admiration and shared interests.[52] Romantic friends kissed and even slept together, but it was not a sexual relationship, she says, and was rarely perceived as such. She argues that close relationships between women were not sexually defined until the beginning of the twentieth century following the work of Freud and the sexologists. Romantic friendship was condoned and respectable. Even when elopement occurred – as with the Ladies of Llangollen – this did not necessarily violate codes of respectable behaviour. Faderman quotes a family friend of Sarah Ponsonby, who said that Sarah's 'conduct, though it has an appearance of imprudence, is I am sure void of serious impropriety. There were no gentlemen concerned, nor does it appear to be anything more than a scheme of Romantic Friendship.'[53]

Faderman describes the loving words written in the Ladies' diary and the references to their sharing a bed, but argues that while this was a committed, devoted, loving relationship, it was probably not a sexual one: 'it is unlikely that as eighteenth-century women, educated in the ideal of female passionlessness, they would have sought genital expression if it were not to fulfill a marital duty'.[54] She further asserts that: 'Women dreamed not of erotic escapades but of a blissful life together. In such a life a woman would have choices, she would be in command of her own destiny . . . .'[55] While conflating the nature of passionate friendship with 1970s lesbian-feminism, Faderman does acknowledge that late twentieth-century lesbianism was more likely to be expressed sexually. But she goes on to assert – and this places her position firmly in the 1970s and early 1980s – that most contemporary lesbians do not see their lesbian identity as a *primarily* sexual phenomenon. She emphasises the similarities across the centuries: two women sharing their lives, trusting each other, always there for each other, creating a powerful emotional tension and bond, i.e. a relationship of intense romantic love.[56]

In the mid-1980s, however, there was a paradigm shift in lesbian theory and lesbian history: a movement away from emphasising the political nature of lesbianism, and back to celebrating the sexual.[57] On the face of it, the Ladies of Llangollen did not fit easily into this kind of history. However, the publication, in the late 1980s, of Anne Lister's diaries was of timely assistance to early nineteenth-century lesbian history. The decoded passages demonstrated that despite the outward show of romantic female friendship, she did indeed have full sexual relationships with her women lovers. In their representations of both Anne Lister and the Ladies of Llangollen, we can see that lesbian historians were searching for continuities, and finding women who 'felt like us'. But the nature of that cross-century identification changed. For Faderman, it was the romantic friendship couple she found in the Ladies. For slightly later historians it was the explicit lusts, intrigues and messy relationships of Anne Lister.

This did not, however, mean the eclipse of the Ladies as important for lesbian history. Even the respectable Ladies could be recouped for a more sexualised lesbian narrative in the 1990s, and they are certainly important for progressing historical debates about lesbianism. Marjorie Garber's book *Vested Interests* (1992) reflected a growing interest in the 1990s in issues of transgender and cross-dressing as part of 'queer' politics and academic debate. In a rather astonishing reading of the evidence, Garber describes Eleanor Butler and Sarah Ponsonby as 'the two cross-dressing Ladies of Llangollen' and quotes the 1790 *General Evening Post* story about them (and other caricatures) as straight reportage (see above).[58] She uses the Ladies as an example of cross-dressing female marriage to support her argument about gay appropriation of heterosexual models: 'their dress and appearance, while in some sense "male", were also sufficiently "singular" to make them legible as "keeping the middle", as identifiable cross-dressers rather than women passing for men'.[59] Concentrating on only part of the evidence, Garber thus reappropriates the Ladies as radical queer transvestites.

Back in mainstream lesbian history it was Emma Donoghue who really challenged Faderman's asexual reading of romantic friendship and the Ladies of Llangollen. As the title suggests, in *Passions Between Women: British Lesbian Culture 1668–1801* (1993) Donoghue was concerned to reinstate sexual passion in eighteenth-century lesbian history. Her general argument is that in a wide range of texts from this period – medical literature, pornography, novels, ballads, court cases – there can be found a knowledge, language and culture of sex between women. The notion of romantic friendship as lifelong emotional partnership is often considered to be in opposition to or incompatible with lesbian love, by Faderman and others she notes. But, Donoghue argues, many romantic friends might have shared sex, and she reminds us of the historical specificity of what constitutes 'sex'. Romantic friendship was seen as sexless because it had nothing to do with men – the sexual gender. But in reality passion between women might well have included physical caresses which today we would certainly term 'sex', yet could be seen at the time as chaste.[60] She uses the newspaper attack on the Ladies in 1790 as evidence not about the nature of their actual relationship, but to show that the idea of sex between women did have currency in eighteenth-century England, especially when certain factors were found in combination: romantic friendship, rejection of marriage and masculinity in women either in dress or role.[61] Donoghue also cites Liz Stanley's work in uncovering previously unknown letters by Mrs Hester Thrale Piozzi, a contemporary diarist who knew the Ladies well and who privately wrote of them as 'damned Sapphists', claiming that women were reluctant to spend the night in their cottage unless accompanied by men. In this period romantic friendship could thus at the same time be idealised and acceptable *and* sometimes associated with unnatural sexuality.[62] This discussion, then, opens up more complex debates, not simply about the sexual practice of the Ladies, but about the extent to which their contemporaries saw close female friendships as acceptable, and about the historical moments at which cultural evidence of what we would now call 'lesbian identity' can be located.[63]

Conclusion

The historical 'myths we live by' illustrate the importance of the past for our present-day concerns. This chapter has discussed the changing ways in which the Ladies of Llangollen have been represented by various lesbian writers over the 200 years since their lifetime. These depictions include Anne Lister's 1820s' speculation on whether their partnership was a sexual one, Anna Seward's contemporary aspiration to coupledom, the rewriting of them as feminist New Women by Mary Gordon, and their enlistment in the 'lesbian sex wars' of the 1980s. These representations demonstrate the shifting elements of what was felt to be important for lesbian identity for different generations of women who loved women, in different historical periods, and for varied groups and individuals. In particular, histories of the Ladies highlight the stress laid on sexual desire and expression (or not) as part of lesbianism and the relationship (or lack of it) with feminism. Lesbian historians may sometimes appear to be creating myths based on their own politics, prejudices and experiences. But in the process they are combating the heterosexual bias of history-writing, widening the variety of ways in which we can conceptualise lesbianism in history, opening up important historical questions and debates, and composing a multifaceted picture of lesbian lives in the past.

Further reading

L. Bland and L. Doan, eds, *Sexology in Culture: Labelling Bodies and Desires* (Polity Press, Cambridge, 1998).

E. Donoghue, *Passions Between Women: British Lesbian Culture 1668–1801* (Scarlet Press, 1993).

M. Duberman, M. Vicinus and G. Chauncey, eds, *Hidden From History: Reclaiming the Gay and Lesbian Past* (Penguin, 1991).

L. Faderman, *Surpassing the Love of Men: Romantic Friendship and Love between Women from the Renaissance to the Present* (Women's Press, 1985).

Hall Carpenter Archives Lesbian Oral History Group, *Inventing Ourselves: Lesbian Life Stories* (Routledge, 1989).

E. Hamer, *Britannia's Glory: A History of Twentieth Century Lesbians* (Cassell, 1996).

Lesbian History Group, *Not a Passing Phase: Reclaiming Lesbians in History 1840–1985* (Women's Press, 1993).

A. Oram and A. Turnbull, *The Lesbian History Sourcebook: Love and Sex between Women in Britain 1780–1970* (Routledge, 2001).

Notes

My warm thanks go to Barbara Brookes, Laura Gowing and Sarah Waters for their generous contributions to this chapter from their own research findings. I am also very grateful to Clare Midgley and the editors for their helpful comments.

1. E. Mavor, *The Ladies of Llangollen: A Study in Romantic Friendship* (Michael Joseph, 1971).

2. 'Introduction', in Lesbian History Group, *Not a Passing Phase: Reclaiming Lesbians in History 1840–1985* (Women's Press, 1993), pp. 1–4. Conventional biography has been censured by lesbians for representing women's lives and relationships only within a heterosexual model. Elizabeth Mavor's 1971 biography of

the Ladies continued this tradition in refusing to link them to present-day lesbianism, though in other respects it is a scholarly and useful source. Mavor, *Ladies of Llangollen*, pp. 10–11.

3. See D. Lowenthal, *The Past is a Foreign Country* (Cambridge University Press, 1985), pp. 41–4 for discussion of the importance of a personal sense of history.

4. L. Gowing, 'History', in A. Medhurst and S. Munt, eds, *Lesbian and Gay Studies: A Critical Introduction* (Cassell, 1997), p. 63; S. Waters, 'Out and about: lesbian and gay historical fiction', *History Workshop Journal* 47 (Spring 1999). See, for example, R. Collis, *Portraits to the Wall: Historic Lesbian Lives Unveiled* (Cassell, 1994).

5. E. Carpenter, *Love's Coming-of-Age* (Methuen, 1906), p. 134.

6. Lesbian History Group, *Not a Passing Phase*; Hall Carpenter Archives Lesbian Oral History Group, *Inventing Ourselves: Lesbian Life Stories* (Routledge, 1989).

7. J. Tosh, *The Pursuit of History* (Longman, 1993), p. 3; Lowenthal, *The Past is a Foreign Country*, pp. 44, 57, 61–2, 213; Lesbian History Group, *Not a Passing Phase*, 'Introduction'; M. Grever, 'The pantheon of feminist culture: women's movements and the organisation of memory', *Gender and History* 9/2 (1997).

8. Gowing, 'History'; A. Oram, ' "Friends", feminists and sexual outlaws: lesbianism and British history', in G. Griffin and S. Andermahr, eds, *Straight Studies Modified: Lesbian Interventions in the Academy* (Cassell, 1997).

9. D. Beddoe, *Discovering Women's History: A Practical Manual* (Pandora Press, 1983), 'Introduction' and pp. 1–16.

10. L. Faderman, *Surpassing the Love of Men: Romantic Friendship and Love between Women from the Renaissance to the Present* (Junction Books, 1981); Lesbian History Group, *Not a Passing Phase*; M. Vicinus, *Independent Women: Work and Community for Single Women 1850–1920* (Virago, 1985).

11. Lesbian History Group, *Not a Passing Phase*, 'Introduction'.

12. Tosh, *Pursuit of History*, Chapter 7.

13. J. Baxendale and C. Pawling, *Narrating the Thirties. A Decade in the Making: 1930 to the Present* (Macmillan, 1996), p. 6.

14. See Oram, ' "Friends", feminists and sexual outlaws'.

15. M. Gordon, *Chase of the Wild Goose: The Story of Lady Eleanor Butler and Miss Sarah Ponsonby, known as the Ladies of Llangollen* (Hogarth Press, 1936).

16. Mavor, *The Ladies of Llangollen*, *passim*, esp. Chapters 8 and 9.

17. Ibid., pp. 177, 194–6.

18. Ibid., pp. 81–5.

19. Faderman, *Surpassing the Love of Men*, pp. 121–2, 132–8. Mavor puts less stress on Seward's envy of the Ladies and describes her romantic obsession with a clergyman as well as with other women friends apart from Sneyd. Mavor, *The Ladies of Llangollen*, pp. 95–7, 126–7.

20. Faderman, *Surpassing the Love of Men*, p. 137.

21. H. Whitbread, ed., *I Know My Own Heart: The Diaries of Anne Lister (1791–1840)* (Virago, 1988); H. Whitbread, ed., *No Priest But Love: The Journals of Anne Lister from 1824–1826* (Smith Settle, Otley, 1992); J. Liddington, ed., *Female Fortune: Land, Gender and Authority. The Anne Lister Diaries and Other Writings, 1833–36* (Rivers Oram, 1998). Jill Liddington has illustrated the gradual 'outing' of Anne Lister, analysing the changing versions of her life presented by successive local historians, in *Presenting the Past: Anne Lister of Halifax 1791–1840* (Pennine Pens, Hebden Bridge, 1994).

22. Whitbread, ed., *I Know My Own Heart*, p. 196 (14 July 1922). Eleanor Butler was 83 years old in 1822, Sarah Ponsonby 67.

23. Ibid., p. 204 (23 July 1822).

24. Ibid., p. 210 (3 August 1822).

25. A. Clark, 'Anne Lister's construction of lesbian identity', *Journal of the History of Sexuality* 7/1 (1996).

26. Mavor, *The Ladies of Llangollen*, pp. 203–4.

27. Gordon, *Chase of the Wild Goose*, p. 11.

28. Ibid., pp. 12–13. As well as *The Hamwood Papers*, however, Gordon also made use of a highly embellished and dramatised version of the Ladies' story published by Charles Penruddock in 1897. Mavor, *The Ladies of Llangollen*, pp. 201–2.

29. Gordon, *Chase of the Wild Goose*, p. 35. The issue of marriage refusal here evokes the position of some suffrage feminists including Christabel Pankhurst and Cicely Hamilton.

30. Gordon, *Chase of the Wild Goose*, p. 135, and see p. 127.

31. Ibid., pp. 121–2.

32. Ibid., pp. 136–7.

33. Ibid., p. 137.

34. At several points in her book Mary Gordon echoes a perspective developed by other contemporary Jungian feminist writers by representing the Ladies as spiritual forerunners of the higher development of womanhood, symbolised by single women in particular. See M. E. Harding, *The Way of All Women* (Longman, 1933); A. Oram, 'Repressed and thwarted or bearer of the new world? The spinster in inter-war feminist discourses', *Women's History Review* 1/3 (1992).

35. Gordon, *Chase of the Wild Goose*, pp. 243–71.

36. Ibid., p. 267.

37. Ibid., p. 266.

38. Ibid., pp. 269–70.

39. Ibid., pp. 270–1.

40. I am very grateful to Barbara Brookes for sharing with me her research on Agnes Bennett, a New Zealand woman doctor who was a friend of Mary Gordon. In her letters to Agnes Bennett Mary Gordon referred to her studies with Jung and to the problems in her relationship with Frank. Letters from Mary Gordon to Agnes Bennett, 11 December 1920, 5 December 1922, in Agnes Bennett Papers, MS 1346:179, Alexander Turnbull Library, New Zealand.

41. Gordon used the profits from her book to commission a plaque depicting the two Ladies for Llangollen church and reputedly had the Eleanor Butler figure made in her own likeness. Mavor, *The Ladies of Llangollen*, p. 206. Gordon's biography of the Ladies has also been discussed by Deborah Turton, who argues that the book functions partly as her own autobiography. D. Turton, '"That enchanting unique": representations of Plas Newydd and the Ladies of Llangollen', unpublished paper.

42. T. Castle, *The Apparitional Lesbian: Female Homosexuality and Modern Culture* (Columbia University Press, New York, 1993).

43. See A. Oram, '"Sex is an accident": feminism, science and the radical sexual theory of *Urania*, 1915–40', in L. Bland and L. Doan, eds, *Sexology in Culture: Labelling Bodies and Desires* (Polity Press, Cambridge, 1998).

44. Review by Basil de Selincourt in *The Observer*, quoted in *Urania* 121 and 122 (Jan–April 1937), p. 3.

45. A. O. Bell, ed., *The Diary of Virginia Woolf. Volume III: 1925–1930* (Hogarth Press, 1980), p. 131. My thanks to Sarah Waters for alerting me to this reference to the Ladies.

46. S. Raitt, *Vita and Virginia: The Work and Friendship of V. Sackville-West and Virginia Woolf* (Clarendon Press, Oxford, 1993), p. 18 and Chapter 1.

47. S. Pinney, ed., *I'll Stand By You: Selected Letters of Sylvia Townsend Warner and Valentine Ackland* (Pimlico, London, 1998), p. 62 n. (27 March 1931). I am very grateful to Laura Gowing for these references.

48. Ibid., p. 106 (19 September 1932).

49. The French writer Colette also published her version of the Ladies' story, as part of her exploration of women's erotic and emotional life, in *Ces Plaisirs* (Paris, 1932). Since it was not published in English until 1968 (as *The Pure and the Impure*), it is not considered here as being part of British lesbian historiography.

LIVERPOOL JOHN MOORES UNIVERSITY
LEARNING SERVICES

50. S. Jeffreys, 'Does it matter if they did it?', in Lesbian History Group, *Not a Passing Phase*.

51. Faderman, *Surpassing the Love of Men*, p. 18.

52. Ibid., pp. 84–5.

53. Ibid., p. 75.

54. Ibid., p. 123.

55. Ibid., p. 117.

56. Ibid., p. 142.

57. Exemplified by J. Nestle, *A Restricted Country* (Sheba, 1987); M. Vicinus, ' "They wonder to which sex I belong": the historical roots of the modern lesbian identity', in D. Altman et al., eds, *Homosexuality, Which Homosexuality?* (Gay Men's Press, 1989); Oram, ' "Friends", feminists and sexual outlaws'.

58. M. Garber, *Vested Interests: Cross-Dressing and Cultural Anxiety* (Routledge, 1992), p. 139 for quote; also see pp. 143–5.

59. Ibid., p. 145.

60. E. Donoghue, *Passions Between Women: British Lesbian Culture 1668–1801* (Scarlet Press, 1993), pp. 109–11.

61. Ibid., pp. 11, 107–8.

62. Ibid., pp. 143, 149–50; Liz Stanley, 'Romantic friendship? Some issues in researching lesbian history and biography', *Women's History Review* 1/2 (1992), pp. 196–7.

63. For debates about the emergence of a modern lesbian identity which cite the Ladies of Llangollen see, as well as Faderman and Donoghue already discussed, T. Hitchcock, *English Sexualities, 1700–1800* (Macmillan, 1997), Chapter 6; R. Trumbach, 'London's sapphists: from three sexes to four genders in the making of modern culture', in J. Epstein and K. Straub, eds, *Body Guards: The Cultural Politics of Gender Ambiguity* (Routledge, 1991); Vicinus, ' "They wonder to which sex I belong" '.

LIVERPOOL
JOHN MOORES UNIVERSITY
AVRIL ROBARTS LRC
TITHEBARN STREET
LIVERPOOL L2 2ER
TEL. 0151 231 4022

CHAPTER THREE

'A little, decent-looking woman': violence against nineteenth-century working women and the social history of crime

SHANI D'CRUZE

Feminist scholarship, interdisciplinarity and the question of violence

In 1891, 21-year-old Isabella Fitton told the Middleton, Lancashire, petty sessions that her illegitimate child had been fathered by Robert Woodcock (aged 16). She claimed that he had 'connection with me three times. I did not want him to do [*sic*], he got me on the floor in the kitchen . . .'.[1] From my broader study of Middleton I know that this hearing would have taken place in a purpose-built courtroom adjoining the police station and that witnesses entered the court in turn and retired when their evidence had been given. Consequently Isabella's supporting witnesses, her family and neighbours were probably not in the room itself but waiting outside. Her initial statement to the court opened:

> '. . . Bob Woodcock is the father of my child – He took me on the floor – on a Thursday afternoon – child born 6th January on Tuesday morning – I never told Marshall – did not tell Sam anything . . . I did not tell Mrs Marshall that Sam Williams was the father – did not tell her that Williams had put me on Betty's bed on Sunday afternoon – never said the child was Sam Williams' – she's telling lies – I never knew Woodcock a long long time – I have gone with him – Woodcock has touched me and spoken to me – Yes he has – No one told me to tell this tale – no one said I was to say this – he came Wednesday and Thursday in summer time. I know what a month is – it was the 6th January – Tuesday morning – He sent Lizzie Woodcock out – three times – He knows his [*sic*] done it – He always did it – when he was looking after me – Thursday afternoon – I don't understand you.'

The sense of historical realism encapsulated in these brief and frag-mented sentences is at first sight compelling. Isabella seems on the defensive and vulnerable. She faced questions which sought to represent her as sexu-ally promiscuous and thus not respectable. She claimed that the sex was unwanted – something that had been done *to* her, against her will. This is not, of course, evidence that was strictly called for since this was a hearing to establish paternity, not a criminal trial for rape or indecent assault. She countered allegations that another man was the father, but did this by invoking another representation of sex as something imposed upon a woman (*putting her* on a bed). (Sam Williams, incidentally, said that he was not the father as he had been impotent since rupturing himself in 1877.) Other people had told lies about her. The testimony seeks to represent her as the victim of importunate male sexuality. This is but one of very many com-parable accounts buried in the records of nineteenth-century courts from working women, called upon to stand up in a public, male-dominated courtroom and narrate details of violence or unwanted sex. A key purpose of this chapter is to consider exactly what kinds of meanings a feminist historian can draw from such accounts.

Feminist work in both history and other disciplines has repeatedly demon-strated that violence by men against women is but one of a composite of strategies by which power relations by gender are worked out, not in isola-tion, but as part of a nexus of power relations by age, class and race as well as gender. It is a necessary part of feminist academic practice that violence against women (while obviously a serious topic in itself) should not be read in isolation from other uses of violence against subordinated groups and individuals in past and present societies.[2] One of the achievements of fem-inist scholarship is to have inserted the question of interpersonal violence onto the research agendas of a number of academic disciplines including sociology, criminology and history. The recent work that underpins this understanding has in general taken its inspiration from second wave fem-inist writings of the 1960s and 1970s. Susan Brownmiller's *Against Our Will*, while by no means the only work that addressed the question of sexual violence, was important in establishing rape as a strategy of patriarchy – as an issue of power rather than only of sex.[3] Brownmiller's radical feminist stance tended to produce a trans-historical (effectively de-historicised) account of sexual violence. Nevertheless her consideration of sexual violence as a strategy of warfare in institutional and social settings and as a metaphor in literary and cultural representations of masculinity and femininity clearly demonstrated that sexual violence should not be theorised as a private matter but seen as essentially political.

Feminist work on domestic violence likewise highlighted abusive behaviour against women, which was normatively rendered invisible by the notion of domestic privacy. Of course, second wave feminists were not the first to do this. Domestic violence was an area of activism for the nineteenth-century women's movement. Frances Power Cobbe's campaign against 'wife torture' took a very middle-class view of working-class domestic violence.[4] Nevertheless the work of Cobbe and other feminists very publicly called abusive men to account for their domestic conduct and achieved real legislative changes that were seized upon by very many working-class women seeking a separation from violent husbands. Feminist scholarship has repeatedly demonstrated how institutions whose notional duty it is to protect the individual and to discipline the perpetrators of violence actually condone or even become party to such violence through their own attitudes and practices.[5] For the feminist historian, such tendencies have theoretical and methodological implications in the location of and the interpretation of sources. These are issues that I will develop below through further consideration of the representation of Isabella Fitton and other working women who encountered the courts in the nineteenth century.

To account for women's historical subjection to male violence and their poor treatment at the hands of the police and judiciary by the workings of patriarchy should not constitute a view of patriarchy as an ahistorical conspiracy. Nor should gender analysis lead to explanations based on crude phallocentrism, though it certainly is possible to cite instances where men and male institutions used women's reasonable fears to endorse their power over both specific women and women as a group.[6] Neither should feminist interpretations represent women as (blameworthy) victims. Feminists working in criminology and in particular in victimology are dealing with political and theoretical problems associated with this contemporary tendency.[7] Feminist historians also face evidence that much nineteenth-century domestic violence (for example) was tolerated under the rubric of 'legitimate punishment', even by the women who were subjected to it. Furthermore, those same women may well also have used physical violence as 'legitimate punishment' of their own children. Feminist analysis should not try to circumvent the historical evidence of women's own violence and cruelty, nor indeed to try to explain it away as some kind of false consciousness. What is required is an appreciation of the historical meanings of both men's and women's violence, both in terms of social relations and of the ways that violence was constituted in (for example) legal, journalistic and colloquial discourses.

Feminism offers multiple theorisations of violence against women. In my own research I have found some of the feminist appropriations of poststructuralism the most useful.[8] The work of post-structuralists, particularly Foucault, has been rightly criticised for its lack of attention to gender, and some feminist academics vehemently dispute its relevance in feminist analysis.[9] Taking due note of these reservations, however, I do find myself on the more optimistic side of the argument. Particularly in its later formulations, Foucault's view of 'shifting, fracturing, unstable power relations'[10] can help interpret a good deal of the material I have used. I have been encouraged to pay attention to the textuality and intertextuality of these sources. The sense of immediacy in Isabella Fitton's evidence was in no small part brought about by the circumstances through which it was generated. The clerk of the court was writing down Isabella's answers to questions posed probably by a solicitor but also possibly by the magistrates and even occasionally by the defendant. The silent questions are represented in this text by dashes. The account is therefore by no means a free one. It is one that can be read sympathetically by a modern feminist historian. However, it might well have been read by the magistrates, the public gallery or by the readership of the local newspaper that reported court proceedings as illustrating deviant and promiscuous working-class female sexuality. Likewise, notions of surveillance, of the way that bodies and the spaces between bodies are both an expression of and a mechanism of disciplinary power, have helped me understand the 'theatre' of the nineteenth-century courtroom. The dashes constrained and structured Isabella's responses in the text as the formal space of the courtroom did her body and voice. On the other hand, those same dashes opened up the spaces that her words filled as the courtroom specified the position where she stood and from which she could speak.

The idea of power/knowledge as differentially constituted in multiple discourses offers ways into reading documentary sources, though (as Cain argues) feminist analysis must refuse to subsume all social relationships under those that are discursively constituted.[11] Indeed, in my own research I have coined the notion of 'puzzlement' to express the difficulties that women and men encountered in describing kinds of violence and abuse which prevailing ideologies found it difficult to name. This addresses the same basic problem.[12] Cain cites Liz Kelly's work on sexual violence which found that all interview respondents, including those who had not originally declared themselves to have experienced sexual violence, had in some measure experienced 'pressurised sex' and recognised it only when the process of research enabled them to name it.[13] It might be that 'pressurised sex' was what Isabella Fitton was attempting to describe in 1891, although for her, the need to convince the court and gain weekly maintenance made her search for language to name her experience. I fully subscribe to the approach that invites us as researchers to understand difference, to reject naturalism, fundamentalism and biological determinism and to view proximate bodily experiences as historically situated. Nevertheless, a feminist politics still requires us to acknowledge and deplore such hurt and harm.[14]

And I think that the historical record amply demonstrates that Victorian working women were clear that certain kinds of violence, at least, were intolerable, unjust and amounted indeed to 'crimes of outrage'.[15] Furthermore, the representations of working women in the records of nineteenth-century courts and in the press reports of their proceedings could recognise these women's arguments, even though they did so in unstable and contingent ways. Isabella Fitton was awarded 2s. 6d. a week maintenance for her baby.

The social history of crime

The historical investigation of interpersonal violence has generally been undertaken as part of the social history of crime, which over the last 30 years has radically revised older institutional histories. While meticulous in detail, these gave a progressivist account of the enlightened development of the law and police, particularly since the eighteenth century.[16] The approaches taken by historians from the 1960s were part of a broader 'new' social history, which came to be known as 'history from below' and was generally underpinned by theorisations of class, particularly Marxist or socialist ones.[17] My own approaches owe a clear debt to undergraduate training in this kind of social history which is still widely practised although in the twenty-first century the theorisation of culture, of gender and of race come to contribute other, overlapping frames of analysis.

Particularly in the 1960s, 1970s and 1980s, social historians sought to write a history of the lower classes rather than the better documented elites and viewed the political and economic through the lens of the social. Interpretation was aided by insights borrowed from notions of culture (particularly popular culture), ritual and symbolism drawn from social anthropology.[18] This was to be a history of social movements and of the working classes in political action, hence the history of social protest featured alongside labour history among social history's priorities. Much important work, concerned with the historical significance of the 'poor bloody infantry of the industrial revolution',[19] addressed the period before the mid-nineteenth century. Particularly under the inspiration of E. P. Thompson, crime and disorder were understood as socio-cultural phenomena. The notion of 'social crime' explained (for example) smuggling or poaching as protest against perceived incursions against property rights. Thompson's notion of the 'moral economy' interpreted riot and other kinds of disorder as social protest.[20] Without ignoring work that, for example, demonstrated women's active participation in food and market riots, or the importance of the feminine among the symbolic language of protest,[21] women's agency was often subsumed under the notion of 'community' with very little analysis of how this term, too, was gendered.[22]

Further, if violence was predominantly represented as class struggle, it was located in the public arena: of class, work, politics, or indeed of 'community'. This was not the public of the high political histories. The new social history in many ways reconstituted the notion of the public as an historicised space for working-class political and economic activity. However, in so doing it implied a 'private' which remained very much equivalent to nineteenth-century bourgeois ideologies of separate spheres. Thus, family or everyday violence remained largely ahistoricised. There was little perception of the power relations underpinning violence in what was generally thought of as 'the private'. No wonder, perhaps, since the legal systems that generated many of the historical sources actively concealed the violence of middle- and upper-class men.[23] Consequently the perpetrators of documented violence were usually the working men whom the new social history sought to rescue 'from the enormous condescension of posterity'.[24] It was second wave feminist historians such as Nancy Tomes, Ellen Ross or Anna Clark, recuperating the history of the first wave, who disclosed and theorised this kind of interpersonal violence.[25] This work has influenced research agendas in the history of crime, where an increasing amount of recent work considers interpersonal violence and does include an awareness of gender in its approaches.[26]

Between the medieval and the modern periods recorded violent crime as indexed by homicide seems to have declined.[27] The later Victorian period was thought of as seeing the broad capitulation of working people to the logic of industrial capitalism. Hence crime and violence became more to do with deviance than with incipient revolution. From the mid-nineteenth until the mid-twentieth century, offences against the person declined overall, though drunkenness and assaults increased as against property crime in more prosperous periods.[28] For some historians a narrative of progressive 'civilisation' could account for these apparent trends. However, the abilities of these statistical series actively to reflect the historical incidence of crime and violence are now being more rigorously interrogated.[29] Reported domestic violence declined at the end of the nineteenth century. However, changes in the powers of police courts, enabling them to grant marital separation, helped limit recorded prosecutions for assault. The Matrimonial Causes Act of 1878 and the Summary Jurisdiction (Married Women) Act of 1895 led to the bench arbitrating over many unsatisfactory working-class marriages,[30] and until the inter-war period police courts still dealt with a good deal of domestic violence.[31]

A more thorough and nuanced understanding of the processes and practices of the police and courts shows that repeated discriminations according to judgements about the social and moral character of the protagonists shaped charges, verdicts and penalties.[32] These kinds of reservations have particular resonance for the history of physical and sexual violence against women. Let us take as an example the history of sexual violence. Feminist historians have demonstrated that cases of sexual violence were decided as much by judgements about the sexual chastity of the woman as about the violent conduct of her attacker.[33] Both the fact of a sexual assault and the requirement to speak of it in open court potentially compromised a woman's reputation and thus her plausibility as a witness. Under-reporting of sexual violence in the criminal statistics is often noted by historians of crime, but not effectively accounted for. Emsley and Philips are among those who suggest that 'embarrassment' might have deterred an attacked woman from pursuing a case. I do not mean to imply a deliberate intention to trivialise these offences – in most cases at least. However, it seems that 'embarrassment' is called upon to serve in the place of a developed analysis of gender relations. Which it doesn't.[34]

By the 1860s key legislation had altered the face of local justice and policing. The County Police Act of 1856 followed a few years after the adoption of magistrates' summary jurisdiction over lesser crimes and the regularisation of petty sessions through the Summary Jurisdiction Acts (1847– 51), the Indictable Offences Act (1848) and the Petty Sessions Act (1849). By that period magistrates had acquired jurisdiction over much interpersonal violence (short of felonies) and domestic life.[35] English magistrates' courts were the 'point of entry' into the legal system for much interpersonal violence and can be demonstrated to have minimised and effectively hidden much sexual and physical violence against women by reclassification or acquittal. In general there seems to have been an attitude shared by both courts and perpetrators that violence (sexual or physical) which was not 'excessive' and did not target the weak or innocent was not a particularly grave offence.[36] Recent social histories of crime also suggest both ruling-class confidence in social stability and, by the later nineteenth century, a broad social acquiescence in the rule of law tempered by selectivity in the use of the courts and the police by working people.[37] Working-class women used these courts tactically – to frighten a violent husband, to gain a separation or maintenance. Most importantly, they used the forum offered by the court to re-establish their respectability before the law and before their friends and neighbours, which the experience of violence had potentially compromised.[38]

Sources and representation

The register

Courts generated two main kinds of surviving records. An abundance of tabulated registers listed the names of the people involved, the nature of the offence, the outcome of a court hearing, the nature of the punishment. Though their survival is very partial, large numbers of such bound volumes are currently gathering dust in county record offices without being disturbed overmuch by historians.[39] Their uneven survival and the sheer volume of the material that would have to be processed to get any kind of meaningful answers to research questions – questions which anyway would remain remote from the lived experience of interpersonal violence – make them difficult sources to work with. These difficulties meant that I too decided early in my research to abandon any systematic exploration of court registers. However, revisiting my notes in preparation for writing this essay with questions about representations at the forefront of my mind, I was confronted again by the significance of these texts. If the legal and policing institutions were highly discriminating in their decisions and categorisations of violence depending on social judgements about respectability and status, registers were the discursive site where such contingencies were reified and thus mystified. It became very clear that these texts were actively engaged in representing the individuals they listed through processes of examination and subsequent 'normalising judgement'. Each individual listed – those who had experienced *and* perpetrated violence or had engaged in certain kinds of transgressive sexual activity – was constituted in the register as a 'case'. The register's purpose was one of naming and defining 'the individual as he [*sic*] may be described, judged, measured, compared with others, in his very individuality; and it is also the individual who has to be trained or corrected, classified, normalized, excluded etc.'.[40]

In one sense, of course, the women who had experienced violence or who were in court because they had an illegitimate child were normalised in these documents as victim or as deviant. However, the registers do not have a column labelled 'victim'. These women were named by the legal process and recorded in the registers as the 'complainant'. They had a grievance. They were there to complain about it: this is not a passive status. The productive effect of the disciplinary power which enmeshed them named them as active participants. As Jennifer Davis points out, a good many cases of violence that came before the magistrates' courts appeared due to a summons taken out by the complainant. A summons cost 2s. – a significant but not impossible charge on a working-class domestic budget. Police prosecutions depended on a police officer having witnessed the violence or the injuries caused. Even in this latter case, there remained a role in fetching the policemen, and sources describe women doing so.[41] Consequently even such bald and bureaucratic sources actively produced representations of working women subjected to violence that were certainly patriarchal but which nevertheless potentially acknowledged these women's grievances.

Minutes

Magistrates' courts also produced minute books, such as the one in which Isabella Fitton's testimony was recorded. Although some survive from rather earlier, these have their statutory origin in an 1848 requirement that witnesses' responses to questions in court should be recorded. Minute books are handwritten accounts of witnesses' evidence, written down as it was delivered in court. Despite their limitations, the minutes provide pretty direct access to the voices of working-class women at a time before the reach of oral history and for which we have very, very few working women's autobiographies or other writings. Where minutes record a case fully they provide competing representations of women in court.

The initial impression of Isabella Fitton as an isolated voice is substantially modified by the several pages of cramped writing which follow her statement in the Middleton minutes as other witnesses had their say.[42] Principal among these was Ellen Mooney, a neighbour and married woman. Ellen Mooney provided the main corroborating evidence for Isabella's story, and it is largely through her observations and actions that the case came to court. To this extent Ellen Mooney was acting as a female advocate for Isabella: the role of many women witnesses in court records. Ellen's testimony gives a very assertive self-representation of an individual who was autonomous yet well rooted in her local social networks. She was a respectable married woman and a good (if nosy) neighbour. Ellen had repeatedly observed Bob Woodcock going to a stable at the back of his father's house on May and June evenings in 1890, ostensibly to feed rabbits that he kept there but also to meet Isabella. Ellen clearly felt she was justified in intervening:

> 'I told him I had seen him in the stable and if I saw him there again I should tell his Mother. He never spoke. On the 1st May (18)90 I went to the stable and a light inside was put out.'

She had also observed the couple on other occasions. Bob Woodcock had a key to his married sister's house and, according to Ellen Mooney, would go into the house to light the fire in the early evenings before his sister and her husband came home from work in the mill:

'. . . He went in on the 4th June (18)90 – He got in with the key – I saw him go in at about 10 past 5 and I saw him come out about 20 to 7 p.m. It was light. I saw comp(lainan)t go in on the same evg at in [*sic*] about three minutes after he did – I was stood at my door and watched – I was dubious – I saw no one else go in. When she went in she shut the door. I saw def(endan)t when inside pull the blind down before my face.'

This certainly provides a more complex representation of Isabella Fitton. She was living at the time of the court hearing with her married sister Elizabeth Williams (whom she helped in the house) and her husband. Isabella did not herself go out to work (as would have been normal for a 21-year-old woman in a mill town) because, as well as the baby born on 6 January, she had another illegitimate child. None of this actually refutes Isabella's accusation that Bob Woodcock had forced himself upon her, of course. It might, however, indicate why Ellen Mooney was keeping a particular eye on the couple: less, perhaps, to support Isabella and more to defend the reputation of the street and of her neighbours, the Woodcocks.

In fact, the minutes give a far clearer and more obviously self-authored representation of Ellen than they do of Isabella. Ellen positioned herself in the classic pose of the late Victorian housewife, observing the street from her doorstep. She claimed the authority to adjudicate the proper and improper uses of neighbourhood space. Her affront was clear when Bob (presumably) pulled down the house blinds 'before my face'. Not only was Ellen quite unabashed to recount in court the extent of her surveillance and intervention: within the community itself she identified herself with this story and used it as a basis for social interaction with both families. She took it upon herself to communicate her knowledge to the families and a confrontation took place '. . . in his sister's house – his Mother, his (?) Brother and his wife and his sister were all present – I told my tale same as now and what I have told now'.

The tale was *her* tale – not Isabella's, nor indeed Bob's. Although Isabella was there, she is not recalled as having made much contribution. Likewise, Bob is reported by both Ellen and the array of other family witnesses as being markedly silent. Salient details emerged in court through other people's stories. In the minutes, the information that '. . . he had laid her on the floor, the sofa and in the kitchen against the Boiler' emerges as part of Isabella's sister's evidence, not in Isabella's own statement. In fact the evidence of family and neighbours moves rapidly away from considering the chief protagonists as individuals and deals with the pregnancy as far more of a family and neighbourhood problem. To this extent, the discrete agency of individuals (particularly Isabella and Bob) was subsumed into the collective identity of this social network.[43] A decision was taken (perhaps suggested by

Bob's adult brother, perhaps by Isabella's sister) to try to procure an abortion. The brother went out to the druggist for tincture of steel and gin which was administered to Isabella by her elder sister.

The court decided that Bob Woodcock was the father of Isabella's child and awarded her 2s. 6d. per week for its upkeep. Its decision was predicted through the text by minor inconsistencies in the defence evidence: the Woodcocks attempted to argue that the tincture of steel was fetched to cure a cold, but not all of them remembered to include this in their evidence. Also, of course, the previous sexual conduct of Isabella and the lack of any other medically creditable candidate for the paternity meant that she gained her maintenance. The court did not necessarily believe that she had been coerced into intercourse. As many other cases show, it was virtually impossible for a young, unmarried woman – particularly one with an illegitimate baby – to prove sexual assault in court against a man she knew and had been alone with. Judgments in such cases were made on the basis of the reputations of men and women, and women's sexual reputations were frequently very hard to defend. However, the fact that she had made this argument in the first place (whether it was true or not) does indicate that for Isabella herself, the status of her relationship with Bob Woodcock was problematic. To claim forced intercourse implies that she was not courting with him in the accepted sense.[44] Isabella gained a material advantage from the hearing and had her version of events vindicated but emerged with her respectability uncertain. She was already an unmarried mother and had had to demonstrate her lack of sexual restraint in open court.

The issues around Isabella's sexual reputation apparently had wider resonances in the street and the family. The fact that Bob was only sixteen and five years younger than Isabella may well have provoked this reaction. At this period late in the nineteenth century, it is argued, the sexual mores of working-class culture had become stricter.[45] This is an argument that needs careful qualification and depends on sometimes very localised variables. Nevertheless, the extent of family and neighbourhood involvement in this specific case, the relative silence, defensiveness and marginalisation of the couple themselves in the presentation of the evidence, and the dominant way in which the actions and concerns of Ellen Mooney in particular emerge here, do seem to indicate that local codes of respectability had been challenged by events and were being policed and enforced – in particular by neighbourhood married women. The fact that the court hearing happened not at the time of the baby's birth, when lying-in expenses would have been incurred, but nine months later also seems to indicate that neighbourhood attempts to stabilise the situation, firstly by unsuccessful attempts to procure an abortion and presumably subsequently by an informal agreement for the payment of some maintenance, had at first been tried but eventually found wanting. Jennifer Davis makes the point for London that in cases of theft and common assault at this period, the magistrates' court was only one of a composite of strategies adopted by working people to gain restitution and solve disputes. The decision as to whether to resort to legal or informal means was, she argues, invariably strategic and contingent on the particular circumstances.[46] This case is one of many I have read which demonstrate working women's active roles in making these decisions and their ability to make tactical use of the legal institutions available to them. The court's own records, while being problematic texts in many ways, multiple-authored and giving only very contingent historical evidence of the events they describe, nevertheless do demonstrate active and often success-ful attempts at self-authorship by women in court, very often hinged around contested definitions about respectability and reputation.

Newspapers

Because of the partial survival and often very poor legibility of magistrates' court minutes, a good deal of recent historical research on these courts has used newspaper reports of court proceedings. Victorian local newspapers by no means provide a complete account of court proceedings. However, they did regularly use such reports as good cheap and entertaining copy and also included cases from higher courts (quarter sessions and assizes) as well as not infrequently reprinting particularly sensational cases from other parts of the country. Journalists frequently apparently directly repro-duced large sections of witnesses' evidence and were capable of filling col-umns of newsprint with the testimony of multiple corroborating witnesses. They nevertheless also provided their own descriptive gloss, giving a sense of the atmosphere of the courtroom and the mood of the public gallery. Journalists also inserted assessments of the reputation and respectability of both the women and the men in the courtroom, which were frequently expressed through descriptions of demeanour, appearance and behaviour in court.

In a case of incest in Middleton, William Jagger, 'a debauched charac-ter', was accused of 'attempted . . . criminal assault' by his adolescent daugh-ter, Jane Ann, 'an innocent looking girl'. In the view of the magistrate Jagger 'deserved horsewhipping'. Jagger's wife, Mary Ann, was described by the newspaper as 'a little, decent-looking woman'. The reputation of the mother was under examination as much as that of the daughter and the husband. The daughter's testimony became inconsistent at a subsequent hearing and William Jagger was acquitted, whereupon 'disappointment seemed to stamp every feature' present in the hot, crowded courtroom.[47]

The newspaper report is both melodramatic and sensational. Although historians of the press tend to dismiss these kinds of reporting styles as crowd pleasing aimed at filling columns and entertaining the readership, new approaches in cultural history have demonstrated that melodrama provided a rhetorical device available to a range of different political and social causes, including feminist ones.[48] It was certainly the sensationalist genre employed most readily when newspaper accounts chose to elaborate at length in cases of violence – particularly sexual violence – against women. The heightened emotion of melodrama helped evoke sympathy for the victim and sometimes for her assailant. The stereotypes of this genre provided a grid of character types to facilitate readers' comparisons with the facts of the case being presented, or with the real life individuals known to them first, second or third hand through the mechanisms of neighbourhood gossip. This is not to argue that newspapers invariably used the techniques of melodrama, nor that they always used it to its fullest. Sometimes just a lurid headline would preface a brief description, sometimes the usage was merely formulaic. Sometimes melodrama was rejected altogether. Kim Stevenson argues that *The Times* used deliberately restrained language as a strategy to marginalise the harm done to women in the cases of sexual violence that it reported.[49] Silence, formalism and closure were alternative journalistic practices particularly where a case evoked distaste, for example in some cases of child sexual abuse. In a brief mention of an affiliation case involving 'an elderly man', the *Middleton Albion* remarked only that 'The usual amount of "unfit for publication" material was gone through . . . .'.[50] Other historians have found this kind of censorship to be more widespread than I have.[51] For example, one case of child sexual abuse that the newspaper reported in considerable detail but without melodrama involved William Bell of Crewe. Bell argued that Mary Alice Cope (aged eleven) came repeatedly to his shop and he gave her pennies and apples in exchange for sexual access. He said:

> 'She was continually coming, and I could not keep her away. She kept sending other children asking for straw, or something like that. I told her to keep away, and not be sending children there. One time she said if I did not give her a penny she would tell the missus. I had to give it to her to keep her quiet'.[52]

However we may view this litany of excuses, it is clear that there is no press agenda to protect the identity of the child. It may be that news was slow that week. On the other hand, I would argue that this kind of publication was a means of scrutinising an incident that contradicted ideals both of manliness and of childhood in a community and a family both represented as respectable. Plain prose – but long, long columns of it – was an effective way of doing so. A fair proportion of William Bell's customers must have been children running errands for their mothers. Linda Gordon comments on the 'ordinariness' of incest. Much the same could be said of most interpersonal violence which arose out of mundane and ongoing struggles about resources, reputation, sex and power.[53] This is why these cases offer such an insight into women's and men's roles in late nineteenth-century working-class culture.

The journalistic uses of melodrama or elaboration of detail were generally partnered by other techniques which sensationalised what were fairly commonplace events. The tendency to reprint items from other newspapers that were similar to a local story, or to juxtapose related items on the page, could organise ephemeral items into a broader view. The original report of the Bell case appeared alongside reports from other nearby police courts, headlined 'Abominable Assault upon a Farmer's Wife at Northwich', 'A Cruel Husband', 'Threatening a Wife'. Even though the (plainly reported) Bell case is headed simply 'Alleged Criminal Assault' it is nevertheless presented as part of a composite narrative of unacceptable, sensationalised, and yet everyday male violence.[54] The newspaper constantly repeats itself, piling one cheap thrill upon another, but each item depends on its own fragmented specificity. Stories and anecdotes become 'sensations' because they describe the ways in which the exceptional can suddenly intrude on the everyday, how order can be unexpectedly inverted into disorder. Thus sensation is exciting because of its potential to transform the mundane and is shocking because it can disrupt ordinary lives. Sensation speaks to insecurity and subversion, but to do so it relies heavily on shared perceptions of the normal.[55] These print techniques of accumulation, repetition and emotionally heightened prose (a horrific crime; a brutal assailant) resonate with some of the patterns of informal oral communication (gossip).[56] Ellen Mooney's story about the sexual irregularities between Isabella Fitton and Bob Woodcock transferred readily from the neighbourhood to the courtroom – and doubtless back again. Such sayings and tales could be used as metaphor to reflect upon and imaginatively to police the normative boundaries of respectability in popular culture. Newspaper reporting of physical and sexual violence can only have fuelled the gossip and discussion that was not only a pleasurable leisure occupation but also attributed judgements about the respectability of the parties involved. Oral and print culture were interactive. Press coverage of sexual and physical violence cases can be thought of as providing working people with narratives 'to think with'.[57] Thus reading/ listening practices involved interaction between the social and the imaginary.

Such effects were heightened when the press repeatedly reported certain types of cases. Joanne Jones has demonstrated that in the later nineteenth century, at a time when the crime statistics show a clear drop in the numbers of prosecutions, the Manchester press coverage of domestic violence cases in the newspapers increased significantly.[58] Perhaps press coverage deterred some women from summonsing their husbands in order to avoid the 'embarrassment' of publicity. Certainly, the press kept an ongoing, composite and often sensationalised narrative of working-class (domestic) violence and disorder before the newspapers' readership, both middle and (respectable) working class. Likewise, the 6 July 1881 issue of the *Chester Courant* described no fewer than four cases of family and domestic violence. William Moore, a labourer, kicked and beat his wife, accusing her of living with another man though they had been separated for more than four years and he himself was living with another woman. The Jinks family (husband, wife, father, sister-in-law, uncle and a neighbour) fought a large-scale street brawl and broke windows one Sunday afternoon. The fight started with a husband's attack on his wife; then he involved his own kin. A drunken butcher, Philip Owen, beat his wife and turned her out of the house. Thomas Jones, a hawker, had also locked out his wife in a drunken fit and tried to strangle her. Two similar cases were also reported in the 13 July edition of the paper, one on 20 July, two on 3 August including one attempted wife murder heard at the Cheshire assizes, two on 10 August, and so forth.

Returning to the 6 July cases, the reporting discriminates in the ways in which it represents the women and men involved, making normalising judgements around axes of respectability and non-respectability based not on entirely middle-class stereotypes of femininity and masculinity but on norms rooted far more strongly within working-class culture. Both Mrs Owen and Mrs Jones are associated closely with their home responsibilities. It is the drunken husbands who have transgressed by putting them out on the street and thus reneging on their responsibilities as breadwinners. Mary Moore, separated from her husband, is represented chiefly as mother but also as wage earner and through her earnings as a good mother to her two children. She is reported as stating that:

> . . . in consequence of her husband's ill treatment she left him between four and five years ago, and had since maintained herself and two children without any assistance from him, and she never asked him to contribute towards their support.

The Jinks women appear far less respectable. Both in the events and in the telling of them their femininity, veracity and respectability are undermined. The reporting uses another common technique: that of low comedy. In the text, laughter in the court is reported in brackets, the magistrate calls the affray a 'Sunday afternoon's amusement', and a woman fighting her husband in the street is said to be 'sparring like a man'. These textual devices mirror 'plot' details, such as the neighbour's refusal to help the women and Sarah

Jinks's error in applying for a warrant for assault against her husband when 'on that occasion' he had 'only threatened her'.

This last point introduces a second theme that interweaves these separate cases into a composite narrative about domestic violence: working women's interaction with the courts. In the period between the Matrimonial Causes Act (1878) and the Summary Jurisdiction (Married Women) Act (1895), these women are reported as using the court tactically. Neither Mrs Owen nor Mrs Jones was keen to press the charges against her husband. Mrs Owen might have been intimidated but probably thought the summons was sufficient warning to a husband.[59] Mrs Jones is reported as saying 'she did not want him sent to prison, but wished the Magistrates would grant a separation order'. Mrs Moore was likewise not keen to press the charge 'if he would promise to leave her alone. What she wanted was a protection order.' 'Protection orders' did not in fact exist, but Mary Moore was not the only working-class wife to ask for one.[60] Each of these women seems to have been using the court to remedy the specific problems of her own situation. Because their cases were reported in this detail they formed part of broader debates about working-class respectability.

Violence and the later Victorian working class

The violence and drunkenness of later nineteenth-century working-class men was often interpreted in dominant ideologies as part of a more generalised 'disorder'. Of course, disorderly conduct was not the sole province of working-class masculinity. Prostitution, drunkenness and violence were thought of as 'moral crimes' that jeopardised working women's very identity as women.[61] Class privilege concealed the violence of other men from the attentions of the legal system. Legal or journalistic descriptions of violence against women by working men informed part of a critique of a composite behaviour pattern which contributed to a public negotiation of the boundaries between 'rough' and 'respectable'. If a broader reformulation of working-class culture by the later nineteenth century in the direction of respectability is accepted, then whether that culture is characterised as 'reformism', 'populism' or a 'culture of consolation', inevitably the working class itself had direct interests in debating and distinguishing the rough from the respectable.[62] Such negotiations took place across class as well as gender. Women seeking justice to some extent colluded with dominant projects of disciplining disorderly working-class masculinity. Press reports publicised accounts of violence to a broader audience. The scope of much press coverage was local, and I am committed to the view that local differentiation of patterns of culture and social relations remain important within over-arching class or national cultures.

A feminist understanding of gendered social identities can inform an inter-pretation of the often uncomfortable role of physical and sexual aggression in working-class masculinities. It can also pinpoint the ways in which working women could draw on their domestic and neighbourhood roles to counter implications of un-chastity and non-respectability. The significance of 'Family' to later nineteenth-century working-class men is increasingly being researched. Anna Clark has established the importance of the family to working-class politics by the Chartist era, though she argues that this model implicitly sowed the seed of ongoing domestic conflict since material resources were not necessarily sufficient or stable enough to underpin the social role of the working-class breadwinner.[63] Autobiographies, dialect poetry and other sources have all been used to emphasise men's affective investment in family and kinship relations.[64] Keith McClelland sees the ability to support family dependents as a crucial component of the social identity of the 'self-respecting artisan'. The evidence for this is, if anything, stronger in the second half of the nineteenth century, as sources multiply and as industrial society solidified. Kirk has argued that in this period respectable domestic-ity was an important component of 'reformism', whilst Joyce sees affective family relations as contributing positively to cultures of populism.[65]

Much recent work on working-class masculinities has in various ways emphasised the difficulties conflicting social roles posed for aspirationally respectable working men. Andrew Davis argues that a 'hard' masculine role was most attainable and relevant to young adult men and that this form of masculinity became the logic which underpinned a whole culture of territ-orial gang violence in late nineteenth-century Manchester and Salford.[66] Indeed, men of all ages faced models of masculinity that involved physical strength, hard drinking, and sexual prowess as well as codes of respectabil-ity that emphasised sexual restraint, promise keeping, obligation to depend-ants, sobriety and Smilesian self-help. If domestic life and family formation was an important site of construction of the social and cultural identities of working women and men, an orderly domestic life was not easy to achieve, very often (if not exclusively) because of the material uncertainties of working-class subsistence. Violence and sexual behaviour that resulted in court appearances often reveal moments when these incipient tensions threatened domestic or neighbourhood order. Men's responses could include a violent assertion of domestic privacy against the extended kinship network that women saw as an important component of family life.[67] The sexual violence that is revealed in some affiliation cases arguably indicates sexual predation as an integral part of at least some men's leisure practices under the guise of 'courtship'.

A study of violence contributes to the recent feminist interventions in the history of the nineteenth-century working class and the gendering of its distinctive culture. Where such approaches are allied to feminist praxis, such inaccessible and fragmentary records as the minutes of nineteenth-century magistrates' courts can illuminate the always problematic spaces between women's historical experience (of violence) and the ideologically constructed sources that are all that remain to us of the patriarchal legal institutions that working women had to deal with. A discriminating reading informed by feminist praxis reveals Isabella Fitton, for example, to have been neither a working-class Jezebel nor an innocent victim. She did not conform to middle-class ideas of femininity, yet was sufficiently respectable according to working-class codes to retain the support of friends, neighbours and family. She clearly exercised agency in shaping her social and sexual relationships. Nevertheless because her social identity (and that of Bob Woodcock) was rooted in proximate social networks, its agency was ultimately diffused among those broader associations as steps were taken to solve the social and material problems the pregnancy posed. Overall, these sources represent women in contradictory ways, but such unevenness itself was part of the terms of a wider debate about gender and respectability in working-class culture. Working women were represented as subjected to violence and coercive heterosexual sex, certainly, but not all women in these sources were victims and all of them resisted – even those whose lives were extinguished by violence. The court cases almost invariably associated women with home and neighbourhood and as having areas of autonomy within those arenas. Such autonomy can be seen to differ over the life cycle – there was certainly a role for older women – as mothers, kin or neighbours. Younger women are represented as having the capacity for pleasure, leisure and shrewd if not always successful sexual bargaining.

Over the last 30 years, by its careful attention to the voluminous and difficult sources of regional, local and higher courts and its interpretations of criminal or violent activity grounded in social context, the social history of crime has certainly provided much published work of interest to feminist historians. More recently this history has in some quarters overcome the gender-blindness that marked much of the earlier work. Feminist theory can now offer multiple and sophisticated theorisations of power relations by gender. The interdisciplinarity inherent in feminist scholarship enables feminist historians to build their interpretations on a broader base, which can reveal the nuanced complexities of representations of women. Most certainly insights from feminist work in sociology and in cultural studies have provided my own research with ways of understanding the difficult yet compelling accounts of women's experiences of violence in nineteenth-century lower court records.

Further reading

M. Arnot and C. Usborne, eds, *Gender and Crime in Modern Europe* (1999).

P. Bartley, *Prostitution: Prevention and Reform in England, 1860–1914* (2000).

A. Clark, *Women's Silence, Men's Violence: Sexual Assault in England, 1770–1845* (1987).

A. Clark, *The Struggle for the Breeches: Gender and the Making of the British Working Class* (Berkeley, Calif., 1995).

C. Conley, 'Rape and justice in Victorian England', *Victorian Studies*, 29 (1986), pp. 519–36.

Andrew Davies, ' "These viragoes are no less cruel than the lads": young women, gangs and violence in late Victorian Manchester and Salford', *British Journal of Criminology*, 39, 1 (1999), pp. 72–89.

A. Davies and G. Pearson, eds, 'Histories of Crime and Modernity', *British Journal of Criminology*, special issue, 39, 1 (1999).

Andrew Davies, 'Youth gangs, masculinity and violence in Late Victorian Manchester and Salford', *Journal of Social History*, 23 (1998), pp. 251–68.

J. Davis, ' "A poor man's system of justice"; the London police courts in the second half of the nineteenth century', *Historical Journal*, 27 (1984), pp. 309–35.

J. Davis, 'Prosecutions and their context: the use of the criminal law in later nineteenth-century London', in D. Hay and F. Snyder, eds, *Policing and Prosecution in Britain, 1750–1850* (Oxford, 1989), pp. 379–426.

S. D'Cruze, *Crimes of Outrage: Sex, Violence and Victorian Working Women* (1998).

S. D'Cruze, ed., *Everyday Violence in Britain, 1850–1950: Gender and Class* (2000).

C. Emsley, *Crime and Society in England, 1750–1900* (2nd edn, 1996).

C. Emsley, 'The history of crime and crime control institutions', in M. Maguire, R. Morgan and R. Reiner, eds, *The Oxford Handbook of Criminology* (Oxford, 1994), p. 61.

M. Feeley and D. L. Little, 'The vanishing female: the decline of women in the criminal process, 1687–1912', *Law and Society Review*, 25, 4 (1991), pp. 719–57.

V. A. C. Gatrell, 'Crime, authority and the policeman-state', in F. M. L. Thompson, ed., *The Cambridge Social History of Britain, 1750–1950*, 3: *Social Agencies and Institutions* (Cambridge, 1990).

L. Gelsthorpe and A. Morris, eds, *Feminist Perspectives in Criminology* (Oxford, 1992), pp. 26–40.

A. James Hammerton, *Cruelty and Companionship: Conflict in Nineteenth-Century Married Life* (1992), pp. 47–56.

J. Hanmer and M. Maynard, eds, *Women, Violence and Social Control* (1987).

F. Heidensohn, 'Gender and crime', in M. MacGuire et al., eds, *Oxford Handbook of Criminology* (Oxford, 1994).

Louise Jackson, *Child Sexual Abuse in Victorian England* (2000).

Jan Lamertz, 'Feminists and the politics of wife-beating', in H. L. Smith, ed., *British Feminism in the Twentieth Century* (1990), pp. 25–46.

E. Ross, ' "Fierce questions and taunts"; married life in working-class London, 1870–1914', *Feminist Studies*, 8 (1982), pp. 575–602.

C. Smart, ed., *Regulating Womanhood: Historical Essays on Marriage, Motherhood and Sexuality* (1992), pp. 53–77.

E. A. Stanko, *Intimate Intrusions: Women's Experience of Male Violence* (1985).

N. Tomes, 'A "torrent of abuse": crimes of violence between working-class men and women in London", *Journal of Social History*, 11 (1978), pp. 328–45.

C. Weedon, *Feminist Practice and Poststructuralist Theory* (Oxford, 1987).

L. Zedner, *Women, Crime and Custody in Victorian England* (Oxford, 1991).

L. Zedner, 'Victims', in M. MacGuire et al., eds, *Oxford Handbook of Criminology* (Oxford, 1994), pp. 1207–46.

Notes

1. Middleton, Petty Sessions Minutes, Lancashire Record Office, PsMi/1/5, 17 September 1891.

2. C. Sumner, 'Foucault, gender and the censure of deviance', in L. Gelsthorpe and A. Morris, eds, *Feminist Perspectives in Criminology* (Oxford, 1992), pp. 26–40.

3. S. Brownmiller, *Against Our Will: Men, Women and Rape* (1975); S. Griffin, 'Rape: the all-American crime', *Ramparts* 10 (1971).

4. C. Bauer and L. Ritt, ' "A husband is a beating animal": Frances Power Cobbe confronts the wife-abuse problem in Victorian England', *International Journal of Women's Studies* 6 (1983), pp. 99–118; *idem*, 'Wife-abuse, late Victorian English feminists, and the Legacy of Frances Power Cobbe', *International Journal of Women's Studies* 6 (1983), pp. 195–207.

5. S. Elstrich, *Real Rape* (Cambridge, Mass., 1987); J. Hanmer and M. Maynard, eds, *Women, Violence and Social Control* (1987); E. A. Stanko, *Intimate Intrusions: Women's Experience of Male Violence* (1985).

6. J. Walkowitz, 'Jack the Ripper and the myth of male violence', *Feminist Studies* 8 (1982), pp. 543–74.

7. C. Smart, 'Feminist approaches to criminology, or postmodern woman meets atavistic man', in Gelsthorpe and Morris, eds, *Feminist Perspectives in Criminology*, pp. 70–84; S. Walklate, 'Can there be a progressive victimology?', *International*

Review of Victimology 3 (1994), pp. 1–15; T. McCartney, 'Rethinking theories of victimology: men's violence against women', in S. Cook and J. Besant, eds, *Women's Encounters with Violence: the Australian Experience* (California, 1997), pp. 127–44.

8. C. Ramazanoglu, ed., *Up Against Foucault: Explorations of Some Tensions Between Foucault and Feminism* (1993); C. Weedon, *Feminist Practice and Poststructuralist Theory* (Oxford, 1987); J. Sawicki, *Disciplining Foucault: Feminism, Power and the Body* (1991); L. McNay, *Foucault and Feminism* (Cambridge, 1992).

9. See, for example, J. Hoff, 'Gender as a postmodern category of paralysis', *Women's History Review* 3 (1994), pp. 149–68, and the subsequent debate in *Women's History Review* 5 (1996); S. Clegg, 'The feminist challenge to socialist history', *Women's History Review* 6 (1997), pp. 201–15.

10. Ramazanoglu, ed., *Up Against Foucault*, p. 17.

11. M. Cain, 'Foucault, feminism and feeling: what Foucault can and cannot contribute to feminist epistemology', in Ramazanoglu, ed., *Up Against Foucault*, pp. 73–99.

12. S. D'Cruze, *Crimes of Outrage: Sex, Violence and Victorian Working Women* (1998), pp. 43, 164.

13. Cain, 'Foucault', p. 83, quoting L. Kelly, *Surviving Sexual Violence* (Cambridge, 1988).

14. C. Euler, 'Josephine Butler and Frances Power Cobbe: strategic uses of the body in c19th campaigns against violence', in S. D'Cruze, ed., *Everyday Violence in Britain, 1850–1950: Gender and Class* (2000).

15. D'Cruze, *Crimes of Outrage*.

16. L. Radzinowicz, *A History of English Criminal Law*, 4 vols (1948–68).

17. J. Sharpe, 'History from below', in P. Burke, ed., *New Perspectives on Historical Writing* (Cambridge, 1992), pp. 24–42.

18. For example, P. Burke, *Popular Culture in Early Modern Europe* (1978).

19. E. P. Thompson, 'History from below', *Times Literary Supplement* (7 April 1966), p. 280.

20. E. P. Thompson, 'The moral economy of the English crowd in the eighteenth century', *Past and Present* 50 (1971), pp. 76–136; J. Stevenson, *Popular Disturbances in England, 1700–1870* (1979); E. and S. Yeo, eds, *Popular Culture and Class Conflict, 1590–1914: Explorations in the History of Labour and Leisure* (Brighton, 1981); J. Rule, ed., *British Trade Unionism, 1750–1850: The Formative Years* (1988); J. Rule and R. Wells, *Crime, Protest and Popular Politics in Southern England, 1740–1850* (1997).

21. J. Walter and K. Wrightson, 'Dearth and the social order in early modern England', *Past and Present* 71 (1976), pp. 22–42; J. Bohstedt, 'Gender, household and community politics: women in English riots, 1790–1810', *Past and Present* 120 (1988), pp. 88–122.

22. Catherine Hall, 'The tale of Samuel and Jemima: gender and working-class culture in early-nineteenth-century England', in her *White, Male and Middle Class: Explorations in Feminism and History* (Cambridge, 1992).

23. Vic Gatrell, 'Crime, authority and the policeman-state', in F. M. L. Thompson, ed., *The Cambridge Social History of Britain, 1750–1950*, vol. 3: *Social Agencies and Institutions* (1990).

24. E. P. Thompson, *The Making of the English Working Class* (1965), pp. 12–13.

25. N. Tomes, 'A "torrent of abuse": crimes of violence between working-class men and women in London', *Journal of Social History* 11 (1978), pp. 328–45; E. Ross, '"Fierce questions and taunts": married life in working-class London, 1870–1914', *Feminist Studies* 8 (1982), pp. 575–602; A. Clark, *Women's Silence, Men's Violence: Sexual Assault in England, 1770–1845* (1987); S. D'Cruze, 'Approaching the history of rape and sexual violence: notes towards research', *Women's History Review* 1 (1992), pp. 377–96.

26. A. Davis, 'Youth gangs, masculinity and violence in late Victorian Manchester and Salford', *Journal of Social History* 23 (1998), pp. 251–68, and his '"These viragoes are no less cruel than the lads": young women, gangs and violence in later Victorian Manchester and Salford', *British Journal of Criminology* 39 (1999), pp. 72–89; C. Conley, 'Rape and justice in Victorian England', *Victorian Studies* 29 (1986), pp. 519–36; M. Arnot and C. Usborne, eds, *Gender and Crime in Modern Europe* (1999).

27. L. Stone, 'Interpersonal violence in English society, 1300–1980', *Past and Present* 101 (1983), pp. 22–33; *idem* 'A rejoinder', *Past and Present* 108 (1985), pp. 216–24; J. A. Sharpe, 'The history of violence in England: some observations', *Past and Present* 108 (1985), pp. 206–15; J. S. Cockburn, 'Patterns of violence in English society: homicide in Kent 1560–1985', *Past and Present* 131 (1991), pp. 70–106.

28. D. Jones, *Crime, Protest, Community and Police in Nineteenth-Century Britain* (1982), p. 4; V. A. C. Gatrell and T. B. Hadden, 'Criminal statistics and their interpretation', in E. A. Wrigley, ed., *Nineteenth-Century Society: Essays in the Use of Quantitative Methods for the Study of Social Data* (Cambridge, 1972), pp. 336–96; C. Emsley, 'The history of crime and crime control institutions', in M. Maguire, R. Morgan and R. Reiner, eds, *The Oxford Handbook of Criminology* (Oxford, 1994), p. 61.

29. H. Taylor, 'Rationing crime: the political economy of criminal statistics since the 1850s', *Economic History Review* 51 (1998), pp. 569–90.

30. T. Skyrme, *A History of the Justices of the Peace*, vol. 2 (Chichester, 1991), p. 181; Ross, '"Fierce questions"'; A. James Hammerton, *Cruelty and Companionship: Conflict in Nineteenth-Century Married Life* (1992), pp. 47–56; J. Davis, '"A poor man's system of justice": the London police courts in the second half of the nineteenth century', *Historical Journal* 27 (1984), pp. 309–35.

31. L. Gordon, *Heroes of Their Own Lives: The Politics and History of Family Violence: Boston 1880–1960* (1989); L. Jackson, 'Women professionals and the regulation of violence in interwar Britain', in D'Cruze, ed., *Everyday Violence*, pp. 119–35.

32. C. Conley, *The Unwritten Law: Criminal Justice in Victorian Kent* (Oxford, 1991).

33. Ibid.; Clark, *Women's Silence, Men's Violence*; Joanne Jones, 'Violence against women in late nineteenth-century Manchester', and K. Stevenson, '"Ingenuities of the female mind": legal and public perceptions of sexual violence in Victorian England, 1850–1890', in D'Cruze, ed., *Everyday Violence*, pp. 89–103.

34. C. Emsley, *Crime and Society in England, 1750–1900*, 2nd edn (1996), p. 147; D. Philips, *Crime and Authority in Victorian England* (1977), p. 269; J. M. Carter, *Rape in Medieval England: An Historical and Sociological Study* (New York, 1985), p. 153.

35. Skyrme, *A History of the Justices of the Peace*, p. 175; Conley, *The Unwritten Law*, pp. 49–53.

36. Philips, *Crime and Authority*, p. 257.

37. Jones, *Crime, Protest*, pp. 3–4; Philips, *Crime and Authority*, p. 284; Davis, '"A poor man's system of justice"'; *idem*, 'Prosecutions and their context: the use of the criminal law in later nineteenth-century London', in D. Hay and F. Snyder, eds, *Policing and Prosecution in Britain, 1750–1850* (Oxford, 1989), pp. 379–426.

38. Hammerton, *Cruelty and Companionship*; Ross, '"Fierce questions"'; D'Cruze, *Crimes of Outrage*, p. 70.

39. See, for example, Blackburn registers in Lancashire Record Office, Ps/Bl 1880–1940, plaint book 1876–1915, Lancaster registers 1889–99, 1907–15, 1918–21 at Ps/La.

40. M. Foucault, *Discipline and Punish: The Birth of the Prison* (1991), p. 191.

41. Davis, 'Prosecutions'; D'Cruze, *Crimes of Outrage*, p. 93.

42. See n. 1 above.

43. R. Smith and D. Valenze, 'Mutuality and marginality', *Signs* 13 (1988), pp. 277–98.

44. For the relevance of courtship as a context for pre-marital sex, see D'Cruze, *Crimes of Outrage*, Chapter 5.

45. J. Gillis, *For Better, For Worse: British Marriages, 1600 to the Present* (Oxford, 1985).

46. Davis, 'Prosecutions', p. 419.

47. *Middleton Albion*, 7 July and 14 July 1866.

48. L. Brown, *Victorian News and Newspapers* (Oxford, 1985), p. 96; P. Joyce, *Visions of the People* (Cambridge, 1991), pp. 123–4; R. Williams, 'The press and popular culture: an historical perspective', in G. Boyce, J. Curran and P. Wingate, eds, *Newspaper History from the Seventeenth Century to the Present Day* (1978), pp. 44–80; J. Walkowitz, *City of Dreadful Delight* (1992), pp. 87–8, 93–4.

49. Stevenson, '"Ingenuities"'.

50. *Middleton Albion*, 20 June 1862.

51. Philips, *Crime and Authority*, p. 269.

52. *Crewe and Nantwich Chronicle*, 19 January and 26 January 1889.

53. Gordon, *Heroes*, p. 227.

54. *Crewe and Nantwich Chronicle*, 19 January 1889.

55. Joyce, *Visions*, pp. 293–304.

56. M. Tebbutt, *Women's Talk: A Social History of Gossip in Working-Class Neighbourhoods, 1880–1960* (Aldershot, 1995), p. 5.

57. Williams, 'The press and popular culture', p. 45; V. Berridge, 'Popular Sunday papers and mid-Victorian society', in Boyce, Curran and Wingate, eds, *Newspaper History*, pp. 247–64; Brown, *Victorian News*, pp. 50–1; R. Darnton, *The Great Cat Massacre*, p. 70, quoted in Joyce, *Visions*, p. 6.

58. Joanne Jones, *Male Violence against Women in Manchester and its Representations in the Local Press, 1870–1900*, PhD, Lancaster University, 1999, and her '"She resisted with all of her might": sexual violence against women in late nineteenth-century Manchester and the local press', in D'Cruze, ed., *Everyday Violence*, pp. 104–18.

59. See n. 18 above.

60. *Chester Courant*, 26 October 1881, Wm Wilding assault on Elizabeth Wilding; Davis, 'Prosecutions', p. 419.

61. L. Zedner, *Women, Crime and Custody in Victorian England* (Oxford, 1991), Chapter 1.

62. N. Kirk, *The Growth of Working-Class Reformism in Mid-Victorian England* (1985); Joyce, *Visions*; G. Stedman-Jones, *Languages of Class: Studies in English Working-Class History* (Cambridge, 1983).

63. A. Clark, *The Struggle for the Breeches: Gender and the Making of the British Working Class* (Berkeley, Calif., 1995).

64. J. Burnett, *Destiny Obscure* (1982); D. Vincent, *Bread, Knowledge and Freedom* (1980); Joyce, *Visions*.

65. K. McClelland, 'Masculinity and the "representative artisan" in Britain, 1850–80', in M. Roper and J. Tosh, eds, *Manful Assertions: Masculinities in Britain since 1800* (1991), pp. 74–91; Kirk, *Working-Class Reformism*; Joyce, *Visions*.

66. Davis, 'Youth gangs, masculinity and violence'; J. White, *The Worst Street in North London: Campbell Bunk, Islington, Between the Wars* (1986), Chapter 6.

67. *Crewe and Nantwich Chronicle*, 9 November 1889.

PART TWO

The process of representation: visibility and invisibility

LIVERPOOL
JOHN MOORES UNIVERSITY
AVRIL ROBARTS LRC
TITHEBARN STREET
LIVERPOOL L2 2ER
TEL. 0151 231 4022

CHAPTER FOUR

Feminist historians and challenges to imperial history

CLARE MIDGLEY

Over the past two decades feminist historians have begun to make critical interventions into one of the most male-dominated areas of historical scholarship: the history of imperialism. Their challenge to the gender-blind paradigms of imperial history has not been a straightforward process, however: it has involved disagreements among feminist historians themselves, as they have engaged in broader political and scholarly debates. In the first place, feminist historians have become engaged in contests over the writing of histories of imperialism between the 'old school' of Western-based imperial historians, Third World scholars writing from an anti-colonial nationalist perspective and post-colonial theorists seeking to analyse and undermine imperialist forms of knowledge and power. Secondly, they have participated in, and been affected by, black and Third World women's critiques of Western feminism as an 'imperial feminism' which takes white, middle-class, Western women's experiences as the norm, viewing all women 'through Western eyes' and failing to respect their differences or take account of inequalities in power shaped by racism and imperialism.[1] These scholarly and political debates have taken place in the context of continuing inequalities in access to resources for researching and representing the past: inequalities which are themselves one of the legacies of imperialism.

Given this contested terrain, a number of questions have arisen concerning the writing of feminist histories of imperialism. When scholars write woman-centred accounts of empire, which women are they putting at the centre? In seeking to rescue white women in the colonies from the derogatory stereotypes of male imperialists and imperial historians, are white women writers in danger of creating plucky feminist role models while ignoring their complicity in imperialism? Does taking gender as the central category of analysis produce distorted accounts which fail to explore the complex interactions of gender with race and class in colonial contexts? In making use of colonial archives, are researchers unwittingly replicating the views of colonisers towards indigenous women and men? Are Western-based scholars adopting an 'imperial feminist' perspective and presenting colonised women as a homogeneous group of passive victims, or assuming that any resistance to patriarchal oppression which they articulated was derived from Western influence?

In this chapter I want to explore the nature of feminist historical writing on women, gender and imperialism and to examine the extent to which this has challenged the paradigms of traditional imperial history. I confine myself to Britain and its empire, since this is the material with which I am most familiar. A brief outline of the contested field of the history of imperialism is followed by discussions of both woman-centred and gender-based approaches by feminists to rewriting the imperial past. The final section comprises a case study discussing my own work on the origins of feminism in imperial Britain. By contributing to an exploration of the ways in which Western feminism has been implicated in imperialism, this section is intended to shed further historical light on the problems of rewriting the history of imperialism from a feminist perspective.

Early imperial history was produced in British universities during the period of 'high' or 'new' imperialism (1880s–1914) by scholars involved in the education of future colonial officials and in imperial policy-making. It was marked by a preoccupation with policy and administrative matters, reflecting not only the overall bias towards political history at the period, but also of the practical investments of this particular group of scholars. Written at a time when feminist demand for the vote was challenging masculine political authority at home, it was highly masculinist: empire was presented as a 'boy's own' sphere. It was also based on an assumption that, overall, the British empire was a good thing. With the end of formal empire and the development of social history after the Second World War this type of imperial history became somewhat marginalised from the historical mainstream in Britain, but it attempted to update itself and maintain its viability under the new label of imperial and commonwealth history.[2]

The main challenge which this hegemonic imperial history faced between the 1950s and the 1970s was from anti-colonial nationalist histories which began to be written with decolonisation and the emergence of newly independent nations. These histories stressed the negative impact of imperialism on their countries' development, and replaced the white male heroes of traditional imperial history with new male heroes in the form of the nationalist elites and their forefathers. While attempts were made to rectify this elitist bias by radical social historians, notably the Subaltern Studies

Group in India, these scholars, while restoring peasants to history, continued to marginalise the experiences and contributions of women.

A new challenge to imperial history appeared in 1978 with the publication of Edward Said's influential study *Orientalism*. Considered by many to be the founding text of post-colonial theory, it explored the way Western discourse had constructed knowledge of the East in order to dominate it. One of the great strengths of the work of Said and his followers is that it has exposed European imperial historiography as a key form of such colonial discourse. One of its weaknesses from a historian's viewpoint is its literary bias and ahistoricism: its preoccupation with texts to the exclusion of economic conditions and the materiality of lived experience, and its tendency to generalise across time and erase the specifics of colonial contexts. The presentation of a homogeneous view of colonial discourse has also led to a disregard for gender differences.[3]

Feminist scholarship has responded to exclusions in all these three bodies of scholarship: it has attempted both to place women within histories of imperialism and to explore how taking gender into account alters our understanding of the imperial past. In so doing, it has engaged with wider debates concerning the subject-matter and purpose of feminist history as well as becoming involved in the critiques of Western 'imperial feminism' discussed at the opening of this chapter.

Changing the subject: bringing women to the centre of histories of imperialism

In the 1980s there was an outpouring of writings about colonial white women. Many came from outside the discipline of history, and they ranged from the popular to the scholarly.[4] What they had in common is that they were recuperative in their aim. These are 'woman-centred' texts – written by white women and centred on the experiences of white British women in colonial contexts. In seeking to insert women into the story of empire they make a generally positive evaluation of their achievements in difficult circumstances, and seek to demolish the myth of white woman as 'the ruin of empire': racists whose arrival on the colonial scene was destructive of good relationships between male colonisers and colonised peoples. Such studies were valuable in that they drew attention to the important roles played by women in imperial contexts, and highlighted the value of studying the social and cultural as well as the political and economic dimensions of imperialism. However, they were marred by over-identification with their subjects. As Jane Haggis has pointed out, this led them to downplay the racial privileges and power women acquired by virtue of their whiteness in colonial contexts, and to relegate colonised women and men to the role of a silent and undifferentiated backdrop against which Western women's lives were staged.[5]

Such critiques of the recuperative approach in the early 1990s marked the beginnings of a new phase of more critical analysis of white women and imperialism, exploring both the complicity in and resistance to imperialism by women disadvantaged by their sex but privileged by their whiteness, and paying particular attention to the relationships between colonising and colonised women. As research has progressed, generalisations about women colonisers have become increasingly hard to make: the stereotype of the memsahib, leading a life of leisure and idleness under the British Raj, has been replaced by a complex picture involving an enormous range of women, varying in their personal backgrounds, motivations and experiences and in terms of the specific historical and geographical contexts of their lives in the empire. They ranged from evangelical missionaries such as the working-class Scot Mary Slessor, who hoped to convert, educate and civilise 'native' women, to adventurers and travellers such as Mary Kingsley, who sought to escape from the stifling confines of respectable Victorian society; from doctors and nurses who found better opportunities in the wider field of empire than in Britain itself, to political activists such as theosophist Annie Besant, who became involved in nationalist and feminist politics on the international stage; from the 'incorporated wives' of colonial officials in West Africa, to working-class emigrants seeking a better life in the 'white settler' colonies.[6]

Study of white settlers shades over into the histories of women in those self-governing nations which emerged in North America, Australia and New Zealand. Here the struggle to place women within the heroic male narratives of pioneers and the frontier is being replaced by a more critical deconstruction of these narratives, which stresses the role of both men and women in displacing the indigenous inhabitants of the lands they settled and attempting to wipe out their cultures. These white settler women were, as Marilyn Lake has pointed out, both coloniser (with respect to indigenous peoples and their lands) and colonised (with respect to living under British colonial rule). They were supposed to domesticate white men, produce children to ensure the continuity of the white race and set an example of civilised life and respectable femininity to the 'natives'.[7]

Increasingly, there has been a concern not only to explore colonial contexts but also to look at the empire 'at home' and examine the impact of imperialism on women's lives within Britain itself. Previous neglect of this topic reflects both the parochial outlook of much British social history and the tendency among imperial historians to view imperialism as something that happened 'out there'. Since the mid-1980s, however, work has begun on exploring the importance of empire to the shaping of British society and culture.[8] Most recently, work has stressed the importance of studying the interaction between metropolis and colony rather than seeing them as two separate analytic fields: as Ann Stoler and Frederick Cooper have stated, 'Europe was made by its imperial projects, as much as colonial encounters were shaped by conflicts within Europe itself.'[9] Feminist historians have played an important part in these developments, examining topics such as empire and the shaping of white English gender identities, race and sexuality, imperialism and motherhood, women as consumers of imperial produce, women anti-slavery campaigners, female emigration societies and the relationship between feminism and imperialism.[10] Huge gaps in this literature remain, however, with work concentrated mainly on the late Victorian and Edwardian periods, and we are far from being able to put together a full picture of the shifting impact of empire on women's everyday lives in Britain.

Study of the empire 'at home' has also involved an examination of the experiences of women migrants to Britain from its empire, and their impact on British society: these included black slave-servants during the period of colonial slavery, Indian ayahs (nurses) in the days of the Raj, Irish women who came seeking work in the post-Famine era, and a number of prominent individuals who made an impact on British society. Among the latter group was Mary Seacole, Jamaican 'doctress' and Crimean heroine; Cornelia Sorabji, an Indian who became the first woman to qualify as a lawyer in Britain; and Una Marson, Caribbean writer and BBC radio presenter in inter-war London.[11] Exploration of the lives of these and other women and men has helped to demolish the myth that black and Asian immigration to Britain was an exclusively post-war phenomenon. This later and much larger-scale immigration, too, was of course the product of empire. Despite new studies, however, there is unfortunately still a tendency for histories of 'immigrants and minorities' to marginalise women and for histories of women to ignore the multicultural dimensions of British women's past.[12]

Women who came to Britain as temporary or permanent migrants from the empire provide a bridge between the worlds of colonised and coloniser. The 'colonised' represent an even more diverse group than the 'coloniser', united only by the experience of living under British imperial rule. Not only did the lives of women in pre-colonial societies vary immensely; the impact of British rule on women's lives varied a great deal, depending on the form that rule took and the nature of the interaction between British intruders and indigenous society. Studies also diverge according to whether they are seeking to insert women into new national histories – of India for example; whether they are seeking to recover the experiences of indigenous women who have become minorities in their own lands – aboriginal women in Australia, for example; or whether they focus on transnational aspects of colonialism – such as the impact of the slave trade and colonial slavery on women of African descent. Among the diverse studies now appearing, attention is being paid to the impact of imperialism on all aspects of women's lives, from their economic activities to their legal rights and family and community lives, and to the variety of women's responses and resistances to imperialism.[13]

In all this work the problem of historical sources has loomed large. It has proved very hard to get direct access to women's own understandings of their lives for a number of reasons: often the main source is colonial archives, which reveal more about the attitudes of British colonial officials than the lives of colonised women; many societies had oral rather than written historical traditions; and colonised men who left records tended to be male elites whose lives were far removed from the majority of women's. While any historical narrative tells us as much about its writer's present concerns as about a 'real' past, women's limited power to represent themselves in patriarchal colonial societies makes it hard for the historian effectively to check her represention against the traces of the past. This problem has been the subject of particular debate in the case of Indian women, and has centred around Gayatri Spivak's controversial question 'Can the subaltern speak?' As she points out, the debate of *sati*, or widow-burning, in colonial India was a contest between white men and brown men over brown women, in which women themselves had no space to speak. This leads to the question of colonised women's agency. Spivak's views have been criticised as dangerously pessimistic: Lata Mani has pointed out that it is possible to gain some sense of the women's own experiences and attempts to assert agency through a reading of colonial accounts of *sati*, while Ania Loomba has made the important point that not all women in colonial India can be collapsed into the figure of the widow silenced by death.[14]

It is much easier to get at colonised women's experiences from the late nineteenth century onwards, when educated women began to organise and agitate for their rights. Important work has also been undertaken into the development of women's movements at this period, and into their relationship to anti-colonial nationalist movements. Third World feminisms have been shown to be a complex web of ideas and practices shaped by indigenous women themselves in the context of imperial rule and resistance to that rule, developing in response to the shifting position of women in the particular areas concerned, drawing on local traditions of organisation and protest, and also making use of elements of Western thought – just as the development of Western feminism was itself impacted on by its imperial contexts.[15]

Changing the approach: gender and rewriting histories of imperialism

Attempts to insert women into the subject-matter of histories of imperialism have been complemented by scholarship which has introduced gender as a category for analysis into the study of imperialism. Feminist scholars working in the fields of literary and cultural studies have challenged the gender-blindness of much colonial discourse analysis and explored the extent to which Western women's representations of empire differed from those of men. This difference has been ascribed by some to the fact that women were positioned outside the formal institutions of imperial and metropolitan power. This, it is argued, made them more willing to criticise aspects of imperialism, more likely to identify with the colonial 'other', and more prone to explore non-Western cultures as a way of gaining critical perspectives on their own social subordination. Women might also gain access to parts of the colonised society from which white men were excluded, and represent these in very different ways: thus the interior of the harem becomes a woman-dominated domestic space in British women's eyes, rather than the centre of the exotic and sexually available 'oriental' woman of Western male erotic fantasies. Nevertheless, it is important to remember that the Western women were still operating within the colonial system, that they benefited from the privileges that whiteness bestowed in colonial contexts, and that they in the main held on to a sense of racial superiority.[16]

One important insight of colonial discourse analysis has been that knowledge about empire was not only circulated in explicit and direct ways but that it also imbued cultural products in Britain in a far wider sense. Many of the key nineteenth-century novels that Said has discussed in this regard were written by women, as feminist scholars have pointed out. Charlotte Brontë's *Jane Eyre* has been a widely discussed text in this context. Spivak in particular has drawn attention to the way in which black and brown women function in the text to highlight the emergence of the English woman's struggle for individuality and independence.[17]

Gender has also become one of the central categories of analysis in the new imperial histories that are now being written.[18] Studies have revealed just how central gender issues were to contests between coloniser and colonised over questions of culture, custom and law, and have proved crucial to increasing our understanding of the social dimensions of imperialism. Scholars have, for example, examined how British interference in patterns of land ownership impacted on the sexual division of labour in West Africa, how contests between indigenous and colonial patriarchies played out in debates over the age of consent in India, and how missionaries attempted to shape gender relations in black families according to middle-class British ideals of femininity and domesticity in the post-emancipation Caribbean.

Some of this work has focused on men and the construction of masculinities in imperial contexts, deconstructing the male imperial hero. There is huge potential here, but important markers for the direction of future work have been laid out in such studies as Catherine Hall's ongoing work into imperialism and middle-class English masculinity and Mrinalina Sinha's study of the construction of the 'manly Englishman' and the 'effeminate Bengali'.[19] Sinha's study drew attention to the fact that gendering the history of imperialism is about studying power relationships between men as well as those between men and women, and that gender was a key marker of the power relationship between coloniser and colonised. Colonised men have been represented as either effeminate – to negate their power and threat – or as hyper-masculine – to emphasise their sub-human bestiality and their violence towards women and to position white male imperialists as the protectors of female virtue. During the Indian Mutiny, for example, the saving of the Raj was equated in the British press with the protection of white women from rapacious Indian men.

Gender also became a wider metaphor for power in imperial contexts. From the earliest stages of European expansion overseas, imperialists described colonised lands as virgin territory ripe for penetration. Later, anti-colonial nationalists used women as symbolic embodiments of indigenous traditions under threat by imperialism. In analysing such discourses, however, it is important to remember that they are attempts to create hegemonic representations of reality rather than 'reflections' of that reality: colonial discourses erase the rich histories of the indigenous cultures and societies of conquered lands, while oppositional discourses obscure the active contributions made by women to nationalist movements. As feminist historians of imperialism have pointed out, discourse analysis is barren without an accompanying painstaking historical reconstruction of women's actions and experiences in their precise historical contexts.

Case study: imperialism and the origins of feminism, 1790s–1850s

As feminist historians, one of our central concerns is with exploring the nature of women's oppression historically and placing movements for women's rights and women's emancipation within their historical contexts. If we are to do this effectively we must take imperialism seriously as a context, whether we are dealing with women who lived under British imperial rule or women at the heart of empire. In the remainder of this chapter I want to explore what this means with reference to my own work on the development of feminism in imperial Britain. I am particularly interested in the period prior to the emergence of an organised women's movement in Britain and prior to the period of 'high' imperialism, when the substantial impact of empire on British lives and political debates has been relatively widely acknowledged. In other words, I am studying women activists and feminist writers who were the foremothers of those suffragists of the 1860–1914 period who, as Antoinette Burton has shown, represented Indian women as passive victims in need of their help, and pointed to their interventions on the imperial stage to buttress their own claims for political inclusion in Britain.[20] How did empire impact on the origins of modern feminism in Britain? What was particularly 'Western' about this feminism not only in terms of its emergence from a specific set of domestic circumstances within Britain and its indebtedness to European intellectual traditions, but also in terms of its positioning of itself in relationship to the wider world, and in particular to non-Western societies, especially those under British imperial control? The other side of this question concerns the impact of female campaigners on imperial policy-making and the contribution of feminist writers to the development of colonial discourse.

As Christopher Bayly has pointed out, the period between the loss of America in the 1770s and the partition of Africa in the 1880s saw an immense expansion of British dominion overseas, with approximately 150 million people coming under direct or indirect British control between 1790 and 1820 alone, in territories ranging from southern Africa to India, Java and Australasia.[21] It also saw the final stage of English colonialism much closer to home, with the incorporation of Ireland into the United Kingdom under the Act of Union of 1800. It was the period when British colonial slavery was abolished, when British rule in India was consolidated, and when overseas missionary activities steadily expanded. As I will now discuss, such imperial developments provided a significant context for the development of feminist thought in Britain, and for British women's campaigns around questions of female emancipation prior to the emergence of an organised women's movement.

Feminist thinkers of the period between the 1790s and the 1850s, in seeking to highlight the subordinate position of white middle-class women in British society, placed references to non-Western societies at the heart of their arguments.[22] British women's subordination was highlighted by equating their position to that of people in non-Western societies. Early feminist tracts adopted what I have termed a 'triple discourse' of anti-slavery, likening the subordination of British women to black chattel slavery in Britain's

West Indian colonies, to the sexual slavery of women in the harem under 'Oriental despotism' and to the slavish position of women in polygamous, 'savage' societies. In the process feminists combined a critique of the excesses of colonialism represented by the horrors of colonial slavery with the circulation of a set of negative images of non-Western societies.

In the tracts the subordination of women was represented as characteristic of the unchanging despotic nature of Eastern societies, and as a mark of the backward and benighted state of savage societies in Africa and elsewhere. In contrast, female subordination in the West, like the institution of colonial slavery, was represented as an anachronistic and anomalous relic within societies characterised by freedom and progress. Once achieved, black emancipation became to feminist writers the marker of Britain's status as the most progressive Western nation: female emancipation was then presented as the final step along the road to the creation of a fully enlightened society, the culmination of the progress of Western civilisation.

Early feminist tracts which call for the rights of British women thus contributed to creating and widening the circulation of colonial discourse. They reinforced Western views of Eastern countries as despotic, sensuous and corrupt, and represented the societies of the indigenous inhabitants of Africa, America and Australia as living relics of the age of savagery. These feminist propagandists, I believe, helped to consolidate in liberal middle-class circles the sense of Western superiority which came to underpin Victorian notions of Britain's civilising mission. While it was not their main purpose, they contributed to providing the basis for justifications of imperialism in the name of enlightenment and social advance, and, in particular, in the name of female emancipation.

And as they wrote, British women were beginning to engage in just such practical interventions on the imperial stage. Interestingly, despite the production of key feminist tracts over the period 1790–1850, the organised campaigns conducted by middle-class British women at this time were not concerned with their own oppression but rather with the oppression of women living in non-Western countries under British imperial control. The most significant of these was women's involvement in the campaign against colonial slavery, when women focused on the sufferings of black women under slavery in a campaign which marked the first large-scale intervention by middle-class women into the political arena and which was at its height in the period between 1825 and 1838. But another significant intervention, and one hitherto ignored by historians, is women's involvement in the 1810s and 1820s in the missionary-led campaign against the practice of *sati*, or widow-burning, in India. These two campaigns thus tackled different aspects of women's oppression in different colonial contexts: the first was aimed at reform of British colonial practices, the second at reform of indigenous Indian practices. Allying themselves with male-led movements, British women nevertheless made vital and distinctive contributions to both campaigns: as anti-slavery activists they took the lead in organising consumer boycotts of slave-grown sugar, and as opponents of *sati* they became the leading supporters of missionary attempts to educate Indian women so that they would reject the practice of *sati*. Most surprisingly, given that this was a period when middle-class women's sphere was defined as the domestic and the private rather than the public and the political, both groups of female campaigners joined men in petitioning the imperial parliament to pass laws outlawing slavery and *sati*. Indeed these two campaigns represent the first concerted petitioning of parliament by women on questions of women's oppression and female emancipation, taking place some 30 years before the commencement of petitioning for British women's own rights.[23]

What, then, can a study of women's involvement in these two campaigns tell us about the relationship between feminism and imperialism? Can these female campaigners be described as feminists? Just what does it mean to talk of female emancipation within an imperial framework?

The women campaigners expressed their motivation in gender-specific terms which stressed their empathy with the sufferings of other women and their identification with them as mothers across the divides of 'race' and culture. Despite this, the imperial power relationship – control and direction of the lives of the colonised by the coloniser – imbued the relationship between white women and the black and Indian women for whom they campaigned. British women advocated stronger intervention in colonial government by the imperial parliament in the metropolis. They can be seen as promoting projects of imperial social reform: they wished to change imperial laws so that women's position would be improved. They were strong believers in the benevolent and humanitarian potential of imperialism – in the value of a Western civilising mission. Indeed, both sets of campaigners had strong links to Christian missionaries. British imperialism was seen as having the potential to emancipate women.

Women campaigners spoke on behalf of colonised women, whom they represented as passive victims of patriarchal oppression – whether as the 'helpless victims' of abusive white colonial planters in the West Indies, or as 'helpless widows' oppressed by indigenous men and Hindu customs in India. In the case of anti-slavery, this speaking 'on behalf of' took an extreme form which blurred the line between the reality of enslaved women's lives and white women's imagining of these lives: putting the plea 'am I not a woman and a sister' into the mouths of enslaved women, and writing appeals in the form of enslaved women appealing to white women. Clearly this was effective propaganda, playing on women's humanitarian sensibilities and encouraging them to identify with the suffering of other women. In choosing to campaign on behalf of women who had the least opportunity to make their own voices heard, British women helped to make the sufferings of these women visible, but visible through Western eyes.

British women's power to represent other women depended on there being little chance that the women could represent themselves. Female campaigners made little attempt to seek out the views of enslaved or widowed women themselves, content to remain reliant on the representations of male abolitionists or missionaries. Even when the opportunity presented itself for direct contact, British women attempted to fit colonised women's self-representations into their pre-existing colonial frames of understanding rather than revise these frameworks. The publication at the height of the anti-slavery campaign of the autobiography of the Caribbean slave Mary Prince, who presented herself and her fellow slaves not only as victims of slavery but also as resisters and survivors, did not lead to a revision of white women campaigners' representation of black women's passivity.[24] A similar picture emerges from accounts of the first single British woman teacher to travel to India in the 1820s on a mission to educate Indian women and thereby aid the eradication of *sati*. Mary Anne Cooke's supporters claimed with excitement that her work marked the beginning of a dialogue between the women of Britain and the women of India, but Cooke stuck to her pre-conceived ideas about what Indian women needed, insisting on retaining an explicitly Christian focus to her teaching despite the resulting erosion of support from the Bengali Hindu reformers who were her potential allies.

Stress on the passivity of the female victim of *sati* or slavery was accompanied by an emphasis on female degradation. *Sati* was described as 'degrading to the female character', while female anti-slavery campaigners stressed the 'moral degradation' of women under slavery. The connotations of this word – debasement, loss of honour – give an image of women who, in the same way as British prostitutes, were seen as in need of elevation by more respectable and 'pure' women and by contact with Christianity – as in Mary Prince's account of her conversion and realisation that she is a sinner. 'Women's mission to women', defined by female philanthropists at the period, thus had both domestic and imperial dimensions. On the imperial stage, British women simultaneously expressed identification with, and stressed difference and distance from and superiority to, black and Indian women.

Women's critiques of *sati* and slavery tended to be couched in the language of humanitarianism and Christian morality rather than in a language of human rights or women's rights. Their argument was not that enslaved women had a right to be free, but rather that emancipation would relieve their terrible suffering; not that widowed Hindu women had the right to live, or to make a free choice whether to live or die, but rather that *sati* caused them and their orphaned children terrible and unacceptable suffering. The female campaigners saw female emancipation in terms of the abolition of 'barbaric' and unchristian practices, whether these were practised by domineering Hindu men or degenerate colonial planters. Their attack was not on patriarchy in general but rather on abuses of male power which denied to black and Asian women the privileges and protection they claimed to enjoy themselves as British wives, mothers and daughters.

The black woman slave, flogged, sexually abused and torn from her children, and the Hindu widow immolated on her husband's funeral pyre were clearly figures of immense symbolic significance to British women: figures which propelled them to move out of the private sphere into public and political action. However, while campaigners raised issues that were also of concern to the feminist writers analysing British women's own subordination – the sexual exploitation of women, violence against women, the separation of mothers and children, and the legal status of married women – the anti-slavery and anti-*sati* campaigners did not explicitly link the sufferings of non-European women with their own subordination. Rather, they tended to contrast their own position with that of black and Hindu women, and to distance themselves from campaigns for the rights of British women, presenting their public actions as exceptional responses to exceptional circumstances rather than as a challenge to 'separate spheres'.

In the period 1790–1850 middle-class white British women were thus engaged in two parallel and largely distinct projects broadly concerned with female emancipation. First, they created a Western feminist discourse concerned with vindicating their own rights within Britain itself through presenting the subordination of women as out-of-place and out-of-time in such a progressive and enlightened Western society. Second, they were active in campaigning for female emancipation within an imperial frame. In the process, aspects of British imperialism such as colonial slavery were critiqued as incompatible with Western values, while at the same time British imperialism was presented as providing an exciting opportunity for cultural intervention aimed at improving the position of women in non-Western societies. These two strands of early feminism were to come together in the 'imperial feminism' of the years 1860–1914. At the same time the challenge to imperial feminism would begin.

Conclusion

This consideration of the historical roots of British feminism has, I hope, helped clarify the ways in which the development of Western feminism was intimately tied to the development of imperialism. This connection brings us back to the questions raised at the beginning of this chapter concerning the problems that have arisen in the course of Western feminist attempts to rewrite the history of imperialism. Indeed, the features of the imperial frame of reference identified by critics of some Western feminist political activism and scholarship can be seen to have historical roots dating back some two centuries to the origins of modern Western feminism. These features include the taking of white Western women's lives as the norm against which other women's experiences are measured; the homogenising of the diverse experiences of Third World women, and the failure to seek out or take account of their own views and aspirations; the representation of Third World women as passive victims, ignoring evidence of their agency or resistance; and the assumption of the superiority of Western civilisation, associated with a conviction of the need for Western women's leadership to achieve progressive improvement in the position of women worldwide.

In seeking to change representations of the imperial past by placing women at the centre of our studies and making gender an integral part of our conceptual framework, we clearly need to be wary of creating feminist histories that are new forms of colonial discourse. If we can avoid this trap, I believe that the study of women and gender has the potential to provide us with new understandings of the imperial past which may help us to envision more radical feminist and postcolonial futures.

Further reading

Antoinette Burton, *Burdens of History: British Feminists, Indian Women, and Imperial Culture, 1865–1915* (Chapel Hill, NC, 1994).

Nupur Chaudhuri and Margaret Strobel, *Western Women and Imperialism: Complicity and Resistance* (Bloomington, Ind., 1992).

Cheryl Johnson-Odim and Margaret Strobel, eds, *Expanding the Boundaries of Women's History: Essays on Women in the Third World* (Bloomington, Ind., 1992).

Anne McClintock, *Imperial Leather: Race, Gender and Sexuality in the Colonial Contest* (New York, 1995).

Clare Midgley, ed., *Gender and Imperialism* (Manchester, 1998).

Ruth Roach Pierson and Nupur Chaudhuri, eds, *Nation, Empire, Colony: Historicizing Gender and Race* (Bloomington, Ind., 1998).

Kumkum Sangari and Sudesh Vaid, *Recasting Women: Essays in Indian Colonial History* (New Brunswick, NJ, 1990).

Verene Shepherd, Bridget Brereton and Barbara Bailey, *Engendering History: Caribbean Women in Historical Perspective* (Kingston, Jamaica, 1995).

Mrinalina Sinha, *Colonial Masculinity: The 'Manly Englishman' and the 'Effeminate Bengali' in the Late Nineteenth Century* (Manchester, 1995).

Margaret Strobel, *European Women and the Second British Empire* (Bloomington, Ind., 1991).

Vron Ware, *Beyond the Pale: White Women, Racism and History* (1992).

Notes

1. Valerie Amos and Pratibah Parmar, 'Challenging imperial feminism', *Feminist Review* 17 (1984), pp. 3–19; Chandra Tolpady Mohanty, 'Under Western eyes: feminist scholarship and colonial discourse', in C. T. Mohanty, A. Russo and T. Torres, eds, *Third World Women and the Politics of Feminism* (Bloomington, Ind., 1991), pp. 51–80.

2. For critiques of Western history-writing as a form of colonial discourse see: Robert Young, *White Mythologies: Writing History and the West* (1990); Gyan Prakash, ed., *After Colonialism: Imperial Histories and Postcolonial Displacements* (Princeton, NJ, 1995).

3. For a useful overview of the orientalism debate and a thoughtful critique of Said's work, see John MacKenzie, *Orientalism: History, Theory and the Arts* (Manchester, 1995), Chapter 1. For a short introduction to postcolonial theory written from a feminist perspective, see Ania Loomba, *Colonialism/Postcolonialism* (1998).

4. At one end of this spectrum is popular novelist Joanna Trollope's *Britannia's Daughters: Women of the British Empire* (1983); at the other social anthropologist Helen Callaway's *Gender, Culture and Empire: European Women in Colonial Nigeria* (Basingstoke, 1987).

5. Jane Haggis, 'Gendering colonialism or colonising gender? Recent women's studies approaches to white women and the history of British colonialism', *Women's Studies International Forum* 12 (1990), pp. 105–12.

6. Nupur Chaudhuri and Margaret Strobel, *Western Women and Imperialism: Complicity and Resistance* (Bloomington, Ind., 1992); Kumari Jayawardena, *The White Woman's Other Burden: Western Women and South Asia During British Rule* (New York, 1995); Margaret Strobel, *European Women and the Second British Empire* (Bloomington, Ind., 1991).

7. Marilyn Lake, 'Colonised and colonising: the white Australian feminist subject', *Women's History Review* 2/3 (1993), pp. 377–86.

8. Important studies include: John MacKenzie, *Propaganda and Empire: The Manipulation of British Public Opinion 1880–1960* (Manchester, 1984); John Mackenzie, ed., *Imperialism and Popular Culture* (Manchester, 1986); Bill Schwarz, ed., *The Expansion of England: Race, Ethnicity and Cultural History* (1996); James Walvin, *Fruits of Empire: Exotic Produce and British Taste, 1660–1800* (Basingstoke, 1997); Kathleen Wilson, *The Sense of the People: Politics, Culture and Imperialism in England, 1715–1785* (Cambridge, 1995). See also Antoinette Burton, 'Rules of thumb: British history and "imperial culture" in nineteenth- and twentieth-century Britain', *Women's History Review* 3/4 (1994), pp. 483–500.

9. Ann Laura Stoler and Frederick Cooper, 'Between metropole and colony: rethinking a research agenda', in Frederick Cooper and Ann Laura Stoler, eds, *Tensions of Empire: Colonial Cultures in a Bourgeois World* (Berkeley, Calif., 1997).

10. Vron Ware, *Beyond the Pale: White Women, Racism and History* (1992); Anna Davin, 'Imperialism and Motherhood', in Cooper and Stoler, eds, *Tensions of Empire*, pp. 87–151; Clare Midgley, *Women Against Slavery: The British Campaigns, 1780–1870* (1992); Julia Bush, *Edwardian Ladies and Imperial Power* (Leicester, 1999); Antoinette Burton, *Burdens of History: British Feminists, Indian Women, and Imperial Culture, 1865–1915* (Chapel Hill, NC, 1994); Anne McClintock, *Imperial Leather: Race, Gender and Sexuality in the Colonial Contest* (New York, 1995).

11. Gretchen Gerzina, *Black England: Life Before Emancipation* (1995); Rozina Visram, *Ayahs, Lascars and Princes: Indians in Britain 1700–1947* (1986); Ann Rossiter, 'Bringing the margins into the centre: a review of aspects of Irish women's emigration from a British perspective', in Ailbhe Smyth, ed., *Irish Women's Studies Reader* (Dublin, 1993), pp. 177–202; Ziggi Alexander and Audrey Dewjee, eds, *The Wonderful Adventures of Mrs Seacole in Many Lands* (original edn 1857; repr. Bristol, 1984); Delia Jarrett Macaulay, *The Life of Una Marson, 1905–65* (Manchester, 1998); Antoinette Burton, *At the Heart of the Empire: Indians and the Colonial Encounter in Late-Victorian Britain* (Berkeley, Calif., 1998).

12. For an important recent attempt to look at the complex interrelationship of immigrant and indigenous, white and black, women's lives in post-war Britain in the contexts of colonialism and racism, see Wendy Webster, *Imagining Home: Gender, 'Race' and National Identity, 1945–64* (Manchester, 1998).

13. Cheryl Johnson-Odim and Margaret Strobel, eds, *Expanding the Boundaries of Women's History: Essays on Women in the Third World* (Bloomington, Ind., 1992); Kumkum Sangari and Sudesh Vaid, *Recasting Women: Essays in Indian Colonial History* (New Brunswick, NJ, 1990); *Gender and History*, Special Issue: Gendered Colonialisms in African History, 8/3 (November 1996); Verene Shepherd, Bridget Brereton and Barbara Bailey, *Engendering History: Caribbean Women in Historical Perspective* (Kingston, Jamaica, 1995).

14. Gayatri Spivak, 'Can the subaltern speak?', in C. Nelson and L. Grossberg, eds, *Marxism and the Interpretation of Culture* (1988); Lata Mani, *Contentious Traditions: The Debate on Sati in Colonial India* (Berkeley, Calif., 1998); Ania Loomba,

'Dead women tell no tales: issues of female subjectivity, subaltern agency and tradition in colonial and post-colonial writings on widow immolation in India', *History Workshop Journal* 36 (1993), pp. 209–27.

15. Kumari Jayawardena, *Feminism and Nationalism in the Third World* (1986); Mohanty, Russo and Torres, eds, *Third World Women*.

16. Sara Mills, *Discourses of Difference: An Analysis of Women's Travel Writing and Colonialism* (1991); Billie Melman, *Women's Orients: English Women and the Middle East, 1718–1918. Sexuality, Religion and Work* (Basingstoke, 2nd edn, 1995); Reina Lewis, *Gendering Orientalism: Race, Femininity and Representation* (1996).

17. Gayatri Spivak, 'Three women's texts and a critique of imperialism', *Critical Inquiry* 12 (Autumn 1985), pp. 243–61; Antoinette Burton, 'Recapturing Jane Eyre: reflections on historicizing the colonial encounter in Victorian Britain', *Radical History Review* 64 (1996), pp. 58–72.

18. Catherine Hall, 'Gender politics and imperial politics: rethinking the histories of empire', in Shepherd, Bremton and Bailey, eds, *Engendering History*, pp. 48–62.

19. Catherine Hall, *White, Male and Middle Class: Explorations in Feminism and History* (Cambridge, 1992), Part 3; Mrinalina Sinha, *Colonial Masculinity: The 'Manly Englishman' and the 'Effeminate Bengali' in the Late Nineteenth Century* (Manchester, 1995).

20. Burton, *Burdens of History*.

21. C. A. Bayly, *Imperial Meridian: The British Empire and the World, 1780–1830* (1989).

22. The discussion below is based on research into the writings of Catherine Macaulay, Mary Wollstonecraft, William Thompson, Marion Reid, Harriet Taylor and John Stuart Mill, published in Clare Midgley, 'Anti-slavery and the roots of "imperial feminism"', in Clare Midgley, ed., *Gender and Imperialism* (Manchester, 1998), pp. 161–79.

23. The discussion below is based on research published in Midgley, *Women Against Slavery*; Clare Midgley, 'Anti-slavery and Feminism in Britain', *Gender and History* 5/3 (1993), pp. 343–62; Clare Midgley, 'Female emancipation in an imperial frame: English women and the campaign against *sati* (widow-burning) in India, 1813–1830', *Women's History Review* 9/1 (2000), pp. 95–121.

24. Moira Ferguson, ed., *The History of Mary Prince, A West Indian Slave, Related by Herself* (original edn 1831; repr. 1987).

CHAPTER FIVE

The stigmata of 'widowhood' and Indian feminism: expanding the boundaries of international feminism

PARITA MUKTA

Representations, discourses and political contestations surrounding the plight of the upper-caste widow in India remained implicated within the questions of religious salvation, family honour and community construction throughout the pre-modern period. Here, markers of widowhood stood for the visibility of the control exercised over women, this itself betokening the higher social status of a community in an intensely hierarchical caste society. During the period of British imperialism, the status of widows became caught up within acrimonious disputations between colonial officials and members of the Indian male elites, where the colonial 'civilising mission' utilised the index of Indian women's lack of liberties to legitimate its own rule. Simultaneously, both the control over widows and the emergent attempt to grant them legal rights became part of a historical formation whereby the rising Indian elites reformulated the boundaries of caste and religion, thus retaining and consolidating social privilege over the subordinate castes, and over the other religious communities (Muslim and Christian). Throughout all this, the vivid voices of widows themselves remained marginal, and it has been the task of feminist historiography to retrieve the expressions, articulations and pain of widows, thereby stamping this world with the names, utterances and strivings of those women whose experiences arch across the sky from the past to reach the present.

However, it has also been the task of Indian feminism to be self-critical of the history of women's reform, particularly given that the nationalist assertions that were so much a hallmark of the nineteenth century gave rise to the specific construction of a dominant (upper-caste) Hindu community which rose up in violent contestation over the lower-caste communities, and in genocidal acts against Muslims and Christians in India towards the end of the twentieth century.[1] The question of the upper-caste widow's lack of rights, and the construction of a dominant religious community in and through the discourses of widow reform therefore have to be taken together in order to understand the fraught history of women's lack of liberties, the history of nationalism and the genealogy of modern-day violence.

This chapter will begin with an analysis of the ways in which feminist historiography has shifted the terrain of envisioning the past, through bringing into relief women's voices which have challenged dominant notions of wifehood and widowhood in the pre-modern world. It will progress to the representations of widowhood in the period of British imperial rule in India, from the late eighteenth to the nineteenth and early twentieth centuries. It will then argue that profoundly political concerns of the present, centred around the rise of Hindu authoritarian assertions, and the growth of religious nationalisms in the Indian sub-continent, particularly from the 1980s onwards, have pushed feminist historians to return to the early period of 'social reform' (within which the question of the rights of women to personal liberties is embedded), and to assess anew the changing configurations surrounding issues of women's oppression and the link between woman, community and nation. Throughout the discussion, the arguments will shift from dominant representations to their role in buttressing emerging political formations to the strivings of widows themselves. In this sense, then, changing the past entails changing paradigms, perspectives, and the very lens of enquiry, so that past epochs are scrutinised with newer questions in mind, at the same time ensuring that these do not become distorted through presentist assumptions.

The sacral and the dreaded

The ancient Laws of Manu are often quoted to demonstrate the duality of faithful wife/sacralised widowhood as found in high Brahmanical (priestly) culture. While one must be careful about taking the Laws of Manu as representing lived norms, the dominant Brahmanical discourse undoubtedly represented the attempts to make widowhood sacred while (simultaneously) controlling the sexuality of widows within a rigid disciplinary regime guarded by family and community. A woman whose husband died was deemed to be inauspicious: indeed she was considered to have lacked the religious virtue necessary to ward off the call of Death. Manu is clear about the code of conduct enforceable on a woman at the death of her husband:

A virtuous wife should never do anything displeasing to the husband who took her hand in marriage, when he is alive or dead . . . When her husband is dead she may fast as much as she likes, [living] on auspicious flowers, roots and fruits, but she should not even mention the name of another man. She should be long-suffering until death, self-restrained and chaste, striving [to fulfil] the unsurpassed duty of women who have one husband . . . A virtuous wife who remains chaste when her husband has died goes to heaven just like those chaste men, even if she has no sons.[2]

It is clear that the whole body of law and scriptural texts (of which Manu is the best example) strained and laboured to contain the disciplined figure of a woman (uncoupled from her husband through death) within the very prison of upper-caste domestic existence. While many feminist historians have been quick to point to the excessive strictures placed on an upper-caste widow's life, one wonders whether this heralded rather the weakness of a structure which, while overbearing, had to contend with very different norms existing within the mass of labouring and artisan communities. As priestly ritual practitioners and as the *literati*, Brahmans, together with the Rajput warrior brotherhoods which kept women fiercely secluded, held ideological authority, and one important way of demarcating themselves from the rest of the populace was through the visible and tight control of women within these particular communities.[3]

For feminists who cut their teeth on the women's movement of the 1970s and 1980s, the question of women's resistance, and women's subversion of orthodox, dominant practices, was crucial in providing historical forebears of free spirits and thinkers. The aim was nothing short of changing the landscape of representation, of transforming the static and ahistorical view which continued to see women's suffering as a sign of their virtue and stoical purity. Since the guardianship of upper-caste widows was so centrally conjoined with dominant religious ideology, it was then perhaps not surprising that voices of resistance were sought and found in the eclectic and unorthodox devotional movements which swept India in the medieval period. A vibrant feminist scholarship arose which pored over written devotional literature, recorded songs sung in the devotional movements, and compiled the fragments of women's writings available in various religious and social traditions. This labour of love did much to represent women as mediating oppression in complex and socially powerful ways. It shifted analysis away from monolithic structures of power to seeing ways in which these were contested. The wife and the widow appeared in this not as flat, crushed figures who were overdetermined by the structures of domination, but as people who had felt the tyranny of subjugation, and who had transmuted their desires into songs and poems.

The tenth anniversary issue (1989) celebrating the continuing output of *Manushi* (one of the first regular publications on women and society in

India) was dedicated to affirming the large, creative output of women in the devotional movements.[4] Feminist engagement with the richness of this cultural expression achieved a number of important transformations in historical understandings, even at the same time as it differentiated the terrain of debate regarding the relationship between religious beliefs and the nature of salvationist politics.

First of all, it mapped out the distinctive and gendered forms of liberation and salvation sought by women in the heterodox religious movements. While the life-world of the women *bhaktas* (devotees) and the idioms utilised by them were bound up within the realm of religious expression, the songs also commented on the world of social relationships. Questions pertaining to love and desire for God as the Beloved, yearnings and seekings which broke the fetters of existing man–woman relationships were mirrored evocatively in the words of the women *bhaktas*. The songs, transmitted over time through networks of devotees, formed an expressive domain which kept alive the legacy of the women *bhaktas*. The devotional movements provided a space for women (and widows in particular) to speak of their yearnings for the Beloved in ways which both subverted the sexual hierarchy, and retained alternative articulation within the spiritual realm.

The heterodox devotional movements which challenged orthodox Brahmanical religion (not to mention the institution of caste) also carried the seeds of the transformation of gender and caste relationships, whereby large numbers of women carved out a space for themselves within the diverse efflorescence of sects, detaching themselves from the strictures and confines of wifehood and widowhood. Non-elite women joined these sects too, which provided a viable living space for widows who had subsequently had children, poor prostitutes who wanted an entry out of that profession, and women who had lost all their relations.[5]

Second, the exploration of this historical momentum raised salient questions as to the reach, limitations and boundedness of salvationist movements which, while leaving a strong imprint on the society around them, failed to mark a radical rupture in the institutions of caste and patriarchy. The representations of visionary relationships by the women *bhaktas* provided tantalising glimpses of possibilities and promises which remained out of the reach of the majority of women while acting as a marker of possibilities for women in the past and the future. In the enormity of making the shift from being governed by Brahmanic scriptural norms to experiencing tense and fraught ways of representing their aspirations and yearnings, women *bhaktas* succeeded in prising open the world of sacralised oppression. The (changing) structures of caste and endogamous units, however, could not be dislodged by cultural assertions alone, and persisted in providing a stubborn bedrock to both community and (later) nationalist formations.

The momentum of the feminism of the 1970s and 1980s did much to recuperate women's voices, and to document the myriad ways in which women had transgressed and thus resisted social norms. The statement that there were histories (and life) before imperialism was a simple yet necessary intervention which stretched both the imagination and the focus of understanding. While this was not enough to shake off the weight of the colonial legacy, it drew attention to that dense and complicated past which has been collapsed under the concept of 'feudalism', within which women lived, struggled and made courageous attempts to carve out dignified exit points. The emphasis on the pre-colonial period was important to Indian feminism, for it demonstrated that women were historical agents seeking liberties long before the colonial state intruded.

Imperialism, social reform and nationalism

That the colonial 'civilising mission' laid a particular emphasis on the amelioration of the status of women, and that this was firmly embedded within an extension of British rule in India in the first part of the nineteenth century, is by now a well-explored field of studies in feminist history. While the work done by certain feminists in the West has been exemplary in challenging imperial history (see for example Clare Midgley, this volume), newer political constellations have crystallised which require one to look at the past with different and harder questions. This is becoming increasingly clearer within Indian feminism and Indian feminist writings on the past. The tension, however, lies in incorporating these understandings within international and global perspectives. I will outline the substance of the arguments, before going into the detail of representations.

British (colonial) ideologues took the position that the oppression of women in the colonies served as a measure, an index, of that civilisation, which was then placed within an international hierarchy suffused by social Darwinism. The embeddedness of Victorian feminism within the process of consolidating empire (with India at its centre) has also been laid bare by anti-imperialist feminists. The Indian woman stood for an emblematic enslavement against which British feminism gauged its own progress. The representation of Indian women (and in particular the upper-caste widow) in Victorian feminist writings reified the oppression of women and objectified Indian women. The construction of racialised imaginings created a dominating Western feminism which asserted itself in and through the colonised Indian woman (widow).[6]

While the critique of the history of British feminism has been necessary to challenge the imperial thrust of sections of this movement, Indian feminism today is itself concerned with a set of questions and dilemmas which go well beyond challenging imperialism and the representations of Indian women by Victorian feminists, and it is to this that I now turn. I will proceed to argue that the boundaries of international feminism need to be enlarged in order to incorporate an understanding of the nature of imperialism and the shape of nationalism that was subsequently engendered. The post-independence experience, as well as the more recent period of globalisation (together with the imposition of structural adjustment, a new world order and a significant rise in ethnic nationalisms), has brought into sharp relief questions of economic development, political identities and citizenship rights. An engaged international feminism can ill afford to ignore these issues if it is to build a viable and sustainable future. But to return to the nineteenth century first (a period which was formative in configuring unequal international relations).

Colonial rule transformed the political economy and social relationships within India, where the nature of identities based around religion and caste acquired more politicised forms. The imbrication of caste and religion within the political process gave these a virulent new lease of life. Religious and caste identities held a complex relationship to the emergent class formation and to the nature of nationalism both in town and countryside. Indian feminists thus have had to take into account, simultaneously, the workings of colonialism and its attendant depredations. The politicised forms of religion and caste, and the newly configured structures of patriarchy which arose in this period, cast a shadow on the future of social relationships in the sub-continent and have had to be contended with. Both feminist analysis and the practices that have flowed out of this ferment have thus had to look at the colonial roots of identity formations.

These identity formations began to wield an independent life of their own, and since the dismantling of formal empire, the creation of an independent nation-state in 1947, and the rise of religious nationalism from the 1980s onwards, a very different set of questions has arisen in relationship to the past. This has entailed a critical look at the nature of the community formation that took place in the nineteenth century. It is thus not adequate for Indian feminism to study colonialism by itself, and I would suggest that international feminism needs to engage with these political constellations too, particularly in an epoch that has seen the rise of violent ethnic nationalisms throughout the world. For Indian feminism this has required taking seriously the workings of both imperialism and nationalism, as well as the forces of communal violence they unleashed. If Western feminism has had to reckon with the shadow of imperialism and racism within its very inception, Indian feminism has had to confront and face up to the forces of communal (inter-religious) and caste violence which have so devastated the social landscape.

The reconstitution of gender relationships in the nineteenth century was predicated on the 'reform' of the status of women. In earlier analysis, the political contestation over the right of a widow to remarry, property rights for women, and the proper age of consent had been seen in terms of a middle class (upper caste) coming to modernise itself within the ambits of coloniality. Contemporary scholarship today emphasises this 'reform' movement to be more a class assertion within which the contours of a religious community were being redrawn, implicating an upper-caste patriarchy inside the workings of a combative (and anti-imperialist) state formation. For the purposes of our discussion on widow reform, it is important to note that the political debates, the literary ventures, and the fictional representations of upper-caste Hindu widows by upper-caste men fed in significant ways into the making of a reconfigured upper-caste (communal) fold.[7] Tanika Sarkar has argued that

> The Hindu woman became a political resource for a militant Hindu chauvinism that was composed, from the late nineteenth century onward, largely of ideologues from Bengal, Punjab, and Maharashtra . . . In a variety of ways, reimaging the women within the community helped Hindu social leaders to reach out to women of their castes/class as active and consenting constituents of the community. The community came to be vested with a political self-image that cast itself as threatened, weakened and embattled, and, at the same time, inherently superior to non-Hindus.[8]

The contemporary rise of authoritarian Hindu politics in India (with minority Muslim and Christian communities bearing the brunt of violent attacks in the recent period) has entailed a closer look at the constitution of the 'Hindu' community in the nineteenth century. This has called for a significant shift in feminist scholarship. The reconfiguring of patriarchies in the colonial period reconstructed notions of wife and mother and conflated these with the emergence of a distinctive 'Hindu' community. The assertion of a rightist Hindu nationalism today has shifted the debates away from the singular focus upon the nature of the colonial state to the processes whereby the reconstitution of gender relationships went hand-in-hand with the making of an upper-caste, middle-class elite which defined itself through the reforms initiated within its midst.

One of the most cogent cases for the ways in which colonial laws legitimated the domain of sacred texts and the power of priestly interpretations came from Lata Mani in 1986. Mani argued that the 'official discourse' on widow immolation was conducted very much through an interpretation of elite sacred texts, whereby the liberal reform of tradition was based on the utilisation of sayings and injunctions which posited the austerities of widowhood as being more meritorious than widow immolation.[9] Mani's work challenged the earlier history, which had emphasised the impact of Western education and ideals of modernising reforms onto an emergent middle class which led the impetus for legislation on the issue of widow immolation, and subsequently the right of widows to remarry. Mani's scholarship also fed into a wider body of work which saw the structuring of legislation pertaining to matters of divorce, maintenance, separation and child custody enshrined into what became known as 'personal law'. The enshrining of law into Hindu, Muslim, and Christian personal law meant that legal representation tied a woman to a particular religious community.

The institution of widowhood, however, proved remarkably resilient. One reason perhaps is that whereas the wife and the mother remained tied to significant family members (in particular to the husband and children that they were entrusted with moulding into moral citizens), the widow remained tangential to both the family and the community, for she was invisible in the theatre of public bonding. She remained visible only as a mark of repressed womanhood which carried the stigmata of imposed inauspiciousness: in the first instance, the tonsure (shaven head), and on the other the wearing of white or ochre brown.

'Widowhood' as a male genre: defending upper-caste patriarchy

A complete genre of male writing emerged in the late nineteenth and early twentieth centuries which spoke for the widow, and often in the voice of the widow herself. *Widows' Laments* was published by the Gujarat Sansar Sudhara Samaj (Gujarat Social Reform Society) in 1906 and was written by a Kavi (poet), Bhavanishankar Narsinharam. It is a series of poems written in the voice of various widows, whereby the stigmata of a shaven head, bare hands (which wear no bangles) and white clothing appear as constant markers of powerlessness, abject misery and social death. The conceit of speaking as a widow makes for three gestures. First, the widow is represented as lamenting the loss of the insignia which demonstrate her social status as an auspicious wife with standing in the community. It is thus the impossibility of acquiring any social meaning outside of the marital state that is em-phasised. Second, the widows are made to enunciate a death wish. One of the poems has the refrain 'I now die without death', and the windows are also made to want to immolate themselves.[10] For a tract published by the Social Reform Society, it reads remarkably as laments which cynically romanticise the marital relationship, replete with emblems of an auspiciousness which are deemed to form the apogee of a woman's life. Third (and cumulatively), the poems entitled *Widows' Laments* (written by a man) achieve the feat of raising an aesthetics of a feminised suffering, thus making this into an art form. Widowhood did not act solely as a marker of social contestation of what was permissible and impermissible for a woman divested of what was deemed to be her primary role in the social world. It entered the literary realm, and within male discourse represented a new genre of writing.

The versification, essays and tracts written by men provide a body of cultural artifice within which the personal and social plight of the widow was first revealed and then erased through the social conservatism of the texts. Thus, a tract entitled *Widows' Pleader*, published in 1882, began with a preface which made explicit the fact that widow remarriage (within the caste community) was being advocated in order to preserve the boundaries of this caste formation. It stated that when an upper-caste widow who is denied remarriage within her community runs away with a member of a 'different caste' and thus transgresses her caste boundary, then this 'makes the upper caste people lose their rank'.[11] The author argued, painstakingly, that when daughters of a Brahman

> take a Musulman or a sadhu, the parents still retain their caste status; and those parents who did not let their daughters transgress community boundaries and gave them away in remarriage within their own castes, today find themselves outcasted . . . This demonstrates clearly that Brahmans are not happy to have widows marry within their own Brahman community, but are happy to see them go over to another caste.[12]

This representation of upper-caste widows who remarry outside of an ortho-dox Brahman community, and the remonstrance of a male ideologue who harangues from within to keep widows inside the upper-caste fold, is remarkable for the changes in register it portrays in matters of choice. It is the women themselves who are represented as being responsible for 'taking a Musulman or a sadhu', while those parents who married their widowed daughters within the Brahman community are deemed to have done so in order to stop the women from crossing across the caste barriers. One is a woman who chooses to break rank, the other is one who is brought back from this brink. Given the continuing hostility of Brahman communities to widow remarriage, the loss of 'daughters' to communities defined as foreign in their otherness loomed very large.

I am not sure that loss of numbers and retention of 'Hindu wombs' for pro-creation of more Hindu children adequately encapsulates the late nineteenth-century and early twentieth-century milieu.[13] The fear of miscegenation (*varnasankara* in indigenous discourse) was indeed profound, and here the demarcation is of an upper-caste Brahmanical boundary – outside of which lie the Musulman, the sadhus (well known in popular culture as sexual enticers, and 'Hindu' spiritual men to boot) and castes of lower ranking. It is rather, I think, to the ability to demonstrate control over women in the family while at the same time displaying loyalty to caste bonds and to the public theatre of caste configuration that the answers seem to point. These 'upper castes' (*uncha gnati*) stood for dominant moral authority, outside of which lay the domain which was constructed as abhorrent as it breached every Brahmanical norm. The fear of the transgression of widows was acute. Thus, the social reform agenda emphasised moral panic caused by 'caste-crossing, abortion, and infanticide', which would be averted through widow remarriage (within the caste community). This would result in uncountable merit to 'all you righteous people' (*tamo dharmatmaone*).[14]

'All you righteous people' are of course the men of the community, entrusted with ensuring the future moral health of that milieu through control over women. It is extremely instructive that the cause of widow remarriage is argued through the benefits that would accrue to the making of a tight-knit, moral community: infanticide and abortion would be prevented; the numbers of bachelors and widows would go down; widows and bachelors would cease to cross caste by establishing relationships outside of the caste boundary based on 'lust'; those Brahmans who married their daughters to 'Brahmans of lower rank', and thus diluted this 'Brahmagnati' (Brahman caste), would be stopped; and those widows who were starving would be saved. Thus, the representation of widowhood and the amelioration of the plight of widows was closely linked to the construction of the boundaries of 'community', 'self' and the 'other', whereby the 'widow' was sought to be freed from a lifetime of woeful (and enforced) asceticism by being retained within the grip of the upper castes.

It is significant that 'remarriage' itself is construed as remarriage *within* the caste community. Other forms are referred to as 'bad deeds' (*kuda kaam*). The tract refers to various examples of these deeds, with precise details of place and date: a widow who was disgraced in the centre of Vagheshwari; a Brahman widow who 'took a Baniya man and ran away with him'; a child widow who 'ran away taking an Arab with her'; and all these women, moreover, had been seen crossing the Brahman *chora* (square) at night, and no one had intercepted them. One indeed had been seen carrying a bundle of ornaments.

Think you Brahmans. How much of your worth has been left to you?[15]

The pamphlet ended with a stirring call to take up the sword in defence of righteousness (*dharma*), to protect this through vindicating the widow's unhappiness and thereby preserve *dharma*. Those men who did not rise to the challenge were represented here as emasculated: more like women whose wrists jingled with bangles.

While the Brahman men of the caste community are constructed as not manly enough to rise to the challenge of widow reform (and thus strengthen its own community boundary), the widows here are represented as those entrapped within their sexual desire, unable to find a legitimate expression (within the community of Brahman men), and, concomitantly, as brazen women who take an 'Arab' or a 'sadhu' and set up house with him. Not only were religious and caste barriers broken by these widows, but so were boundaries of marriage, for it appears clear that these relationships were not always socially formalised. There were thus diverse and differentiated ways in which upper-caste widows attempted to mediate hierarchies of religion, caste, sexual relationships and economic hardships.

Building on a factual, evidential base, the writer of the *Widows' Pleader* made out a case in order to reach out to the college-educated teachers, administrators and clerks within his own caste community, to convince them of the evils of not accepting widow remarriage. A particular caste–class configuration is taking place here, where the self-image of those who have set themselves up to bring about social transformation has found it necessary to propagate the message of caste–class renewal through shaming strategies. What became occluded here was not only the desires and wishes of the widows themselves, but the material deprivation experienced by widows who lacked a secure social base which gave them access to the food bowl.

Writings by widows

The above discussion has had as its focus the representations of widows in elite sacred texts, and in the discourses of men of the upper castes in nineteenth-century India, of colonial officials and of Victorian feminists. I now turn to writings by widows.

The writings by widows themselves followed two main trajectories. One was that they were acutely aware of the lack of spaces in which they could actualise themselves in the Brahmanical culture, despite the changes wrought within this through the onset of colonial modernity. Widows who either ran away or established unorthodox liaisons with men outside of the caste and religious community they inhabited were clearly a salient part of the social world, and Brahman men attempted either to turn a blind eye to them, or to bring them back into the fold. It was to stem the flow of this that some male social reformers dedicated themselves to writing and propagating. Those widows who took a less individualistic and more public route of action did not, by and large, explicitly argue for the right of exit out of the caste community. The devotional movements which had earlier provided a domain for women to step out of the caste barriers and seek a measure of spiritual and personal freedoms through heterodox cults had congealed in their forms and were not open to innovation as they had been earlier. The political milieu necessitated a different social response, and this was forthcoming from within the body of widows who had gained literacy, and who were strategically placed within the sphere of debate and contestation. They took up the pen, and their writings demonstrate both a profound unease with, and pitiless criticism of, the hierarchies of caste and patriarchy that they inhabited.

Dhankor has gone down in the history of Gujarati social reform as the 'first' woman to enter into a remarriage. This took place on 2 May 1871. Since this was a remarriage *within* the caste, Dhankor and the social reformer Madhavdas Rugnathdas (whom she married) were both put out of caste and suffered many hardships. They were, however, supported by the political and intellectual milieu (which included the protection of the colonial police), and Dhankor, in her article entitled 'The Pitiful Condition of Hindu Widows', placed responsibility squarely on the parents who followed caste traditions, and on those who stood for the preservation of dominant religious norms. Describing the tonsure of a child widow, and other practices imposed on women, she said:

> What oppression! What cruelty! Oh pitiless parents, those who do this in the name of upholding *dharma* and those preachers of the *dharmashastras* and leaders of the community, do they have no feelings? . . . A widow should not look at the face of a man. She has to sit in a dark room with her eyes closed. She cannot talk alone with even her son, her brother or her father. She has to sleep on the floor. She has to eat dry and tasteless food on a leaf plate once a day, she is not allowed to eat on a plate . . . What a strict watch! Even the Russian prisoners in Siberia could not be experiencing such difficulties . . . There are some heroes who care for a widow's salvation and who pay no heed to caste restrictions. My late husband Sheth Madhavdas was one such.[16]

Dhankor's writings point to an intellect which had undergone the fire of resistance, and which had found support within a political ambience where the colonial state could be turned to for redress against the caste community. Dhankor's writing appeared in a women's journal which was dedicated to 'her most gracious majesty, Queen Alexandra, Empress of

India'. In pointing this out, I am neither endorsing imperialism nor (some) Indian women's loyalism to the imperial crown: rather, I am seeking to understand the various levels of pressure points that were accessible to Indian women at a particular time to make for interventions that brought about changes in their lives.

To marry of one's will outside of the community entailed both an exit out of this community and ostracism; to remarry within this community often entailed being outcaste; to live the life of a widow was tantamount to a social death. While one will never know the reach of the first of these forms of wresting of liberty, whereby women sought personal fulfilment in diverse other communities which nurtured both themselves and their children, it is clear that large numbers of women endured the last. The second form of grasping for personal happiness brought women and men centrally into conflict with power hierarchies within the community. Here, reform from 'within' was strongly contested, to the extent that very few upper-caste widows remarry even today. The dismantling of caste hierarchies remains a crucial task for the future, and the histories of widows who broke rank remain central.

The most spectacular example of this is provided by Pandita Ramabai (1858–1922), an activist reformer who wrote and gave lectures on the plight of widows in India, thus coming into conflict with male preachers such as Vivekananda who sought to portray both Indian civilisation and Indian women as the noblest in the world (in the process representing the position of women in the West as being degenerate). Ramabai stood out as a beacon against intellectual obfuscation, and the public, political stands that she took brought her into conflict not just with the elites of Indian society, but with the hierarchies of the Anglican Church, as well as with the cruel bureaucracy of the colonial state at the time of the 1897 plague.

The ways in which Ramabai's history has been written by two contemporary feminists, Antoinette Burton and Uma Chakravarty, illustrate well the tensions in emphasis and political intent between Western feminism and Indian feminism. Burton has provided a meticulous and admirable reading of Ramabai's time spent as a student in Cheltenham and Wantage, framing this within the context of understanding 'colonial encounters' at the 'very heart of the empire'.[17] Having taken seriously the critique of Western feminism as being embedded within an imperial nexus, Burton is at pains to show the grid of race, gender and colonial power as these affected Ramabai's sojourn in England between 1883 and 1886. She does this through an analysis of the relationships between Ramabai (a public advocate of women's reform in India) and Sister Geraldine (Ramabai's spiritual guide at Wantage), and between Ramabai and Dorothea Beale (educationalist, reformer and the headmistress at Cheltenham Ladies' College, where Ramabai studied).

Burton's work is exemplary in its exploration of the nature of the colonial encounter. It focuses upon the overburdened significance put upon Ramabai's conversion to the Christian faith and the subsequent surveillance she underwent in order to ensure that she remained faithful to both religious dogma and the Church authorities. The Anglican Church required Ramabai to return to spread the faith and do the work of a faithful evangelist in India. Ramabai's intellectual exploration of Christian teachings and her spiritual explorations were frowned upon by Sister Geraldine and the bishops. Burton argues that the former's infantilising of Ramabai, her reduction of Ramabai's spiritual doubts as due to 'a great want in the Hindu mind',[18] was a struggle for authority in the imperial context, and that Ramabai understood that evangelical orthodoxy was a metaphor for imperial power. Burton's emphasis is consistently on the ways in which Ramabai negotiated the axis of a gendered, racist orientalism to carve out her own meanings to social reform for women in India, religious belief and public action. Her point of political exposure is the imperial nature of relationships in Victorian England.

Burton's work provides a finely crafted analysis of the limitations of gender solidarity when relationships between women within a colonial context were suffused by and embedded within the workings of an imperial order. In contrast to Burton, the emphasis in Uma Chakravarty's (equally fine) work on Ramabai is on the relationship between gender, class and nation in nineteenth-century India. Chakravarty concentrates on Ramabai's two major challenges: first, to Brahmanical patriarchy, and second, to the exclusivist Hindu nationalism being forged by men of the upper castes in the imperial epoch. This particular emphasis, with its scrupulous analysis of the materiality of caste and class oppression, and the newly emergent political configurations (within which Ramabai stood as an intellectual and reformer of remarkable stature), converges with Burton in the understanding that Ramabai's relationship to and experiencing of Christianity was uniquely fashioned by her, and could not be reduced to the orthodox imperatives of either the Church or colonial rule. Both Burton and Chakravarty share a desire to put flesh and blood to Ramabai's strivings and struggles, and both succeed in portraying Ramabai in a moving way. Burton concludes by paying tribute to Ramabai's endeavours at the heart of the empire, and again reminds us that 'in the geo-political context of imperialism, encounters between women could not, and indeed cannot, be totally free of its ideological effects'.[19] Chakravarty's conclusions on Ramabai's life and travails are instructive here, and I will utilise both writers to draw some general remarks on the future of feminist historiography. Chakravarty says that Ramabai had rejected a whole set of oppressive practices which she saw as integral to Hinduism and was thus branded a 'betrayer':

Ramabai's conflict with the colonial government, her understanding of the manner in which colonial patriarchy interlocked with indigenous patriarchy to tyrannise women and her conflict with the Anglican Church should indicate that her focus was at all times on the women of India living under oppressive conditions. On our part we need to recognise that it is time to break down the false divide on 'loyalty' to the nation created by those with little concern for its oppressed sections, or those for whom there could be only one oppressive relationship, that between the colonising and the colonised.[20]

The last statement is important. For the boundaries of international feminism to be responsive to newer forms of scholarship and political realities, it is crucial that it should engage with structures of power and authority that are interconnected and not unidimensional. The colonial period of history in India marked an era within which relationships based around gender, caste, class and religion were reconfigured such that they acquired a qualitatively different lease of life. Within this, the representations of widowhood were linked with the demarcation of boundaries of caste and religious communities and led to the formation of an upper-caste, Hindu nationalism which marginalised other social groups.

The late nineteenth century was the high noon of imperialism in India, which provided the particular set of parameters within which society became politicised. In this process, boundaries of religion, caste, community (in later times, of nation) were becoming redrawn at the same time as they were thrown open by internal and external challenges. Questions pertaining to women's lives, life chances and livelihoods became conflated, in indigenous male discourse, with casteist notions of moral community and reproduction of an enclosed boundary. The historical legacies left by this impetus have been profound.

Women's rights to material security, personal liberties and political freedoms became subsumed under the cause of caste, community and nation. The political/historical questions range from the nature of imperialism to the imposition of a specific form of colonial capitalism, to the configuring of an indigenous middle class which was predicated on particular gender, caste and religious identities. If Western feminism has had to be self-critical about its complicity with imperialism and racism, Indian feminism has had to take the question of communal violence – violence directed at members of other religious communities – very seriously, and seek to look at the historical basis of the ways in which the dominant religious community constructed itself in and through control over women, lower castes and other religious communities. These shifts and insights need to be incorporated much more widely for them to have resonance in the international sphere, where the spectre of ethnic genocide and new nationalisms looms very large indeed. The histories that have led to these formations need to be understood in order that the future becomes shorn of violence.

Changing the future thus requires a harder engagement with the past: a sombre one, where some of those more innocent contentions that assumed that the mere act of positive representations of women in the past would provide the liberationary ammunition to stamp the future for women in novel ways need to be looked at again. It will take a long, hard struggle before the connections between the imperial order, the new indigenous elites and the consolidation of their power, indeed the imbrication of women's issues within nationalism itself, are taken seriously and we begin to incorporate these within questions of the international political order with its hierarchies of wealth, power, privilege and differential access to the technologies of violence.

While the task of reshifting international feminist agendas is a mammoth one, we can perhaps start out best by learning from the existing scholarship emanating from Indian feminism, and linking this up with related works which analyse the constitution of the English middle class in terms of its race, class and gender specificities. Just as Victorian feminism was embryonically linked to the British empire and to the construction of the Indian woman, so too was the Indian middle class tied to the self-imaging of it self as upper-caste and Hindu. Linking up these structures and demarcating the boundaries of differences and commonalities would advance our identification of the points of intersection and fracture, thus enabling a deeper political engagement with the past, the present and the future.

Further reading

P. Athavle, *My Story: The Autobiography of a Hindu Widow* (New Delhi, 1986).

U. Butalia, *The Other Side of Silence: Voices from the Partition of India* (London, 2000).

N. Chaudhuri and M. Strobel, *Western Women and Imperialism: Complicity and Resistance* (Bloomington, 1992).

N. Gandhi and N. Shah, *The Issues at Stake: Theory and Practice in the Contemporary Indian Women's Movement in India* (New Delhi, 1992).

C. Jaffrelot, *The Hindu Nationalist Movement and Indian Politics 1925 to the 1990s* (London, 1996).

K. Jayawardena, *Embodies Violence: Communalising Women's Sexuality in South Asia* (Delhi, 1996).

C. Johnson-Odim and Margaret Strobel, eds, *Expanding the Boundaries of Women's History: Essays on Women in the Third World* (Bloomington, Ind., 1992).

R. Menon and K. Bhasin, *Borders and Boundaries: Women in India's Partition* (Delhi, 1998).

T. Nasrin, *Lajja: Shame* (Delhi, 1994).

T. Sarkar, *Women and Right-Wing Movements: Indian Experiences* (London, 1995).

T. Sarkar, *Hindu Wife and Hindu Nation: Gender, Religion and the Pre-History of Indian Nationalism* (London, 2000).

S. Tharu and K. Lalita, *Women Writing in India: 600 BC to the early 20th Century* (New York, 1991).

Notes

1. The demolition of the mosque Babri Masjid on 6 December 1992 marked the ascendancy of the Hindu nationalist party in Indian politics. The attempt to construct the Muslim and Christian citizens of India as 'traitors' to the nation-state was accompanied by violence against specific minority communities, including sexual violence.

2. W. Doniger and B. K. Smith, trans., *The Laws of Manu* (New Delhi, 1992), pp. 115–16.

3. Uma Chakravarty has suggested that the higher castes often imposed the diverse, and less strict, marriage and remarriage patterns on lower castes precisely in order to categorise them as 'low'. See her 'Gender, caste and labour', *Economic and Political Weekly* (9 September 1995). The process of caste formation, however, has been a dynamic and shifting one in India, with boundaries being reconfigured constantly. The concomitant shifting of gender boundaries in the different epochs requires attention.

4. *Manushi, Tenth Anniversary Issue*, Nos 50, 51, 52 (Delhi, 1989).

5. For Bengal, see Ramakanta Chakravarti, *Vaisnavism in Bengal* (Calcutta, 1985), p. 299.

6. The best literature on this is A. Burton, *Burdens of History: British Feminists, Indian Women, and Imperial Culture, 1865–1915* (Chapel Hill, NC, 1994).

7. See for example Sudhir Chandra, 'Communal elements in late nineteenth century Hindi literature', *Journal of Arts and Ideas* (January–March 1984); and Sudhir Chandra, 'Conflicted beliefs and men's consciousness about women: widow marriage in late nineteenth-century Indian literature', *Economic and Political Weekly* (31 October 1987).

8. Tanika Sarkar, 'Woman, community, and nation: a historical trajectory for Hindu identity politics', in Patricia Jefferey and Amrita Basu, eds, *Women's Activism and Politicised Religion in South Asia* (New York, 1998), p. 89.

9. Lata Mani, 'Production of an official discourse on sati in early nineteenth-century Bengal', *Economic and Political Weekly* 26/17 (26 April 1986). See also her *Contentious Traditions: The Debate on Sati in Colonial India* (Berkeley, Calif., 1998).

10. Kavi Bhavanishankar Narasinharam, *Vidhva Vilaap (Vidhva Striona Sankatnu Varnan)* [*Widows' Laments (An Account of Widow Oppression)*] (Ahmedabad, 1906), pp. 4–5, 9 (translation mine).

11. D. Ram, *Vidhvano Vakil* [*Widows' Pleader*] (Ahmedabad, 1882), p. 7.

12. Ibid., p. 29.

13. Sarkar, 'Woman, community and nation'.

14. Ibid., p. 30.

15. Ibid., pp. 31–2.

16. Bai Dhankorbai Madhavdas Rugnathdas, 'Hindu Vidhvaoni Karunamay Halat', *Streebodh and Sansarsudharo Jubilee Memorial* (Bombay, 1908), pp. 114–18 (published posthumously, translation mine).

17. A. Burton, 'Colonial encounters in late Victorian Britain: Pandita Ramabai at Cheltenham and Wantage 1883–6', *Feminist Review* 49 (Spring 1995), p. 29.

18. Ibid., p. 39.

19. Ibid., p. 47.

20. U. Chakravarty, *Rewriting History: The Life and Times of Pandita Ramabai* (Delhi, 1998), pp. 341–2.

CHAPTER SIX

Representing nation: women, obituaries and national biography

WENDY WEBSTER

Perhaps the most extraordinary obituary to appear in *The Times* in the 1950s was that of Amy M. Bradford. She was, it records, 'the mother of four sons', much decorated in the First World War, one posthumously. Three of the four had been killed during the war. The obituary provides details about the second son's 'brave exploits' and the youngest son's 'act of conspicuous bravery and leadership in attack', and the decorations that they won. Apart from the characterisation of Bradford as 'the mother of four sons', the obituary refers to her life only in its final sentence:

On more than one occasion Mrs Bradford took her place at the Folkestone observance of Remembrance Day wearing the two Victoria Crosses and a Military Cross.

Bradford's story becomes that of her sons, her death marked as a result of their own earlier deaths. Absent from her own obituary, she stands in for her dead sons at Remembrance Day, wearing their medals.[1]

In striking contrast, the obituary of Flora Sandes records her decoration 'for conspicuous bravery in the field'. As a member of the St John Ambulance Brigade, Sandes had travelled to Serbia during the First World War with a small nursing unit and subsequently joined the Serbian Red Cross and then the Serbian 2nd Army. As a soldier, her obituary records: 'she fought in every battle until she was severely wounded by a Bulgarian hand grenade in November 1916'. Albeit with many explanations about the particular Serbian context in which Flora Sandes became a soldier, she is celebrated for her courage under fire, on the model of the sons of Amy Bradford.[2]

This chapter focuses on obituary columns in *The Times* during the 1950s and the particular version of national biography that they developed. In many ways Amy Bradford's sketchy presence in her own obituary might be regarded as more emblematic of the ways in which this biography was gendered than the celebration of Flora Sandes's courage. Only a small proportion of *Times* obituaries concerned the lives of women, their notices were generally much shorter than men's and, when they did appear, they were often relegated to the bottom of the column. Women were routinely included mainly as an afterword to men's obituaries which recorded the names of wives and the dates of marriages, coralling women in a short footnote referring to home and family at the end of a long piece about men's public life.

In the history of national biography women had characteristically been furnished with this kind of story – recorded as the wives, daughters, sisters or mothers of important men, on the model of Amy Bradford. In the original *Dictionary of National Biography* (*DNB*), a project begun in 1882 and completed in 1901, only 3.5 per cent of entries were on women.[3] Such lives were often indexed by the instruction to 'see under', subsuming women under men in a particularly explicit form. Even as late as the 1912–21 *DNB* supplement Olive Schreiner's life was indexed as 'Schreiner, Olive, see under Schreiner, William Philip' and recorded under that of her brother, who earned one and a half columns to her half column.[4] The main categories of women included in terms of their own records were actresses and writers. The distinction between public and private provided a fundamental ordering device for biography – common to the *DNB* and *Times* obituaries – which, in orchestrating cultural memory around the notion of important figures, developed a discourse of 'public life' – a key element in masculinity and the category of 'man'.[5] Used to refer to men's activities in a range of metropolitan and imperial settings and a network of institutions, the term 'public life' was dignified and enlarged through its associations with the idea of important service to the nation. By these criteria about what constituted importance, women were for the most part rendered, in Carolyn Heilbrun's term, 'storyless'.[6]

The 1950s is an interesting period in the gendered history of national biography, producing as it did a discourse of the 'public woman'. Such a discourse had begun to develop in the late nineteenth and early twentieth centuries, but was consolidated after 1945 as, alongside the conventional notices of actresses and writers, increasing numbers of biographies and obituaries recorded women entering previously all-male institutions as 'the first woman', or leading segregated female branches of institutions – the auxiliary services of the armed forces, girls' public schools, women's colleges at Oxford and Cambridge. In both cases women were incorporated into a discourse of 'public life'. The term 'public woman' – associated with prostitution – was not used, but obituary columns in *The Times* nevertheless constructed such a category in biographies which mediated the history of the late Victorian and Edwardian periods and the First World War in notices of those who died.[7] Here it is Flora Sandes rather than Amy Bradford who offers a model for consideration, for her obituary depicts an autonomous woman who is not defined mainly in relationship to others. Sandes was unique in receiving a notice as a soldier bearing arms, but by the mid-twentieth century the majority of obituaries of any length resembled Sandes's rather than Bradford's, and offered biographies which conformed closely to the narratives of men in public life.

This increasing attention given to women, however meagre, offers a way of exploring the terms on which they gained access to representation, and the raced and classed dimensions of their incorporation into national biography as represented in *The Times*. The 'public woman' was generally represented as sharing the attributes of elite British masculinity in stories which, far from subsuming her under men's identity, did not make any sharp differentiation between her public life and men's. However, a common thread in many obituaries defined her service to the nation in relation to groups whose interests she was seen as serving and representing. Among these groups were the working classes in the metropolis and the colonised in empire, especially working-class or colonised women. Such groups, in so far as they were visible in obituaries, appeared mainly as aspects of the 'public woman's' work – the objects of her management, superintendence, control, authority, scrutiny or benevolence. Thus while she was represented in terms of agency, the groups whose interests she was seen as serving were shown as passive – in need of her intervention in their interests since they did not speak or act on their own behalf. The process by which she gained access to representation was one by which they were denied it.

Obituaries and national biography

Obituaries have generally been neglected in literatures on life-writing. Although they are published in a variety of contexts, their most familiar setting is in newspapers – local, regional and national – where they function to give notice of a recent death. When they move beyond a simple notice it is usually into the conventions of biography, but a biography which is moulded by the timing of the account. The announcement of death with which they normally begin provides a form of narrative closure, allowing the obituary to stand for some final version of the life. At the same time the recent occurrence of the death means that obituaries often serve as acts of memorialising, honouring their subjects. In the *Times* columns, although tributes from named individuals were sometimes published, obituaries were generally constructed as dispassionate and objective records. The conventions adopted were those seen as appropriate to a public and official context and, like entries in the *DNB*, looked to the future as well as the past, conscious that these notices might be consulted by future historians, including contributors to the *DNB*.[8] Nevertheless, even in *The Times*, obituaries tended towards narratives of exemplary lives, honouring their subjects at death.

Although the *Times* columns might appear to link together a random collection of people from different places and sometimes of different generations through the apparently arbitrary dates of their deaths, cumulatively they built a story of the national past. They included far more non-British nationals than the *DNB* but, as in the *DNB*, the majority of notices represented the story of nation in a familiar form, through the lives of those defined as its most important members. In a collective notice published annually in *The Times* on New Year's Day, recording the names of those who had died in the previous year, this national biography was organised in a way which suggested the story of a family firm – headed by the royal family, flanked by peers, baronets and knights, and then divided into different departments: members of the House of Commons, the armed forces, the legal profession, literature, the medical profession, musicians, journalists, religious leaders, scholarship and science, sportsmen, and stage, screen and broadcasting.

While biographies were generally constructed in ways similar to the *DNB*, the form in which obituaries appeared – on a daily basis, triggered by the deaths of individuals – meant that the *Times* column offered a particular naturalised story of nation unfolding on a continuing basis. Encountered by its audience as part of a daily routine of reading, it gave them an everyday diet of images, events and people from the past in a newspaper which was otherwise mainly concerned with the contemporary. Obituaries published in the 1950s, by their frequent reference to the First and Second World Wars and to the empire, could unfold an everyday narrative which highlighted past glories. In a period of national decline and loss of imperial power – characterised by what Chris Waters has called 'a crisis of national self-representation' – invoking cultural memory could offer the possibility of nostalgia and the reassurance of pride in a shared national past.[9]

In constructing this shared national past political divisions were often collapsed into a common Britishness inclusive of most allegiances. Some which *The Times* opposed in its leaders were dignified in its obituaries through reference to 'the British Labour Movement' or 'the British trade union movement'. However, while such inclusiveness generally extended to feminism, it did not embrace pacifism, communism or 'socialism of an extreme type', or feminists who had espoused such causes, like Sylvia Pankhurst. A

LIVERPOOL
JOHN MOORES UNIVERSITY
AVRIL ROBARTS LRC
TEL. 0151 231 4022

common device used in such notices was to represent the person from the point of view of charges made against them by critics – 'he was looked upon by the conventional-minded as a crank', 'he was sharply criticised in many quarters'.[10] Charges made in courts might also feature, as in the record of Sylvia Pankhurst's fine for 'attempting to cause mutiny, sedition, or dissatisfaction among His Majesty's Forces or the civilian population'.[11] By such devices obituarists could condemn their subjects through the verdicts of others rather than by mounting direct attacks of their own. Homosexuality, although it may have been evident to some readers through coded references, was never mentioned.

Such devices draw attention to the notion of an acceptable narrative. In *Times* obituaries this narrative – and the dominant story of nation that it told – was one of masculine authority. The key words which recur in *Times* obituaries – 'eminent', 'important', 'distinguished' – resonate in relation not only to the lives recorded but also to the particular community constructed in the columns through the relationship between *The Times*, its address to its readership and those who were obituarised. They serve notice that the biographies offered are of public significance and address the readership as members of the same club as the obituarised, as though *The Times* imagines its audience as an old boys' network which will read – and discuss – notices from the comfort of armchairs in gentlemens' clubs.[12] *The Times* both clothes itself in the distinction and importance which it attributes to those obituarised and at the same time constructs itself as the arbiter of such distinction through the selection of those deserving of a *Times* obituary. Thus it legitimises both itself and those memorialised through its construction of their importance.

One key feature of this community was membership of the Establishment – an elite which, for all its individual variety, could be written for the most part as sharing a common biography of important service to the nation. Any divisions of class suggested by the wealth, power and status that were common to most of those obituarised could be evaded by the notion of their special qualifications to represent a shared national past as important members of the nation. Obituary writers were usually at pains to establish that a recognition of Establishment membership had long preceded their subjects' deaths. The notion of distinction which the obituary asserted was reinforced by the detail provided of its acknowledgement in life through the award of a wide range of titles, honours, awards, prizes and medals. The obituary might be regarded as one more inscription on an honours board – the final gong.

Another key feature of this community was its authority. The convention of anonymity in obituary notices meant that they appeared authorless, or more accurately authored by *The Times* itself – not as individual assessments which might be contested, but endowed with the full weight of the newspaper's reputation which stamped with authority both the life recorded and the version of it offered by the obituary. The tone in which biographies of British nationals were written, although often of fulsome praise, was rarely deferential or reverential. Sometimes the importance of their life and work was directly linked to the newspaper, with obituaries recording how their subjects wrote for *The Times*, had prolific correspondence published in *The Times*, or had their books serialised or favourably noticed in *The Times*. The narrative developed thus bore a collective authority – that of the newspaper, the figures it memorialised, and the narratives constructed around them.

The genre was strongly masculinised not only in terms of its subjects but also of its form. The exemplary life – the main form that biographies take – was written as a linear narrative tracing development and progress. Taking as a starting point the notion of distinction and importance, it moved to confirm this through a story of a career achieved through a steady sequence of promotions, or distinction attained through a steady sequence of achievements. The emphasis on masculine virtues was perhaps developed especially for men who might otherwise be understood to have occupied an ambiguous position in relation to masculinity. The obituary of the poet Roy Campbell, for example, stressed his delight in taking risks and characterised him in terms of 'pugnacity'.[13] The subject was men's public life, set in a wide range of institutions, and often making reference to a homosocial world – public schools, Oxbridge colleges, the armed forces, sporting prowess, gentlemen's clubs. This meant that notices were generally denuded of all reference to the world of the home or the personal – beyond a simple statement of date of marriage, name of wife/wives, numbers and names of children. They reinforced the construction of a category of public life to denote masculinity and wrote the story of a shared national past in terms of that category.

The private woman and the public woman

One of the most common forms in which women received notices in *Times* obituaries was through their relationships to important men. These notices were often very short, comprising two sentences – the first recording an identity as wife or widow and the second an identity as daughter, as well as the date of marriage. In this way women were incorporated into the obituary column as people who belonged to an elite through a familial identity which was generally traced through a patriarchal line. In such notices, women were subsumed under the identities of two men, husband and father, and the only event recorded in their lives was marriage. The notion of a woman as 'storyless' is appropriate to these obituaries which had a strong tendency, when they went beyond short notices, to provide details, not of her own life, but of the important man to whom she was connected. A woman's obituary could in this way become just one more notice of a famous man.

However, some notices did elaborate a woman's story as a wife or mother, celebrating her devotion in these roles. In these examples, women's stories were strongly differentiated from men's, characterising their subject in terms of her personal relationships to others, focusing on her private life in private settings, and developing a romantic and domestic plot in which she always figured as a wife, and sometimes as a mother and home-maker. The obituary of Mary Endicott Carnegie, for example, celebrates her as the devoted wife of Joseph Chamberlain, and tells the story of her first meeting with him in 1887, their secret engagement, marriage and honeymoon. Although it begins with her death in 1957, the biography it provides ends on his death in 1914, and, apart from the suggestion of her remarriage through her characterisation as 'widow of Canon W. H. Carnegie', the last 43 years of her long life receive no mention. She is referred to throughout as 'Mrs. Joseph Chamberlain' and celebrated as a good wife 'absorbed in her husband's manifold interests' who, during the last year of his illness, 'never left her husband for more than an hour or two at a time'. Her story, shaped by her relationship to men and foreclosed by the death of her first husband, denies her any autonomy.[14]

The obituary of Mary Endicott Carnegie notes that 'her low, clear voice was never heard on any platform, since she did not play any public or semi-public role, of the kind so often played by the wives of distinguished statesmen'. This notion of a 'semi-public role' is particularly appropriate to women who received obituaries as political hostesses, or through a familial or royal identity, which involved various kinds of voluntary public work. Queen Mary, who earned the longest obituary devoted to any woman in the 1950s, might be regarded as belonging in this category, for although her obituary emphasises the onerous nature of her public duties, it shows her generally performing these at her husband's side as Queen Consort as well as paying tribute to her 'active part in helping the work of any charitable organisation or noble cause'.[15] Lady Mountbatten's obituary portrays a similar role, showing her travelling thousands of miles with her husband, and like Queen Mary working for a range of good causes, radiating *noblesse oblige*.[16]

The majority of women who received obituaries of any length, however, were not represented in this way but included in terms of their own records. In charting women's entry into public life in a range of obituaries *The Times* was engaged in producing a story from categories which were normally regarded as opposed, developing a discourse of 'the public woman'. In a tradition of honouring actresses and writers in national biography, the most common career recorded was on a particular sort of public stage. But *The Times* also charted a wide range of other careers – in the auxiliary armed forces, education, law, medicine, universities, Parliament, engineering, missionary work – depicting women on a wide range of public stages. As the obituary of Violet Markham in 1959 asserted, linking her identity to a more general movement of women into public life: 'Among the many remarkable women whom the great social changes of the last half century have drawn into public life Violet Markham stands preeminent.'[17]

As the peroration to Violet Markham suggests, the discourse of the public woman was strongly gendered, and many obituaries made reference to their subjects as 'the first woman'. In the 1950s this yielded, among many others: 'the first woman to fly across the Irish sea', 'the first woman to be made a Companion of the Institution of Electrical Engineers', 'the first woman to be sworn a Justice of the Peace for the County of London', 'the first woman Assistant Commissioner of Prisons', 'the first woman to attain Ministerial rank', 'the first Indian woman to practise law', 'the first woman to obtain a dental qualification in Great Britain'. When a first could not be claimed women were often recorded as 'one of the first': 'one of the first women pastors in England', 'one of the first women to become a Member of Parliament', 'one of the first women to hold ministerial office in Britain'. The status of women as pioneers was reinforced by continual reference to this term: 'pioneer of women's services', 'pioneer of family planning', 'a pioneer in the training of Indian women doctors'.[18] In the common celebration of such women as 'exceptional', there is some suggestion that the private woman is the norm: the public woman may be admirable, but the inference is that women are not like this.

Despite the strongly gendered character of these obituaries, however, the discourse of the public woman generally celebrated her achievements on a male model. The emphasis on the role of wife or mother – so prominent in the obituaries of Mrs Joseph Chamberlain/Mary Endicott Carnegie and Mrs Amy Bradford – was much less apparent. Obituaries recording the lives of spinsters rarely referred to their marital status, and although the married public woman sometimes earned praise as a good wife and mother who successfully combined private and public life, her narrative was usually linear, with a strong focus on the development and progress of her public career. She was often characterised in terms that did not differentiate her from the exemplary male life. Even in the context of charitable work, the emphasis was less on her compassion than on her determination. Dame Grace Kimmins, for example, obituarised for her foundation of the Guild of the Brave Poor Things, was praised for her 'astonishing energy and driving force', and as 'that rarest combination, a masterful, methodical driving woman with, as one of her candid friends once remarked, "a resolute knowledge of what she wanted and a tremendous belief in her own powers"'.[19] Courage — one of the most common terms used to celebrate men — was frequently used of the public woman, who was also hailed, among other things, as 'heroic', 'intrepid', 'indefatigable', 'forceful', 'tireless' and 'energetic'.

The tributes — often fulsome — to women who entered public life in the late nineteenth and early twentieth centuries were often applied to feminists, and are perhaps a rather surprising feature of obituaries written in a newspaper which was not associated with support for feminism, in a decade when feminists were often stigmatised. It is true that *The Times* does not always unreservedly honour feminists. It frequently notes the distinction between militant and constitutional suffragists, characterising the former as 'extreme'. It also makes distinctions within militant suffragists, offering a more favourable assessment of Christabel Pankhurst, who with other leaders, had 'lent their organisation in the cause of national service' in the First World War, than of Sylvia Pankhurst whose opposition to the war is paradoxically described as 'violent'.[20] It is perhaps characteristic that the longest obituary and the most fulsome praise for 'a life largely devoted to the public service' in the 1950s was reserved for Violet Markham, who had opposed women's suffrage. However, even in Sylvia Pankhurst's obituary it is not her feminism that puts her beyond the pale of Establishment affirmation but her pacifism, especially as this is combined with association with the 'extreme left' and brief membership of the Communist Party.

Thus feminism is constructed as a relatively important and honourable part of national history especially as represented by moderate suffragists. But while it is the subject of so many obituaries of the public woman, it is assigned by *The Times* firmly to the past. The public woman is a sign of the nation as modern, but feminism, which produced such public women, is archaic and old-fashioned. The term itself is represented as outmoded in Christabel Pankhurst's obituary, which describes her parents as among those who 'a generation ago would have been called feminists'. The discourse of the public woman makes many references to discrimination against women and barriers to their entry into public life, but the narrative offered is one of major historical discontinuity, and such discrimination is represented as long since over.

Such discontinuity is also represented in the celebration of progress away from the confinements and restrictions of the Victorian period. Women are occasionally praised for virtues which belong to the Victorian ideal of womanhood — an ideal which had so strongly differentiated women and men — but obituaries which record the lives of women who had grown up in the Victorian period are more likely to insist that their subjects moved away from Victorian ideals. In Beatrice Grimshaw's obituary the bicycle is marshalled as a 'sign and symbol' of what is portrayed as women's 'partial emancipation' in the 1890s – 'the slight lessening of restraints on feminine conduct' – and her own enthusiastic use of this vehicle is celebrated through reference to her creation of a new women's 24-hour record on the road.[21] The obituary of Christine Burrows – Principal of St Hilda's Hall, Oxford, and characterised as 'a firm supporter of women's rights, though never a militant suffragist' – comments that she 'seemed older than her age' having 'imbibed much of her mother's Victorian cast of manners'. But the account quickly moves to affirm that she was 'in touch with modern opinion', and the sign of this is her 'insistence that women should take their proper part in the world'.[22]

The task pioneered by the 'public woman' is thus of modernisation, and this is a task that is represented as fully accomplished. The opposition that feminists faced from male institutions surfaces occasionally but is generally downplayed, and any suggestion of gender conflicts and antagonisms in the present is firmly ruled out. The story that *The Times* tells in its obituary columns is one where feminism is no longer necessary because its project is achieved, and that achievement can be celebrated as a story of progress.

Female authority

In its obituary of Major Agnes McGearey in 1954, *The Times* played with conventional ideas of masculine authority in recording the encounter of a soldier and a nurse. The nurse was McGearey – a member of the Queen Alexandra's Royal Army Nursing Corps who, dying at the age of 45, belonged to a different generation from the majority of those obituarised. The soldier was General Wingate, who became one of her patients when she was 'Matron McGearey', in charge of a hospital in India in 1943, and who discovered that 'for once he had met his match, and was under a discipline as iron as his own'.[23]

This representation of McGearey draws on a stereotype of the matron common in the 1950s. The notion of her authority over a general can be articulated relatively safely since her own version of military discipline was exercised within a feminised sphere, where her command – described as that of an 'exacting superior' – was over women rather than men, and any female control over male patients was limited and temporary. Women's authority over men is rarely referenced in obituaries, although Diana Beck's appointment at the Middlesex Hospital in 1947 is noted as remarkable for being 'the first time that a woman was given the charge of men in a consultant capacity in a major London teaching hospital'. However, women's authority over women is depicted in a range of settings. A major route to women's inclusion in the story of nation as told in *The Times* was through the leadership of women, and this suggests the importance of the formation of women's organisations to women's increasing access to representation.

The depiction of a femisocial rather than a homosocial world is common to many biographies of the public woman which make frequent reference to a women's movement, women's organisations, women's institutions and women's friendships. This femisocial world was sometimes explicitly feminist in references to networks of female friendships and women's groups involved in promoting women's suffrage, women's education and women's entry to the professions. But obituaries also make reference to a very wide range of organisations which were not associated with feminism, including the Girl Guides, the Ladies' Golf Union, the All England Women's Hockey Association, the Women's National Liberal Federation, the Women's Advisory Council on Indian Affairs, the National Federation of Women's Institutes, the Women's Voluntary Service and the Women's Engineering Society. Through such obituaries *The Times* constructs a community of women as important members of the nation – a female Establishment, however tiny, which runs parallel to men's. A number of those obituarised had been educated at girls' public schools and women's colleges at Oxford and Cambridge universities, or earned obituaries through their position as principals or professors at such institutions. Women also attracted obituaries for their leadership of women's organisations and services during the First and Second World Wars, including the Voluntary Aid Detachments, the Women's Legion, the Women's Volunteer Reserve, the Women's Royal Naval Service and the Women's Land Army.

Working-class women are visible in obituaries mainly as the objects of the public woman's superintendence and reforming activities. They are dimly discernible, for example, in Hilda Martindale's obituary, which records her appointment as Senior Lady Factory Inspector.[24] They are rather more apparent in the obituary of Dame Lilian Barker, which records her post as Lady Superintendent of Woolwich Arsenal in the First World War where 'she had control of some 30,000 women and girls employed there, where women had never before been employed'.[25] Violet Markham's obituary portrays her long membership of the Central Committee of Women's Training and Employment, which had organised the training of nearly 100,000 women, chiefly for domestic service. Reforming activities that were recorded, while also concerned with employment, focused especially on motherhood, including campaigns for birth control, family allowances and maternity services. Kathleen, Lady Simon had 'at one time worked as a nurse in the slums of London, after training, because she wanted to see for herself the conditions in which the women in these districts had to bear children'.[26]

Occasionally working-class women are shown acting on their own behalf, notably in the obituary of Margaret Bondfield, which tells a story of their collective organisation in trade unions and has at its centre the figure of Bondfield herself, a woman of working-class family – what *The Times* habitually calls 'humble folk' or 'humble circumstances' – and her devotion to the work of the Women's Trade Union League, the National Federation of Women Workers and the Women's Labour League.[27] However, in the obituary of Annie Kenney – one of the few suffragettes from the working classes – despite the portrayal of her own militant activities, including the hunger strike, working-class women are described as 'downtrodden'.[28]

Colonised women were also visible in obituaries of the public woman mainly as objects of her authority, superintendence or reforming activities. However, colonised women also served to heighten her modernity as an emancipated woman in contrast to their restricted existence, with the institution of the *zenana*, often used interchangeably with *purdah* and the *harem*, used as the main symbol of such constraint. The emancipated woman was signalled not only by her active and energetic role in public institutions, but also by her freedom as symbolised by mobility in contrast to the seclusion of her 'other'. In Zetton Buchanan's obituary, for example, consignment to the *harem* represents her fate when she is taken prisoner in Egypt, and the notice draws on her own autobiographical account of this experience to detail its squalor and the monotonous life of the women who inhabited it who, she had written, 'might fitly be described by the term cat'. But her subsequent life demonstrates her own freedom in opposition to their passivity and incarceration, especially in her 'taste for travel' which she indulges by going round the world three times.[29]

The obituary of Dame Edith Mary Brown provides an example of what thorny ground was involved in the construction of an opposition between the modern British and the benighted colonised woman. Celebrating Brown as 'a pioneer in the training of Indian women doctors and midwives in modern western methods, and the founder and for half a century the principal of the Ludhiana Christian Medical College for Women', it produces a number of emblems of Indian backwardness. They include 'the age-long tradition' which meant that the orthodox Hindu woman would not have the services of a medical man, and her subsequent recourse in childbirth to 'the superstitious *dai*' who was 'unbelievably dirty'. But one important emblem is the situation that Dame Edith Brown is credited with transforming – one where 'trained Indian women doctors or nurses were almost unknown'.[30] *The Times* manages to imply that trained British women

doctors were centuries-old. Yet Dame Edith Brown was of the same generation as Dr Lilian Frazer-Nash, whose obituary, appearing in *The Times*
some six years earlier, also recorded her work in India. Here the sign of
Indian backwardness was *purdah*, and not the absence of trained women
doctors, and it was Frazer-Nash herself who was celebrated as 'pioneer
woman doctor', in a reference not to India, but to Britain.[31]

Cornelia Sorabji's obituary – one of the very few of a non-Western
woman – also indicates the thorny ground involved in constructing such an
opposition. Evoking the notion of modernity against the *zenana* not through
a Western woman, but an Indian woman who had taken a law degree at
Oxford, its account of women in Britain as emancipated comes under some
strain through the continual references to the sex discrimination Sorabji
faced in Britain, including a 30-year gap between taking her Oxford degree
and being called to the Bar. But this is partially resolved through the evoca-
tion of '*purdah* women' in India. Through the representation of Sorabji as
an Indian woman who, through her contact with British education, became
a reformer of her own society, the opposition which the obituary risks
undermining can be propped up. And it is particularly in relation to the
zenana that Sorabji's reforming activities are depicted, not only through her
legal work but also through her writings, which the obituary uses to charac-
terise *zenana* life in terms of 'intrigue, deception, cruelty and oppression'.[32]
In these accounts oppositions between private and public construct differences not between femininity and masculinity but between Eastern and
Western women.

Representing nation

The nation is often represented through the figure of a woman. Imaginary
women serve as symbols, icons or allegories across a range of written and
visual narratives. But real women are rarely included in stories of the nation
and scarcely feature in public memorials, statues and other monuments.
Most monuments of historical women in Britain are of pre-modern times.[33]
A notable exception is Queen Victoria, who also received an entry of 111
pages in the *DNB*, and a 35-column obituary in *The Times*. However, she
was celebrated largely as an exemplary wife/widow and mother. War
memorials, which in the nineteenth century had only inscribed the names
of officers, adopted an increasingly democratic practice after 1918, where
the dead were not identified by rank.[34] But they still excluded most of the
female dead of the Second World War by commemorating only those who

died as members of the armed forces. There is no national memorial to the category in which the largest number of women died in the Second World War – civilians.[35]

The representation of women in national biography also remained sketchy. The volume of the *DNB* for 1951–60 claimed quite accurately that it differed from previous volumes in its inclusion of 'more women'. But as Gillian Fenwick's work has shown, this statement referred to an increase in entries on women from 3.5 per cent of the total in the original *DNB* and an average of 4.8 per cent in supplementary volumes published after 1901, to a mere 7.9 per cent.[36] It was not until the 1981–5 volume that entries on women reached double figures – at 11.8 per cent.[37] The obituary columns of *The Times* were similarly dominated by accounts of men.

Nevertheless women gained limited visibility, and although some were subsumed under men, the majority were shown possessed of independence and agency. They were praised for virtues on the model of men – as courageous, heroic, intrepid, indefatigable and tireless – and shown working in areas which were dominated by men, often through organisations and institutions that were specific to women. War remained a major exception. Although women were included in obituaries for their leadership of women in both world wars, and credited with service to the nation through their role in supporting combatant men, it is perhaps significant that of all the notices of any length, it is Amy Bradford's which manages to exclude her most thoroughly from her own obituary. As Leonore Davidoff notes, the inherent masculinity of war meant that women 'were able to serve their nation only by negation, by giving up what was most precious in the private sphere, that is their fiancés, husbands, brothers and sons'.[38]

The access that public women gained to representation suggests the importance of their agency in the foundation and development of a wide range of organisations. They won political representation, often in the period under discussion in the obituary, and acquired a voice, on public platforms and in public settings. Their abilities as public speakers often attracted comment in obituaries. This access to a voice links meanings of representation which are often separated: the campaigns for representation in Parliament, which are a recurrent theme of obituaries in the 1950s; the access to self-representation through a range of definitions of women's needs and interests produced by the plethora of women's organisations, which is another recurrent theme; and the cultural representations of national biography in which they found a place in *Times* obituaries through the discourse of the 'public woman'.

The voice that is represented in *Times* obituaries, however, is mainly that of ladies – members of a female Establishment. Margaret Bondfield, whose obituary described her devotion to women's trade union activity, recorded working-class women's reactions to 'that kind of voice' in her autobiography:

> Mary [Macarthur] asked me to introduce Susan [Lawrence] to a factory-gate meeting. We went to the East End, where our branch members made a good crowd. But Susan's voice had not been trained for speaking to an East End audience, who treated her as a comic turn and roared with laughter. I felt ashamed of them, to treat a stranger so, but also felt that there was something to be said for the girls, who had never before heard that kind of voice.[39]

In contrast to the East End women, it was 'that kind of voice' that *The Times* endowed with authority. Within the dominant story of nation that it told – one of masculine authority – this female voice was incorporated particularly as it addressed other groups of women. It was constructed as a voice which directed and superintended them or which spoke on their behalf, its commanding and forceful tone rendering them passive and voiceless.

Few people write their own obituaries. Self-representations in autobiographies and letters are sometimes used as sources for notices, but the dead rarely have much control over the way in which they are portrayed. In *The Times* women's lives were filtered through the values of the Establishment, and it seems likely that many biographies were written by men. In some cases this mediation resulted in negative notices. Sylvia Pankhurst, who would surely neither have expected nor wanted a eulogy in *The Times*, might not, could she have read it, have been displeased by hers. Overwhelmingly, however, the 'public woman' was celebrated.

Recent feminist work has drawn attention to the mobilisation of nationalist and imperialist rhetoric by many women's organisations in the nineteenth and early twentieth centuries – both feminist and non-feminist – and the extent to which they promoted their causes by claiming to speak and act on behalf of colonised women.[40] When *Times* obituaries assign pioneers of female emancipation an honourable place in the national past and construct the emancipated woman as a sign of a modern nation, they indicate some correspondences between the discourses on which public women drew for self-representation and those which circulated in *The Times*. When *Times* obituaries incorporate the 'public woman' into their version of national biography as someone who speaks and acts on behalf of working-class and colonised women, they show how far the process by which she gains access to representation is one by which they are denied it. But although obituaries pay tribute to female pioneers in the past, they also represent the project of women's emancipation as one which has been long since completed. In mediating its particular version of late Victorian and Edwardian history *The*

Times manages to imply that in the 1950s, though she is perhaps still rather thin on the ground in its obituary columns, the 'public woman' now floods its news pages, running the country.

Further reading

Trev Broughton, *Men of Letters, Writing Lives: Masculinity and Literary Auto/biography in the Late Victorian Period* (London, 1999).

Antoinette Burton, *Burdens of History: British Feminists, Indian Women, and Imperial Culture, 1865–1915* (Chapel Hill, NC, 1994).

Gillian Fenwick, *Women and the Dictionary of National Biography: A Guide to the DNB Volumes 1885–1985 and Missing Persons* (Aldershot, 1994), p. 18.

Margaretta Jolly, ed., *Encyclopedia of Life Writing* (London, 2001).

Lucy Noakes, *War and the British: Gender and National Identity 1939–91* (London, 1998).

Eileen Yeo, ed., *Radical Femininity: Women's Self-representation in the Public Sphere* (Manchester, 1998).

Notes

1. *The Times*, 9 January 1951.

2. *The Times*, 1 December 1956.

3. Gillian Fenwick, *Women and the Dictionary of National Biography: A Guide to the DNB Volumes 1885–1985 and Missing Persons* (Aldershot: Scolar Press, 1994), p. 18.

4. *Dictionary of National Biography*, 1912–21 Supplement (Oxford: Oxford University Press, 1927).

5. For a discussion of the construction of a political public sphere, see Leonore Davidoff, 'Regarding some "old husbands' tales": public and private in feminist history', in Leonore Davidoff, *Worlds Between: Historical Perspectives on Gender and Class* (Cambridge: Polity, 1995), pp. 227–76.

6. See Carolyn Heilbrun, *Writing a Woman's Life* (Women's Press, 1989), p. 37.

7. For the use of 'public woman' to mean prostitute, see Eileen Yeo, 'Some paradoxes of empowerment', in Eileen Yeo, ed., *Radical Femininity: Women's Self-representation in the Public Sphere* (Manchester: Manchester University Press, 1998), p. 1.

8. The criterion for including subjects in the *DNB*, as defined by Sidney Lee, its sub-editor from 1883 to 1891, was 'the probability that his (or her) career would be the subject of intelligent enquiry on the part of an appreciable number of persons a generation or more hence'. See Fenwick, *Women and the Dictionary of National Biography*, p. 21.

9. Chris Waters, '"Dark strangers" in our midst: discourses of race and nation in Britain, 1947–1963', *Journal of British Studies* 36 (1997), p. 208.

10. These comments appear in obituaries of the Duke of Bedford, who was a pacifist, and the Right Reverend G. K. A. Bell, who opposed the allied bombing of Germany in the Second World War.

11. *The Times*, 28 September 1960.

12. For life-writing in the late Victorian period as a 'highly regulated site of masculine pleasure and exchange', see Trev Broughton, *Men of Letters, Writing Lives: Masculinity and Literary Auto/biography in the Late Victorian Period* (London: Routledge, 1999), p. 21.

13. *The Times*, 25 April 1957.

14. *The Times*, 20 May 1957.

15. *The Times*, 25 March 1953.

16. *The Times*, 22 February 1960.

17. *The Times*, 3 February 1959.

18. The 'firsts' are in obituaries of Lady Bailey, Dame Caroline Haslett, Gertrude Tuckwell, Dame Lilian Barker, Margaret Bondfield, Cornelia Sorabji and Dr Lilian Lindsay. Those recorded as 'one of the first' are Dr Maude Royden, Mabel Philipson and Katharine, Duchess of Atholl. The 'pioneers' are Dame Katharine Furse, Dr Joan Malleson and Dame Edith Brown.

19. *The Times*, 4 March 1954.

20. *The Times*, 15 February 1958; *The Times*, 28 September 1960.

21. *The Times*, 1 July 1953.

22. *The Times*, 11 September 1959.

23. *The Times*, 10 December 1954.

24. *The Times*, 19 April 1952.

25. *The Times*, 23 May 1955.

26. *The Times*, 21 April 1955.

27. *The Times*, 18 June 1953.

28. *The Times*, 11 July 1953.

29. *The Times*, 17 March 1959.

30. *The Times*, 10 December 1956.

31. *The Times*, 13 February 1950.

32. *The Times*, 8 July 1954.

33. John Gillis, 'Memory and identity: the history of a relationship', in John Gillis, ed., *Commemorations: The Politics of National Identity* (Princeton, NJ: Princeton University Press, 1994), p. 11.

34. Ibid., pp. 9–12.

35. See Lucy Noakes, *War and the British: Gender and National Identity, 1939–91* (London: I.B. Tauris, 1998), p. 3.

36. *Dictionary of National Biography*, 1951–60 Supplement (Oxford: Oxford University Press, 1971), p. v; Fenwick, *Women and the Dictionary of National Biography*, p. 18.

37. Fenwick, *Women and the Dictionary of National Biography*, p. 18.

38. Davidoff, 'Regarding some "old husbands' tales"', p. 242.

39. Quoted in Anne Summers, 'Public functions, private premises: female professional identity and the domestic-service paradigm in Britain, c. 1850–1930', in Billie Melman, ed., *Borderlines: Genders and Identities in War and Peace, 1870–1930* (London: Routledge, 1998).

40. See, for example, Antoinette Burton, *Burdens of History: British Feminists, Indian Women, and Imperial Culture, 1865–1915* (Chapel Hill, NC: University of North Carolina Press, 1994); Clare Midgley, 'Anti-slavery and the roots of "imperial feminism"', in Clare Midgley, ed., *Gender and Imperialism* (Manchester: Manchester University Press, 1998), pp. 161–79; Clare Midgley, this volume; Vron Ware, *Beyond the Pale: White Women, Racism and History* (London: Verso, 1992).

PART THREE

Re-presenting the past: reframing women's history

CHAPTER SEVEN

Writing women in: new approaches to Russian and Soviet history

MELANIE ILIČ

The emergence and development of Russian and Soviet women's history has reflected the trends of the broader areas of research and study within the field of women's history.[1] It has attempted to address such issues as chronology and periodisation, the 'exclusion' of women from the standard histories, the range of sources and methodologies available to historians, and the iconographic representations of women. As the scholarship in Russian and Soviet women's history is likely to be unfamiliar to many readers of this volume, I will begin this chapter with an overview of recent historiographical developments before examining in more detail the results of some of my own recent research. My comments here are mostly restricted to English-language material and the Western historiography of the nineteenth and early twentieth centuries, where most of the current research is focused. I have cited monograph literature where appropriate, but it is also important to note that there is an extensive journals literature in the area of Russian and Soviet women's history. There are also a number of useful collections of essays on this topic, many of which are cited in the notes.

Chronology

Recent research in Russian and Soviet women's history has questioned the chronological significance of the Bolshevik revolution in October 1917 on ordinary women's everyday lives. For example, Barbara Clements has argued that 'in Russia, the process of adjusting traditional patriarchy to the more egalitarian ethos of the nineteenth century had begun long before the Bolsheviks took power'.[2] Her findings concerning the impact of the October revolution and civil war on urban women and the family confirm this view.[3] A recent study by McDermid and Hillyar of the lives of Russian working women also emphasises the continuities in their experiences throughout a 50-year period of rapid and dramatic economic, political and social upheaval.[4]

Beatrice Farnsworth has also suggested that the political culture of the Bolshevik revolution had very little impact on peasant women and that those women who did become activists in the villages did so because of personal and familial connections rather than through a commitment to socialist ideology. The patterns of temporary and seasonal male migration and military conscription, specific to the Russian context, meant that peasant women held responsible positions in the agricultural economy and rural households long before 1917, and that the numbers of such 'independent' women increased especially during the First World War. Even the supposedly radical innovations of the new Bolshevik government, such as literacy classes for women and workplace nurseries, predated the October revolution.[5]

From Farnsworth's perspective, the history of Russian peasant women in the early twentieth century is one of continuing modernisation rather than revolutionary upheaval. In most respects, the drudgery of peasant women's everyday lives and rural patriarchal family relations remained untouched by the October revolution. Likewise, the period of the New Economic Policy (1921–8), which is depicted as a golden age in the standard revisionist literature of the early Soviet period, was far from a 'golden age' for women. The restoration of market economic relations and the return of soldiers from the civil war resulted in widespread female unemployment. Prostitution flourished and the funding for a range of social initiatives to ease women's everyday lives (such as public canteens and nurseries) was withdrawn. The new sexual morality and changes introduced in family law created an army of economically destitute single mothers.

Wendy Goldman has explored in more detail the ways in which Bolshevik policies in the 1920s and 1930s, which were designed to emancipate women, often had negative results. The revolutionary vision of the 'withering away of the family' had experienced an almost complete ideological reversal by 1936 with the introduction of the new Soviet constitution and family code. The ideas of free union in sexual relations, which included the removal of the necessity to register marriages and the introduction of 'postcard divorce', left many women abandoned once they became pregnant. There were no legal or administrative structures to enforce court rulings on payments of alimony and child support, which were mostly granted in women's favour. The Bolshevik vision of achieving women's liberation via their participation in the production process only served to reinforce the double burden, particularly on working mothers. There were insufficient financial resources, and political will, to develop a network of communal services that would allow for the socialisation of housework and childcare. Goldman has also demonstrated the ways in which different groups of women stood in differing relationships to male wage earners, and the ideological and political shifts in family policy of the inter-war years.[6]

Exclusion

One of the important functions of women's history, it could be argued, is to challenge the exclusivity of mainstream, traditional history writing. This is certainly the case in the Russian and Soviet example. Beate Fieseler's research has highlighted the absence of women from the standard histories of one of the most written about events of the twentieth century: the Russian revolution. Fieseler has undertaken an analysis of 30 contemporary accounts and standard histories published since the 1970s of the 1917 revolutions. Many of the standard histories of 1917, including the more recent revisionist literature, do not include an entry for 'women' in the index, with the exception of those, Fieseler argues, that were written by female authors and were addressed explicitly to a female audience.[7]

The historiography of women's roles in the 1917 revolutions is reduced to two specific examples: first, the demonstrations in Petrograd on International Women's Day, which are commonly reported as having initiated the February revolution; and, second, the formation of the women's death battalion, the 'Bochkareva amazons', which defended the Winter Palace against the Bolsheviks in October.[8] Fieseler has argued that 'without the persistence of the community of female scholars in the field of Russian history the female majority of the Russian population will never find their past', and she has suggested that 'it is not enough to restore women to history, we have to restore history to women as well'.[9]

Yet much of the early writing of Russian and Soviet women's history can also be charged with exclusivity, not only for its distinctly elite bias, but also for its overwhelming focus on the predominant social and cultural experiences of those women of strictly Russian nationality within the broader, multi-ethnic Russian empire and in the Soviet Union. In a review of a recently published collection of essays, Christine Worobec has noted the paucity of research on the history of women in the Soviet period in particular, and she noted that 'only two articles in the volume focus on Ukraine, another imbalance reflective of the continuing preoccupation with Russian culture, history and politics at the expense of the non-Russian nations and nationalities the Russians colonised'.[10] As Clements has recently pointed out, 'women were, after all, as diverse in ethnicity, religion, social rank and place of residence as were men'.[11]

To its great credit, historical research on Russian 'women worthies' has revealed some extraordinary life stories that have proved informative and entertaining. Several biographies have been published of Russia's most well-known empress, Catherine the Great, and of the famous 'Bolshevik feminist' Alexandra Kollontai. The sexual exploits of these two women, however, have proved to be of as much interest to some researchers and readers as their progressive and reformist social policies. Moira Donald's recent study of the historiography of writings about Alexandra Kollontai has highlighted the ways in which women have often been misrepresented in history. Donald has explored in some detail the ways in which myths about Kollontai's personal life and political career have been formulated and perpetuated. She has also examined, decade by decade, the ways in which women in general have been neglected in the standard histories of the revolutions. Donald has set out to restore Kollontai to the history of 1917 and to identify her important and central position in the Bolshevik party hierarchy.[12]

In Donald's analysis, Kollontai was clearly among the five or six leading figures in the Bolshevik party during the revolutionary year. Her quantitative analysis of references to leading Bolsheviks, including Kollontai, in 22 eyewitness accounts of the Russian revolution supports this view. In qualitative terms, however, Kollontai has received mixed reviews, not only because of contemporary speculation about her personal life but also because of her earlier Menshevik (that is, non-Bolshevik) affiliations. In the secondary literature, Donald has argued, Kollontai has become less visible over time. She has noted that 'Kollontai was in danger of disappearing from view through the unconscious prejudice of historians, but interest in her revived in the wake of the new concern for women's history'.[13]

Employing a technique similar to that used by Fieseler, Donald has also pointed to a slight reversal in the trend of excluding women from the secondary literature on the history of the revolutions from the 1980s:

> Relatively few works published before the 1980s included 'women' in the index; almost all of those published recently did so. Although the number of page references was in some cases disappointingly few, the emergence of women as a category is nonetheless significant.[14]

She concluded:

> the signs indicate that, in this field at least, scholarship in women's history is becoming integrated into more general histories. This development should

not only 'restore women to history', it should also allow us to approach a fuller understanding of both the revolution itself and its historiography.[15]

The life stories of other individual exceptional Russian women have also been published, including (among many others) Russia's own 'military maid', Nadezhda Durova,[16] the aristocratic wife of one of the Decembrists who followed her husband into Siberian exile, Maria Volkonskaya,[17] the revolutionary terrorist Vera Zasulich,[18] and the internationally renowned mathematician Sophia Kovalevskaya.[19]

Surprisingly, prominent and influential Bolshevik women, with the exception of the two women closest to Lenin (his wife, Nadezhda Krupskaya,[20] and his supposed lover, Inessa Armand,[21] who is believed to have influenced Lenin's thinking on 'the woman question'), have received relatively little attention in Western literature compared to their male comrades. In researching her recent study of women in the revolutionary period, Clements employed a database that included 545 female Bolsheviks.[22] The scant attention paid to the female Bolsheviks remains the case despite the existence of an active women's department, the *Zhenotdel*, within the Communist Party in the 1920s, which was liquidated when Stalin declared the woman question resolved in the Soviet Union in 1930.[23]

Here, too, it is important to note that historical research has tended to focus more on the Bolshevik leadership than on women who were prominent and active in the other political parties around the time of the revolutions.[24] The Bolshevik victory in October 1917, therefore, also to some extent predicated its own historiographical exclusivity.[25] The limited Soviet historiography on women tends to have a predominantly empirical foundation and is largely premised on the materialist conception of the repressive policies of tsarism being overthrown by the supposedly liberationist and emancipatory ideology of the Communist Party.[26] It is important to note here also that until recently the subjects of historical enquiry for many Western researchers were partly set by trends in Soviet historiography and the granting of permission to access archival and other primary research materials.

The role of women in the Russian intelligentsia[27] and revolutionary movements[28] provided the focus for much of the initial research in nineteenth-century histories, along with two extensive and critical studies of the broader women's movement[29] and feminism in Russia at the turn of the twentieth century,[30] but the emphasis in these works also remained on the exception rather than the norm. However, the everyday lives approach is reflected in more recent social and economic historical writings concerning Russian and Soviet women. There is now an extensive literature on Russian and Soviet peasant women and their accommodation within and challenge to

the patriarchal culture of the countryside.[31] One recent reviewer of some of
the literature on this topic has concluded that

> an important task for historians of rural Russia is to incorporate the
> history of women into general histories with the aim of producing broader,
> inclusive narratives that reflect the realities of life in the villages rather than
> the dominant culture of patriarchy. . . . All the recent research on women in
> rural Russia demonstrates that the history of Russian peasant society without
> due concern for peasant women is no more conceivable or viable than the
> peasant societies themselves would have been without women.[32]

Detailed research into questions relating to female sexuality is relatively
new in Russian and Soviet studies and tends to be located, with a few
notable exceptions, within the academic disciplines of literature, sociology
and cultural studies rather than in history.[33] In examining the reasons why
questions relating to sexuality, and particularly homosexuality, have been
under-researched in the Russian and Soviet historical contexts, Dan Healey
has suggested that

> In the post-1945 era, the historical problems of Russia's cultural traditions
> and responses to sexual and gender dissidence received little serious attention
> on either side of the iron curtain. Soviet prudery tended to view such
> discussions as 'unscientific' or (paradoxically) 'excessively sexological' and
> therefore unsuitable for history professionals. Western academic squeamishness
> about sexual diversity in Russian culture is a remnant of the rigid orthodoxy
> of the cold war, as well as a reflection of Soviet preoccupations.[34]

Sources

Another area in which women's history has made a significant contribution
to the wider discipline is in defining what counts as evidence. This has
resulted in a broadening of topics deemed suitable for historical analysis.
Feminist research has demonstrated that women themselves are a valuable
resource for the study of history. Women's history has highlighted the importance of both oral traditions and interview methodologies to the study of
the past. However, cold war politics and difficulties of access, communication and candour have, until very recently, restricted the application of oral
history methodologies in the field of Russian studies, and especially Soviet
history. In a recently published collection of eight interviews with women
born before 1917 and raised in the Soviet Union, the editors pointed out

that the predominant emphasis of the state-controlled media on public triumphs and achievements made it difficult for women to recount their own private experiences of failure, loss and personal suffering, and that it would also have been dangerous for them to do so in particular years of the Soviet period. For example, even after the collapse of the Soviet Union, and with no possibility of punishment, the interviewees were reluctant to disclose their own experiences of abortion (recriminalised after 1936) until the interviewer offered her own personal testimony.[35]

Very often the resources available for the study of women's history remain invisible, inaccessible or, more simply, untapped. Robin Bisha has recently provided a list of primary sources which could be used to study women and gender relations in eighteenth-century Russia (an altogether under-researched period in Russian women's history): records of the Holy Synod provide evidence of family and marital relations and sexual irregularities; serf books (*krepostnye knigi*) give indications of property ownership and control by noble-women; criminal and court records detail legal disputes primarily among the nobility and merchant families; the various personal archives (*lichnye fondy*) contain collections of women's letters and personal papers. Bisha has noted also that published sources for this period have not yet been exhausted by historical research. She has concluded that 'we are just beginning to build a body of work that will help us to locate elusive changes and complete a periodization of Russian women's history'.[36]

The source materials available to historians have allowed researchers not only to explore and analyse the changing positions of women within given societies at different epochs, but also to examine the ways in which images and representations of women have served a broad range of political, socio-economic and cultural purposes. Lizzie Waters has argued that 'political iconography presents a fascinating barometer of official attitudes about women'.[37] The iconographic representations of Soviet women in the inter-war years reflect their marginalisation by both contemporaries and histor-ians in the events of the Bolshevik revolution. Waters has noted that 'the Bolsheviks preferred an iconography peopled by men because the revolu-tion was largely a male event and was perceived as such by those who commissioned and those who designed the symbols of the new regime'.[38]

In the example of Russian and Soviet history, images of women have been used allegorically to represent 'freedom', 'the nation' and 'Mother Russia' (or patriotism). In early Bolshevik visual propaganda images of women were often used symbolically to represent what were considered to be the rel-atively backward social groups. For example, the female (backward/rural) peasant was often physically located standing behind or alongside the male (advanced/urban) industrial worker. Here, Victoria Bonnell has argued, 'the roles are unmistakably gender-marked, indicating male domination'.[39]

With the progress of industrialisation and the collectivisation drives in the Soviet Union, and the espousal of the doctrine of 'socialist realism' in the politico-cultural arena, images of women began to take on a more heroic form. Official political iconography represented women as politically conscious, youthful and progressive proponents of revolutionary goals. Bonnell has again noted that

> the smiling woman tractor driver appeared in posters not as an accomplished fact but as an indication of what should be, as an incentive to make it happen. The poster constituted a kind of incantation designed to conjure up the new women who would perform certain roles in a specific spirit and manner.[40]

Not only has the revolution been depicted as a 'male' event, but also in the area of Soviet economic history it could be argued that, from a traditional historical perspective, the formation of the Russian and Soviet working class has also taken a distinctly masculine form.[41] The Western historiography of working-class formation in the inter-war years has been reflected in Soviet political iconography of the period. Despite the fact that women constituted approximately 40 per cent of the industrial labour force in the Soviet Union on the eve of the Second World War, very little attention has been paid in the standard economic histories to the role of women in the Soviet industrialisation process beyond the identification of their traditional low-paid and unskilled status in the labour force and their predominance in the light industrial sectors of the economy.[42]

The standard sources used for the study of Soviet economic history in the inter-war period pay little and scant attention to the role of women workers in the industrialisation process. The official government economic reports, the handbooks and archival records of the individual industrial commissariats, focused sectoral studies, contemporary newspapers and economic journals offer little more than empirical data on women's entry into the paid labour force and their proportional representation among workers in different sectors of industry. Such quantitative data provide a useful starting point, but do not constitute the whole picture. For example, how was women's entry into the industrial labour force encouraged and regulated? What were the processes that lay behind the gendering of jobs and the high level of both horizontal and vertical sex segregation in the industrial labour force by the beginning of the Second World War? How did women respond to the opportunities opened to them and to the restrictions placed on their employment? How did men respond to the mass recruitment of women to paid employment, and especially to heavy industrial labour?

New research

Some of my own recent research on Soviet women workers and protective labour legislation attempts to counter the exclusion of women from the economic and social history of the Soviet Union in the inter-war period and to investigate new sources for the study of women's history.[43] It is directed towards examining the practical impact and popular reception of government policies which were designed to ease the entry of women workers into the production process, as well as to questions relating more generally to the role of women workers in the industrialisation process. This research has involved an examination, among other sources, of the published findings of Soviet scientific research institutes which were given the remit during the inter-war period to investigate women's work capacities and, more specifically, to examine the physiological impact of industrial employment on the female body. The studies conducted in the field of labour hygiene in the Soviet Union resulted in a number of legislative initiatives in the 1920s and 1930s, and these were often accompanied by commentaries and debates in the contemporary newspapers. The Communist Party sponsored women's magazine, *Rabotnitsa* (*The Woman Worker*), has been largely ignored as a historical source in the standard economic histories of the Soviet Union. Yet it provides an indication of the extensive range of women's employment in these years and paints a vivid picture of everyday life in the factories, fields and mines.[44] Similar magazines were occasionally published on a regional basis.

Alongside the published sources, a careful reading of the archival records of the government body responsible for employment issues, the People's Commissariat of Labour (Narkomtrud), and the All-Union Central Council of Trade Unions (VTsSPS [ACCTU]) offer both an official and a shop-floor perspective as well as an analysis of women workers' own attitudes to the notion of their 'equality' in the industrial labour force in the early Soviet period. Taken together, these sources allow for a picture to emerge of debates and directions in official government policy towards women workers, and also women's responses and reactions to the protective labour laws that were introduced supposedly on their behalf.

The research has highlighted a possibly unique example of the labour protection of women workers (the provision for 'menstrual leave') implemented by the Bolsheviks in the 1920s and 1930s and has revealed evidence of issues not openly discussed in the published sources. For example, the published sources detail the regulations prohibiting the employment of women workers in underground work in the mining industry after the October revolution, and from these one is left to believe that the policy was effective. When I started to research this topic more closely, archivists in Moscow voiced their scepticism at my assumptions that the legal regulations were not enforced and they suggested that I would find nothing to support my opinion in their collections. In fact, the archival records revealed that women continued to be employed in underground work in the mining industry, as well as in the construction of the Moscow metro, throughout the period of the official prohibition and that women themselves protested against the restrictions on their work. The official prohibition was lifted in October 1940 and the Soviet Union entered the Second World War in the following year.

Scientific research into the impact of industrial employment on workers was not unique to the Soviet Union in the inter-war period. Nor was women's experience of factory work and heavy labour a specific and direct outcome of the attempts by the Bolshevik government to bring about women's liberation through women's recruitment to and accommodation in the production process. Russian peasant women had a long history of work involving heavy physical labour in agriculture. Women's employment in factories, both in rural settings and in the rapidly expanding urban centres, predated the October revolution by many decades. Soviet researchers were keenly aware of the work undertaken by their European counterparts into a variety of issues relating to health and safety in industrial employment. They also advanced their own research into areas not studied in other countries, by conducting experiments and field studies into a broad range of tasks and conditions in which women were employed.

Women, therefore, became the subjects of scientific research in studies which investigated a range of questions, including, for example, the physiological impact of industrial employment on the menstrual cycle; the potential for the infection of breast milk by women's employment with noxious and harmful substances, such as nicotine; the physical impact on women's reproductive organs of lifting and carrying heavy loads; the seating arrangements for female tractor drivers; and the dangers to women posed by underground work and employment on overtime and night shifts.

Invariably in these studies, and the debates which surrounded them, women were viewed and represented not only in terms of their actual economic role as workers in the production process, but also on the basis of their potential social role as mothers in the reproductive process. Moreover, the woman's body (or the 'female physiological organism' as it was often referred to) was almost without exception framed as weaker than, and therefore inferior to, the man's. This factor is reflected also in the protective labour laws that positioned women in the industrial labour force alongside juvenile and young workers, rather than adult male workers. Women workers themselves contested this alignment.

The published contemporary handbooks on 'the protection of labour', including the more specific texts on the regulations for women workers, provide a detailed, though often incomplete, listing of the protective labour laws in operation in this period. However, they include only limited commentary, if any at all, on the broader economic context in which the protective labour laws were introduced.[45] The secondary historiographical literature, as pointed out earlier, provides economic context, but little insight into the changing roles of women workers in the inter-war Soviet economy.[46]

In fact, the 1920s and 1930s were contrasting decades in respect to women's employment opportunities in the Soviet Union, marking the transition, as categorised in my research on this topic, 'from "protection" to "equality"'.[47] The introduction, evasion and repeal of the various protective labour laws reflected the interests of economic planners and enterprise managers rather than the needs of women workers themselves. The limited effectiveness of Soviet policy-makers in achieving their goals, however, is reflected in my conclusion that 'early Soviet attempts to accommodate women into the industrial labour force through the introduction of legislative regulations provided no more for the "protection" of women workers in the 1920s than they did for their "equality" in the 1930s'.[48] As has been the experience of women workers in other countries and at other times, Soviet women workers in the inter-war period served as a 'reserve army of labour'.

The 1920s, a period of high unemployment and job insecurity during the years of the New Economic Policy, saw the introduction of a number of protective measures which restricted the scope of female employment and explicitly excluded women from jobs deemed injurious to their health. In practice and at the same time, the regulations reserved these occupations, often the most highly paid, for men. However, by the early 1930s, following the transition to the planned economy, the Soviet Union, now in conditions of full employment, was experiencing severe labour shortages in many sectors of the economy. There were retractions in the scope of the official 'protective' policy towards women workers, sanctioned in part by the latest 'findings' of the scientific research institutes: night shift employment was no longer seen as harmful to female workers because women, it was claimed, as mothers were more accustomed to broken patterns of sleep; work by women underground in mines was deemed to be no more difficult or injurious than some of the tasks undertaken by workers in surface jobs. The 'menstrual leave' provisions, first introduced in 1921, proved too complex and expensive to implement and were soon abandoned in all but a few limited examples.

One popular perception of the Soviet Union in the 1930s is that it was a country which, more than any other country in the world, had guaranteed women's equality. Yet this 'equality' was little more than an official construct, predicated on the ideological assumption that the mass entry of women into the paid labour force was the foundation for their liberation. What feminist historical research has revealed is that in reality women laboured under a difficult, and sometimes intolerable, 'double burden'. This consisted of paid work and the exclusive responsibility for domestic labour (which became a 'triple burden' if childcare is also to be taken into account). Soviet women in this period held contrasting opinions on how their own equality was to be best achieved. With great contemporary resonance, some argued that women's equality was located in their ability to work alongside men (that is, in their 'sameness'), while others professed that women's equality could not be achieved without the recognition of their distinct needs (that is, their 'difference').

It is only from a closer reading of a broader range of contemporary sources, such as the proceedings of trade union congresses, investigative reports and letters published in women's magazines, and the accounts offered by foreign visitors to the Soviet Union in these decades, that women's voices come to be heard. These can be supplemented by archival documents, including the unpublished findings of studies conducted by government-sponsored commissions and committees that were established to investigate the realities of female employment and women's everyday lives. These readings reveal that women workers were not simply the willing and passive recipients of paternalistic protection encapsulated in the labour laws. Women workers sometimes vociferously contested the introduction and imposition of protective labour legislation and flagrantly violated the terms of the statutes in many sectors of the economy, most noticeably in the textile industry.[49] This example alone to some extent supports the growing revisionist literature which contests the traditional historiographical view of Soviet society as constituted by a homogeneous and inert, and later terrorised, population. This has been more conclusively illustrated by the studies of peasant women's resistance to the collectivisation drives.[50]

Conclusion

By way of conclusion, it would be wrong to suggest that women's history and the discipline of history as a whole have nothing to gain from retaining a distinct emphasis on making visible the history of women. Women can be 'written in' to history, and thus both 'change the past' and inform the present. There is a wealth of historical source material on women's lives yet to be explored. The women's histories arising from an analysis of these sources will both supplement and complement our existing knowledge, as well as open up completely new topics for historical investigation. They will also, undoubtedly, come to contest long-held assumptions about the nature of the historical process and women's role within it. Moreover, they will reveal that ongoing debates in contemporary feminism are not purely recent considerations – they often have a long history. Feminism itself and the interdisciplinary training offered by a women's studies approach to scholarship have already had a very significant impact on historiography, research methodologies and academia in general. The growing scholarship on women in the field of Russian and Soviet history provides us with an excellent example.

Further reading

A number of review articles which detail developments in the Western literature on Russian and Soviet women's history are available: see, for example, B. A. Engel, 'Women in Russia and the Soviet Union', *Signs* 12/4 (1987), pp. 781–96; B. A. Engel, 'Engendering Russia's history: women in post-emancipation Russia and the Soviet Union', *Slavic Review* 51/2 (Summer 1992), pp. 309–21; and R. Ruthchild, 'Engendering history: women in Russia and the Soviet Union', *European History Quarterly* 24 (1994), pp. 555–62.

Many of the works cited in the notes to this chapter will be of interest to those studying Russian and Soviet women. In addition to these, B. E. Clements, *Daughters of Revolution: A History of Women in the USSR* (Arlington Heights, Ill., 1994) provides a concise overview of the history of Russian and Soviet women. See also J. McDermid and A. Hillyar, *Midwives of the Revolution: Female Bolsheviks and Women Workers in 1917* (1999). General surveys of the Soviet period are provided by G. W. Lapidus, *Women in Soviet Society: Equality, Development and Social Change* (Berkeley, Calif., 1978), and M. Buckley, *Women and Ideology in the Soviet Union* (1989). For women's memoirs and oral histories see also A. Horsbrugh-Porter, ed., *Memories of Revolution: Russian Women Remember* (1993).

Notes

1. I am grateful to Linda Edmondson (Centre for Russian and East European Studies, University of Birmingham), the editors of this volume and participants at the International Federation for Research in Women's History Conference on 'Women and Human Rights, Social Justice and Citizenship: International Historical Perspectives' (University of Melbourne, 1998) for comments on earlier drafts of this chapter.

2. B. E. Clements, 'Women and the gender question', in E. Acton et al., *Critical Companion to the Russian Revolution, 1914–21* (1997), p. 596.

3. B. E. Clements, 'The effects of the civil war on women and family relations', in D. Koenker et al., *Party, State and Society in the Russian Civil War: Explorations in Social History* (Bloomington, Ind., 1989), pp. 105–22.

4. J. McDermid and A. Hillyar, *Women and Work in Russia, 1880–1930: A Study in Continuity Through Change* (1998).

5. B. Farnsworth, 'Peasant women after the revolution', and *idem*, 'Village women experience the revolution', in B. Farnsworth and L. Viola, eds, *Russian Peasant Women* (Oxford, 1992), pp. 137–66.

6. W. Z. Goldman, *Women, the State and Revolution: Soviet Family Policy and Social Life, 1917–36* (Cambridge, 1993). See also E. Waters, 'The modernisation of Russian motherhood, 1917–37', *Soviet Studies* 44/1 (1992), pp. 123–35.

7. B. Fieseler, 'Gender and revolution: Petrograd, Russia 1917', paper presented to IV World Congress for Soviet and East European Studies, Harrogate, 1990. See also B. Fieseler, 'The making of Russian female Social Democrats, 1890–1917', *International Review of Social History* 34/2 (1989), pp. 193–226.

8. R. Abraham, 'Mariia Bochkareva and the Russian amazons of 1917', in L. H. Edmondson, ed., *Women and Society in Russia and the Soviet Union* (Cambridge, 1992), pp. 124–44.

9. Fieseler, 'Gender and revolution', pp. 1, 6.

10. C. Worobec, review of R. Marsh, ed., *Women in Russia and Ukraine* (Cambridge, 1996), in *Europe–Asia Studies* 49/4 (June 1997), pp. 730–1. For notable exceptions on non-Russian women, see M. Bohachevsky-Chomiak, *Feminists Despite Themselves: Women in Ukrainian Community Life, 1884–1939* (Edmonton, 1988); G. J. Massell, *The Surrogate Proletariat: Moslem Women and Revolutionary Strategies in Soviet Central Asia, 1919–29* (Princeton, NJ, 1974); and S. Keller, 'Trapped between state and society: women's liberation and Islam in Soviet Uzbekistan, 1926–41', *Journal of Women's History* 10/1 (1998), pp. 20–44.

11. Clements, 'Women and the gender question', p. 592.

12. M. Donald, ' "What did *you* do in the revolution, Mother?" Image, myth and prejudice in Western writing on the Russian revolution', *Gender and History* 7/1 (April 1995), pp. 85–99.

13. Ibid., p. 90.

14. Ibid., p. 91.

15. Ibid., p. 96.

16. M. F. Zirin, trans. and ed., *The Cavalry Maiden: Journals of a Russian Officer in the Napoleonic Wars* (Bloomington, Ind., 1989).

17. C. Sutherland, *The Princess of Siberia: The Story of Maria Volkonsky and the Decembrist Exiles* (1984).

18. J. Bergman, *Vera Zasulich* (Stanford, Calif., 1983).

19. D. H. Kennedy, *Little Sparrow: A Portrait of Sophia Kovalevsky* (1983), and A. H. Koblitz, *A Convergence of Lives. Sofia Kovalevskaia: Scientist, Writer, Revolutionary* (Boston, Mass., 1993).

20. R. H. McNeal, *Bride of the Revolution: Krupskaia and Lenin* (Ann Arbor, Mich., 1972).

21. R. C. Elwood, *Inessa Armand: Revolutionary and Feminist* (Cambridge, 1992). Recent research tends to confirm the commonly held belief that Armand and Lenin were lovers. For example, see D. Volkogonov, *Lenin: A New Biography* (1994).

22. B. E. Clements, *Bolshevik Women* (Cambridge, 1996).

23. On the work of the *Zhenotdel* and the institutional problems it faced, see E. A. Wood, *The Baba and the Comrade: Gender and Politics in Revolutionary Russia* (Bloomington, Ind., 1997). See also C. Hayden, 'The *Zhenotdel* and the Bolshevik Party', *Russian History* 3/2 (1976), pp. 150–73; R. Stites, '*Zhenotdel*: Bolshevism and Russian women, 1917–30', *Russian History* 3/2 (1976), pp. 174–93; and, more recently, W. Z. Goldman, 'Industrial politics, peasant rebellion and the death of the proletarian women's movement in the USSR', *Slavic Review* 55/1 (Spring 1996), pp. 46–77.

24. See, for example, B. T. Norton, 'Laying the foundations of democracy in Russia: E. D. Kuskova's contribution, February–October, 1917', in Edmondson, *Women and Society*, pp. 101–23. A number of other prominent non-Bolshevik women are listed in Fieseler, 'Gender and revolution', n. 3, and Donald, ' "What did *you* do"?', n. 8.

25. In a study of attitudes towards homosexuality in the early Soviet period, Dan Healey notes that 'Leftist culture was . . . profoundly masculine . . . the dominant line . . . imagined an indivisible proletariat, with a single roster of universalized masculine concerns'. See D. Healey, 'Evgeniia/Evgenii: queer case histories in the first years of Soviet power', *Gender and History* 9/1 (April 1997), p. 86.

26. See, for example, G. N. Serebrennikov, *The Position of Women in the USSR* (1937).

27. B. A. Engel, *Mothers and Daughters: Women of the Intelligentsia in Nineteenth-Century Russia* (Cambridge, 1983).

28. See, for example, B. A. Engel and C. N. Rosenthal, *Five Sisters: Women Against the Tsar* (New York, 1975), and V. Broido, *Apostles into Terrorists: Women and the Revolutionary Movement in the Russia of Alexander II* (1977).

29. R. Stites, *The Women's Liberation Movement in Russia: Feminism, Nihilism and Bolshevism, 1860–1930* (Princeton, NJ, 1978).

30. L. Edmondson, *Feminism in Russia, 1900–1917* (1984).

31. The writing on this topic is now extensive. Farnsworth and Viola, *Russian Peasant Women*, provides a useful collection of essays on a variety of relevant issues. For a valuable contribution to the monograph literature, see B. A. Engel, *Between the Fields and the City: Women, Work and Family in Russia, 1861–1914* (Cambridge, 1994).

32. D. Moon, 'Women in rural Russia from the tenth to the twentieth centuries' (review article), *Continuity and Change* 12/1 (1997), p. 137.

33. For historical studies on issues relating to sexuality, see L. A. Bernstein, *Sonia's Daughters: Prostitutes and Their Regulation in Imperial Russia* (Berkeley, Calif., 1995); E. Levin, *Sex and Society in the World of the Orthodox Slavs, 900–1700* (Ithaca, NY, 1989); L. Engelstein, *The Keys to Happiness: Sex and the Search for Modernity in Fin-de-Siècle Russia* (Ithaca, NY, 1992); and J. T. Costlow et al., eds, *Sexuality and the Body in Russian Culture* (Stanford, Calif., 1993).

34. Healey, 'Evgeniia/Evgenii', pp. 83–4.

35. B. A. Engel and A. Posadskaya-Vanderbeck, eds, *A Revolution of Their Own: Voices of Women in Soviet History* (Oxford, 1998), p. 1.

36. R. Bisha, ' "Engendering" 18th-century Russia', unpublished discussion essay distributed via the Eighteenth Century Russia list from rbisha@hobbes.kzoo.edu. I am grateful to D. Moon for this reference.

37. E. Waters, 'The female form in Soviet political iconography, 1917–32', in B. E. Clements et al., eds, *Russia's Women: Accommodation, Resistance, Transformation* (Oxford, 1991), p. 242. In addressing issues of periodisation Waters also questions the utility of traditional historical narratives for the study of women in Soviet iconography.

38. Ibid., p. 232.

39. V. E. Bonnell, *Iconography of Power: Soviet Political Posters under Lenin and Stalin* (1997), p. 75.

40. Ibid., p. 110. See also S. Reid, 'All Stalin's women: gender and power in Soviet art of the 1930s', *Slavic Review* 57/1 (1998), pp. 133–73.

41. For a study of female industrial workers in pre-revolutionary Russia, see R. L. Glickman, *Russian Factory Women: Workplace and Society, 1880–1914* (1984). See also J. Pallot, 'Women's domestic industries in Moscow province, 1880–1900', in Clements et al., eds, *Russia's Women*, pp. 163–84.

42. Two exceptions here are D. Filtzer, *Soviet Workers and Stalinist Industrialisation* (1986), which devotes five pages to 'the growth of female employment' (see pp. 63–7), and J. Barber, 'The composition of the Soviet working class, 1928–41', unpublished Discussion Papers, SIPS no. 16 (CREES, University of Birmingham, 1978), which includes details of gender composition.

43. M. Ilič, *Women Workers in the Soviet Interwar Economy: From 'Protection' to 'Equality'* (1999).

44. Women's magazines also provide a useful insight into official constructions and changing perceptions of women's roles and femininity. See L. Attwood, *Creating the New Soviet Woman: Women's Magazines as Engineers of Female Identity, 1922–53* (1999).

45. For an early example in English, see S. I. Kaplun, *The Protection of Labour in Soviet Russia* (Moscow, 1920).

46. For two notable, but limited, exceptions, see N. T. Dodge, *Women in the Soviet Economy: Their Role in Economic, Scientific and Technical Development* (Baltimore, 1966), and A. McAuley, *Women's Work and Wages in the Soviet Union* (1981).

47. Ilič, *Women Workers*.

48. Ibid., p. 176.

49. C. Ward, *Russian Cotton Workers and the New Economic Policy* (Cambridge, 1988).

50. L. Viola, '*Bab'i bunty* and peasant women's protest during collectivization', *Russian Review* 45/1 (1986), pp. 23–42, and S. Fitzpatrick, *Stalin's Peasants: Resistance and Survival in the Russian Village after Collectivization* (Oxford, 1996).

CHAPTER EIGHT

New histories of the labour movement

JUNE HANNAM

In all these hard years of fierce struggle for women's political freedom, the women of the country had no greater friends than the members of the Independent Labour Party. From the beginning of its existence the I.L.P. has stood for the political equality of men and women . . . the I.L.P. has never been a men's Party, and therefore never can be exclusive and domineering in the sense in which this may have been true of the older parties hitherto controlled exclusively by men. Women with any personality at all will not lose it here. Women with any ability at all will find scope for it here. Women who have any desire to help directly in the shaping of the Party's destinies can help here.[1]

Ethel Snowden's assessment of the support given by the socialist group, the Independent Labour Party (ILP),[2] to the struggle for women's suffrage and of the possibilities that the party offered to women to influence policies and events was echoed in many other books, pamphlets and articles written by ILP members in the period 1913 to the 1920s.[3] This positive view has then been repeated in mainstream labour history texts right up to the present day, despite the fact that feminist historians have questioned this version of socialist history[4] and have suggested that the ILP's attitude towards women's involvement in socialist politics was far more ambivalent than the retrospective accounts of contemporaries might imply.[5]

Although labour historians make passing reference to the work of feminist historians, they fail to engage fully with the arguments presented. This is largely because women's contribution to the socialist movement and the gender dimension of socialist politics are still seen as marginal in histories of socialism. These concentrate, in the same ways as contemporaries, on the male industrial worker, his struggles at the workplace and the development of class-based politics. It is not surprising, therefore, that the judgements made in contemporary histories are accepted uncritically. And yet the latter were not written in a vacuum. Many were produced at a time when the Labour Party had made an alliance with the National Union of Women's Suffrage Societies (NUWSS) and the relationship between the two was being projected in a positive light.[6] Others were written in the early 1920s in a context in which newly enfranchised women were being encouraged to support the Labour Party.[7]

This version of the ILP's commitment to women's political equality did not go uncontested at the time. Although Isabella Ford, a member of the National Administrative Council (NAC) of the ILP between 1903 and 1907 and a suffrage campaigner, claimed that the ILP uniquely 'put women on an equal footing with men',[8] Margaret McMillan, the educational reformer who was also a member of the NAC, was far more doubtful about the extent to which the ILP gave priority either to women's suffrage or to other issues which affected women's social position.[9] Significantly, Ethel Snowden, who praised the ILP in 1920, was so disappointed with the party's luke-warm support for women's suffrage in the pre-war years that she resigned from the ILP in 1909 and did not rejoin until the First World War.[10]

It is hardly surprising that individual members of the ILP should produce different versions of the extent to which women were on an 'equal footing' with men within the party and of how far the ILP had a strong commitment to women's suffrage. Their experiences of the ILP could be shaped by their own background and position in the party and were subject to change over time. They could also be affected by the characteristics of particular local branches which varied in their attitudes towards female members. Moreover, judgements about the ILP were made in a context in which socialist groups were unusual in placing no formal barriers in the way of women becoming members and holding office in their organisations, whereas other contemporary political parties tended to confine women to a narrow range of activities or to separate groups.

This complexity, however, tends to be overlooked in histories of the socialist movement, where women are usually given only a brief mention and gender issues are not central to the analysis put forward. Thus there is a tendency to accept uncritically the ILP's own version of its past without interrogating the context in which such a history was produced or recognising it as only one among many possible versions.[11] Moreover, women socialists tend to be seen as a single group and differences between them are rarely explored. It is the intention of this chapter, therefore, to examine some of the different perspectives, both of the ILP itself and of some of its women members, towards women's involvement in political activity through an examination of the attitudes towards women's suffrage expressed in selected ILP newspapers between 1906 and 1914.

During this period, when the struggle for the vote was at its height, many of the broader questions about the extent to which socialists should concern themselves with the inequalities and oppression women suffered as a sex and the meaning of women's emancipation were viewed through the lens of suffrage. The suffrage movement brought to the fore underlying tensions about the nature of women's involvement in socialist politics, the importance of party loyalty and the extent to which priority should be given to gender inequalities within a class-based movement. The story of the conflicts that the demand for the vote on a 'limited' basis caused within the labour and socialist movements is a familiar one and does not need repeating at length here.[12] Alone of all the European socialist groups which were affiliated to the Second International, the ILP gave official support at its conferences to the demand for a 'limited franchise', or votes for women on the same terms as men, as a first step towards the achievement of the franchise for all adult men and women.[13] Support for a 'limited franchise' is then seen as an indicator not only of the ILP's commitment to women's political equality, but also of the party's interest in 'women's emancipation' more generally, although this is seldom defined. Thus support for a 'limited' franchise is equated with a commitment to prioritise issues relating to the disabilities women suffered on account of their sex, whereas support for adult suffrage is taken to imply a greater interest in questions of class and a non-feminist outlook.[14]

The ILP played an important role in developing the alliance between the Labour Party and the NUWSS in 1912. Thus it is assumed that, although the party had a close relationship up to 1907 with the Women's Social and Political Union (WSPU), many of whose members also belonged to the ILP, this broke down as the WSPU became hostile to the Labour Party and adopted militant actions which involved the destruction of property. Instead, it is argued that the constitutionalist NUWSS appeared to provide a more congenial ally for the ILP in the suffrage struggle.[15]

And yet what such accounts rarely consider are the range of perspectives put forward by both men and women in the ILP in this period. In grappling with ways to pursue changes in women's social, economic and political position within a socialist framework they adopted a variety of positions which cannot be neatly labelled into categories such as limited/adult suffragist or feminist/non-feminist.[16] It is argued here that these varied perspectives become more apparent when different ILP newspapers are examined and when closer attention is paid to who was writing in the newspapers and their relationship with the editor and with the NAC of the party. This should then allow for a more complex reading of the relationship between suffragism and ILP socialism than is normally found in mainstream texts.

National and local ILP newspapers

The *Labour Leader*, the ILP's national weekly newspaper, has been used extensively as a key source by historians of the ILP. It became the official organ of the party in 1904 when John Bruce Glasier, a member of the NAC, was appointed as the new editor, a position he held until 1909.[17] On the other hand the *Labour Leader* was not the only forum for the expression of views on the burning issues of the day. A number of local newspapers were published by ILP branches in the period 1890–1914. This was a time when socialist journalism flourished because newspapers were seen as crucial for spreading propaganda and for 'making socialists'.[18] It has long been recognised that local branches were a key site for the development of social-ist politics in the pre-war years and that they had diverse characteristics.[19] This was certainly the case in relation to the extent to which women were actively involved in branch life and in attitudes towards female members. It is crucial, therefore, to examine local as well as national newspapers in order to explore the relationship between the ILP and women's political activism.

As well as the *Labour Leader*, therefore, this chapter will focus on two local newspapers, the Glasgow based *Forward* and the *Northern Democrat*, which covered the north-east of England. They were first published in 1906, just as the suffrage movement was gaining far greater publicity through the development of 'militant' tactics, and becoming an increasingly controver-sial issue for the labour movement. Both papers had a considerable influ-ence within their local areas, although *Forward*, which was published weekly, had a more extensive coverage of political events and drew on a wider range of contributors than the *Northern Democrat*, which was a monthly pub-lication. Neither of the areas they represented have received a great deal of attention in relation to socialist women's support for the suffrage. Instead, the focus has been on Lancashire and Yorkshire where national leaders of the suffrage campaign, such as Emmeline and Christabel Pankhurst, Ethel Snowden and Isabella Ford, were based. An examination of these two local papers, therefore, should help to give an insight into the range of views expressed within the ILP.

Forward was edited and partly owned by Tom Johnston, an ILP member who, nevertheless, hoped that the paper would be a forum for the expres-sion of progressive opinion and would be the means to bring together radical liberals and socialists. After 1908 it became far more firmly the paper of labour and socialist thinkers. This reflected the growing import-ance of the Glasgow ILP, which was replacing the Liberals as the 'leading radical force in city politics'.[20] Joan Smith suggests that by 1913 *Forward* was the 'galvanising hub of the entire Glasgow labour movement presenting a distinctive and coherent presence in local politics'.[21] The *Northern Democrat* was edited by Matt Simm, organiser of the North East Federation of the ILP from 1904. Within three years the number of ILP branches in the area had increased from 4 to 76, of which 39 were active. Hopkin suggests that the *Northern Democrat* both reflected and also helped to contribute to this renewed activity and that it was 'an organisational paper, giving regular balance sheets and reporting the transactions of the party's executive committee as well as a journal of opinion and ideas'.[22]

The three papers were very different from each other in tone and content and certainly do not present one ILP voice in their reporting of women's suffrage. The amount of space given to the suffrage question, and the extent to which it was seen as a vital political issue, varied both between the papers and also over time during the period under review. Moreover, a range of different views was expressed about the methods used by suffrage campaigners and their political tactics. These differences can be explained by the outlook of the editors, the views of the regular contributors and changes in the policies of the NAC, all of which were inextricably linked.

Women's representation in ILP
newspapers, 1906–14

Despite the consistent support given to women's suffrage in the House of Commons by individual ILP MPs, in particular Keir Hardie and Phillip Snowden, the *Labour Leader* did not provide a focus for the movement until after 1911 when the editor, Fenner Brockway, a committed suffrage supporter, spearheaded a campaign for political equality. This preceded the alliance between the Labour Party and the NUWSS, which led to a spate of articles between 1912 and 1914 on women's suffrage and the need for a 'democratic' franchise. Many of these were written by well-known ILP suffrage activists, including Isabella Ford, Ada Neild Chew and Annot Robinson, who were keen to foster a close relationship between the women's movement and the labour movement. The theme which ran through their articles was one of admiration for the ILP and its steadfast support for their cause. Annot Robinson, at one time a member of the WSPU before she became involved in the ILP and the Women's Labour League (WLL), an auxiliary of the Labour Party, claimed that:

> The *Labour Leader* has also rendered invaluable service to the suffrage movement, for, through good report and ill, it has never wavered in its steadfast allegiance . . . It is impossible to conclude such an article as this

without saying how indebted we are to the brilliant band of propagandists inside the Party who have worked so hard for Woman Suffrage . . . I am proud of my Party.[23]

This was a very different interpretation from that expressed by women a few years earlier. In *Forward* in particular, which was sympathetic to militant campaigners, there were frequent criticisms in 1907 and 1908 of the lack of energy displayed towards women's suffrage by the NAC and the *Labour Leader*. Teresa Billington, an ILP member and organiser for the WSPU in Scotland, who later founded a new militant group, the Women's Freedom League (WFL), was typical of many in pointing to the gap between rhetoric and practical support in the ILP:

> In the 'Labour Leader' our attitude of independence is challenged by Mr Bruce Glasier, who meantime declares that as in the past so in the future the I.L.P. and the Labour Party generally will stand straight for principles and work for women's enfranchisement, in spite of the errors of its advocates. Mrs Ethel Snowden questions the measure and quality of the support which the 'Labour Leader' and some of the rank and file of the I.L.P. have given to the agitation or the agitators, in the very same issue![24]

This reference to Ethel Snowden provides a timely reminder that it was not just militant supporters who complained about the ILP. Even the suffragist Isabella Ford, a former member of the NAC who was invariably conciliatory in her attitudes and rarely criticised the ILP, was so 'astonished' in 1909 to find that the chairman of the party was an adult suffragist that she warned that if a limited suffrage was no longer official policy 'many of us will be compelled to leave the party for which we care so much'.[25]

Although suffrage activists were still able to express criticisms of the NAC within the *Labour Leader*, very little space was given in the paper between 1907 and 1911 to the question of women's suffrage, and those debates which were conducted from time to time tended to appear on the letters page. The NAC did not give a strong steer on the issue. Many of the leading suffrage supporters had decided to give a full-time commitment to the suffrage campaign in 1907 and therefore were less prominent within the ILP. The NAC contained prominent adult suffragists, and those supporters of a limited suffrage who remained, such as Margaret McMillan, gave priority in this period to child education and welfare rather than to suffrage. The editor of the *Labour Leader*, John Bruce Glasier, and his wife, Katharine Bruce Glasier, who wrote a women's column in the paper between 1906 and 1909 under the name of Iona, were ambivalent in their attitudes to the suffrage campaign. Although they were supporters of a 'limited' franchise for women, John Bruce Glasier became increasingly irritated by the militant actions of the

WSPU and their hostility to the labour movement. Katharine Bruce Glasier claimed that the editor had given her freedom to express her own opinions: '"The Woman's Outlook" is, he says, mine not his. "You are a perfectly free woman", he adds, "so far as the *Leader* is concerned" . . . .'[26] And yet in many respects Katharine Bruce Glasier's views echoed those of her husband. She wrote lively and supportive reports of suffrage demonstrations and activities in her column but did not give women's suffrage priority in her day-to-day politics, and therefore it became one among many issues which were covered in her column rather than the most important.

A very different picture was presented in *Forward*. The editor, Tom Johnston, was a keen supporter of women's demand for the vote and wrote a pamphlet on the subject, *The Case for Women's Suffrage*, which was published in 1907.[27] Editorials on the issue appeared on a regular basis along with lengthy reports of suffrage meetings, in particular when leading campaigners visited Scotland. Considerable space was given between 1906 and 1908 to the debate between adult and limited suffrage positions, in which a variety of points of view were expressed in articles and letters written by male and female members of the ILP. In contrast to 'Iona' in the *Labour Leader*, the women's column that appeared in *Forward* between 1906 and 1909 and from 1913 to 1914 took the suffrage as the starting point for any discussion of issues affecting women and in 1913 was entitled 'Our Suffrage Column'. Although it changed its name and authorship several times between 1906 and 1914, the column gained coherence through the consistency of its support for the WSPU and the WFL. At various times it was edited by Teresa Billington, Lily Bell, Mary Phillips, Janie Allan and Helen Crawfurd, all of whom were active in the WSPU at the time when they edited the column. Tom Johnston was himself sympathetic to the militant movement and, although he increasingly criticised WSPU leaders when they attacked ILP MPs such as Keir Hardie, he was unusual in retaining his sympathy for them even when militancy had escalated and become more violent. As late as 1913, for example, Johnston wrote:

> Have you forgotten the Chartist times, the burning of the hay ricks, the smashing of the weavers' looms? . . . Particular acts we may disapprove of; but surely we can admire and reverence the spirit, the fearlessness and the courage of the Woman Militant who has risen among us; and surely the spectacle of brave women going open eyed to a felon's cell, a hunger strike and a ruined physique for a great cause is not a spectacle that should arouse from an intelligent democracy a medley of sneers, cat calls and abuse?[28]

This positive admiration of the courage of the woman militant can be compared with the more cautious approach to be found in the *Labour*

Leader. The 'militant' was either not represented at all or was supported in a qualified way when reference was made to the brutality of the government. Sympathy with her position was often tempered by criticisms of the counter-productiveness of violent actions and the divisiveness caused by political tactics which led to the disruption of meetings held by Labour Party and ILP candidates for election to parliament.

Some of these ambiguous views can be found in Iona's column. Although she was a leading member of the Women's Labour League, which looked on the WSPU as a rival for the allegiance of working-class women, Katharine Bruce Glasier used her column to attempt to conciliate between the two. She was reluctant to criticise the WSPU leader Emmeline Pankhurst, describing her as one of the 'most faithful and most spirited of women . . . She has a record of genuine service for socialism and for every democratic cause which is simply unexcelled in our movement.'[29] Nonetheless she was uneasy when militancy escalated and feared that the political tactics of the WSPU were divisive for the labour movement. Consistent with her own emphasis on the importance of the struggle for socialism and the needs of working-class women was her criticism of the way in which large sums of money were given to the WSPU. Once, when she noted that they had received £15,000, she regretted that 'pounds come in to them, while pence are given for the teachings of socialism'.[30] Similarly Lisbeth Simm, a WLL organiser in the north-east who wrote for the *Northern Democrat*, was critical that the WSPU collected money in distressed areas and thought that they did not understand the poverty of most women's lives.[31]

As part owner of *Forward* Tom Johnston had a degree of freedom to stamp his own style and outlook onto the paper and did not have to link as closely with the views of the NAC as the *Labour Leader*, which was the party's official national newspaper. Moreover many ILP members in Scotland, in particular in Glasgow, were members of the militant groups, the WSPU or the WFL, rather than the NUWSS which was so closely associated with Liberalism. Most of them retained their links with the ILP and were keen to express their views in its local paper. After 1912 Sylvia Pankhurst became a regular contributor to the paper and introduced her own brand of militant socialist and suffrage politics. It is interesting that when four pictures of women appeared in the paper in 1913 under the heading 'Four Glasgow Suffragists' they were all members of the WSPU.[32] *Forward*, therefore, provided a space in which the voice of militant suffrage campaigners, many of whom retained their commitment to ILP socialism, could be heard. This alternative voice suggests the need to probe more deeply the relationship between the ILP and the militant movement, in particular in the provinces, at a time when the NAC and the *Labour Leader* were giving strong support to the alliance with the NUWSS. Although the political tactics adopted by the WSPU caused difficulties for ILP members, many women in local areas managed to continue to combine their membership of the WSPU with allegiance to the ILP, and in some cases also to the WLL, despite the hostility between the national leaders of all three organisations in the immediate pre-war years.[33]

Female members of the ILP faced considerable difficulty in attempting to reconcile issues which highlighted their grievances as a sex with the struggle for socialism, which emphasised class solidarity and party loyalty. Although they believed that it was only through socialism that women would achieve full emancipation they still had to make choices in their day-to-day politics about what position to take on particular questions and what to see as a priority, both as women and as socialists. Too often these positions have been characterised in terms of polar opposites, such as adult versus limited suffrage. Those who took the former position are seen as putting class before sex in their politics and therefore are characterised as 'less feminist' in their outlook.

It is certainly the case that, at least up to 1908, contemporaries themselves discussed the suffrage in these terms. The stark differences between them are clear in the debate between the two positions in *Forward* in 1907. 'Lily Bell', the pseudonym of Isabella Bream Pearce, who had written a women's column in the *Labour Leader* between 1894 and 1898, was a forceful advocate of the need to push at once for a limited franchise for women. Isabella Bream Pearce had been one of the leading members of the Glasgow Women's Labour Party in the 1890s and in 1907 became treasurer of the Scottish Council of the WSPU. She took over the women's column of *Forward* – 'A Woman's Point of View' – when Teresa Billington was imprisoned in 1906 and was a frequent contributor to the paper over the next two years. She supported a limited franchise on the grounds that 'the evils and dangers of "property qualifications" are less than those of "sex property qualifications" which must at all costs be overturned'.[34] She was criticised by Agnes Pettigrew of the Shop Assistants' Union who claimed that working-class women were not exploited by men of their own class, but by the employing class, and that their interests would be no safer in the hands of propertied women than in those of propertied men.[35]

And yet for many women the issue was not so clear cut. Instead they adopted a range of different positions as they attempted to integrate their socialist and 'feminist' perspectives and took different political journeys over a lifetime. It is not necessarily helpful, however, to see one route rather than another as representing a greater feminist commitment. Margaret McMillan, for instance, was a member of the NAC in 1906 and joined with Isabella Ford in supporting a limited suffrage position. They both sought to conciliate between the ILP and the WSPU when the latter had carried out propaganda against the Labour Party candidate at a recent by-election in Cockermouth.[36] Nonetheless, when Isabella Ford decided in the following year to give a full-time commitment to the suffrage movement, becoming a member of the executive of the NUWSS, McMillan remained as a member of the NAC of the ILP because she believed that the party offered a better platform for her main political agenda, the medical inspection of schoolchildren.[37] She continued, however, to take an interest in the vote and at various times belonged to both the WFL and the People's Suffrage Federation. Katharine Bruce Glasier also accepted a limited suffrage position and believed that the 'professedly Adult Suffrage movement' was 'deeply anti-woman', but she was far more sceptical than many socialist women about how far the suffrage would enable working-class women to improve their position. She argued that working-class men had had votes for a long time but they had 'not used them right . . . Nor will we women when we get them unless we are taught the truth of socialism. That is why I stick by the I.L.P.'[38] In her study of the political partnership of John and Katharine Bruce Glasier June Balshaw suggests that the suffrage 'was always going to be secondary to their work for the socialist cause . . . the paramount task was to spread the religion of socialism and in so doing the inequalities of class and, in theory, gender would be resolved'.[39]

Journalism and personal politics of women journalists

These differences of emphasis, along with changes over time, were reflected in the contributions made by such women to the socialist press. Socialist journalism was closely tied in the period to the personal politics of individuals. Women and men wrote about their own activities and used newspapers to advance the causes in which they were active. Thus the main female contributors to the *Labour Leader* between 1907 and 1912, Margaret McMillan, Margaret MacDonald, leader of the WLL, and Mary Macarthur, leader of the National Federation of Women Workers and member of the NAC, wrote about the education and welfare of children and women's work conditions – which were the areas which concerned them most at the time – and did not focus their journalism on women's suffrage.[40] When Iona's column was discontinued in 1909 there was no longer a space for a discursive and wide-ranging discussion of the 'woman question'. Instead there were one-off articles on specific issues, such as reports of international women's congresses, and a regular column for Women's Labour League Notes which provided a catalogue of events and local meetings. Very little

LIVERPOOL
JOHN MOORES UNIVERSITY
AVRIL ROBARTS LRC
TEL. 0151 231 4022

attention was paid to women's suffrage or issues around women's engagement in socialist politics until the alliance between the NUWSS and the Labour Party had been concluded in 1912.

In smaller newspapers, women's own personal political journeys could make a difference to the way in which the suffrage campaign was represented over time in the ILP press. Only two women, both of whom were prominent socialist propagandists in the north-east, wrote regularly for the *Northern Democrat*. They were Lisbeth Simm, the wife of the editor, who was described as 'a tireless activist for socialism and women's rights', and Florence Harrison Bell, a cook and then schoolteacher who was married to Joseph Bell, secretary of the Amalgamated Union of Labour.[41] As early as 1894 Florence Bell had been involved in organising an ILP Women's Association in Newcastle and in the late 1890s she had been a member of the NAC until her place was taken by Emmeline Pankhurst.[42] Unlike many other local ILP members who started their suffrage activism as members of the WSPU, Florence Bell and Lisbeth Simm were unusual in playing a leading role between 1905 and 1908 in the North Eastern Society for Women's Suffrage, a group which was affiliated to the NUWSS. A third ILP member, Ethel Bentham, joined them as part of the leadership group, which also included the radical liberal Ethel Williams. In contrast to most other NUWSS branches the North East Society, from an early stage, supported Labour candidates and tried to forge a closer link between the NUWSS and the Labour Party.

These interests were reflected in the pages of the *Northern Democrat* in its early years. Lisbeth Simm wrote a column under the pseudonym of 'Ledron' which included items related to women's suffrage, while both she and Florence Harrison Bell also wrote articles which described suffrage demonstrations and the development of the movement at a local level.[43] On the other hand, women's suffrage was never their only, or even main, concern, and they also covered issues such as the feeding of schoolchildren and the legal disabilities of married women. As both women became increasingly involved in the activities of the local Women's Labour League after 1908, they withdrew from active participation in the suffrage movement. Thus in contrast to the *Labour Leader* and *Forward*, references to women's suffrage had virtually disappeared from the *Northern Democrat* after 1909. Lisbeth Simm's column concentrated on education, housing and health and her more discursive style of writing was replaced by straightforward reporting of the day-to-day activities of the WLL.

In debating the franchise men and women socialists were not just concerned about the terms on which the vote should be given, or the methods and political strategies that should be employed, but were also engaged in working out the ways in which women could and should engage in mixed-sex politics. Apart from a small minority who opposed the view that women should be enfranchised, there was general agreement that sex should not be a barrier to the exercise of the vote, which was regarded as a basic human right. On the other hand this support for 'political equality' did not prevent suffrage activists from also basing their claims on women's difference from men, which was a thread running through much of the debate in the socialist press during the period. The significance of difference, however, was interpreted in varied ways. Committed suffragists such as Isabella Ford and Annot Robinson agreed that women would bring special qualities to political life and argued that they would 'purify politics'.[44] On the other hand they demanded the vote so that women could take a full part in political life on the basis of their common humanity with men. Since neither of them believed that men in the Labour Party and the ILP could be relied on to fight for women's rights, they hoped that political equality would help women to ensure that the labour movement was proactive in challenging other inequalities and wrongs that were faced by women.[45]

Many members of the WLL, including Katharine Bruce Glasier and Lisbeth Simm, approached the question of women's special qualities in a different way. They argued increasingly that women needed the vote so that they could bring their distinct perspective as wives and mothers to labour politics and thereby add weight to demands for social reforms which would benefit women and children. Criticising educated women for looking down on domestic work, Katharine Bruce Glasier argued that 'one of the chief aims of a Socialist woman's life ought to try to be to alter that. Very few of us can work for Socialism on the platform or with our pens; but we can all try to work out our home life problems from a Socialist standpoint . . .'.[46]

A different analysis could be found in *Forward* in which the masculine nature of socialism and the oppression of women by men in the socialist movement was frequently raised. Lily Bell, for instance, complained that socialist men often ignored women as 'essentially inferior . . . Listen to the average Socialist discussing women either privately or in public debate and you will find, usually, that his attitude of mind, as far as women in general are concerned, differs little from that of any other man.'[47] Tom Johnston emphasised the importance of motherhood and the home, but he also saw women's political equality as having a broader significance and likely to alter existing gender roles. He argued that it would mean the end of sex dominance and that there would be 'altered conditions of married and single life . . . And these altered conditions, what will they produce? They'll produce almost different women.'[48] This was not a welcome message to most socialist men who feared any disruption to the existing gender divison of labour in the workplace and the home and was rarely represented in the pages of the *Labour Leader*. Indeed, once the alliance had been made between the Labour Party and the NUWSS in 1912, the emphasis within the ILP was on the importance of men and women co-operating to bring social change. This argument was put forward by some of the most active suffragists, such as Isabella Ford, Annot Robinson and Ada Neild Chew, and was the perpective which permeated the *Labour Leader*.[49]

Conclusion

It has been argued here that newspapers are an invaluable source for understanding the relationship between ILP socialism, the struggle for women's suffrage and the nature of women's involvement in socialist politics in the decade before the First World War. In order to understand the complexity of this relationship, however, it is crucial to make a detailed reading of local as well as national newspapers. These reveal that a wide range of views existed within the ILP and that the positions taken were more complex than conventional wisdoms would allow. This should encourage historians to consider the arguments put forward by women and men in the ILP from their perspective as socialists and to understand them in their own terms rather than fitting them into neat categories such as limited suffragist/ feminist and adult suffragist/non feminist.

A variety of positions were adopted as women attempted to integrate their feminism and their socialism, although these are not necessarily all to be found in one single newspaper. Moreover, newspapers did not simply represent the views of ILP members at large. The lack of interest in women's suffrage in the *Northern Democrat* after 1909 reflected the position of Lisbeth Simm and Florence Harrison Bell, but in the immediate pre-war period the local ILP took an active part in the suffrage campaign and worked closely with the North East Society for Women's Suffrage.[50]

Eleanor Gordon argues that *Forward*'s sympathetic attitude towards women's suffrage, along with its emphasis on the importance of social and political as well as industrial struggles played a part in the success of the local ILP in attracting women members. On the other hand there was still an emphasis on raising the status of motherhood and 'reasserting the ideology of separate sexual spheres', although in a context in which women should have greater economic independence and freedom from the drudgery of domestic labour.[51] Discussions of the 'woman question', therefore, were ambivalent. Women were rarely selected as candidates for elections and Tom Johnston complained that socialist males did not put their formal commitment to equality into practice in their everyday lives. But, as Gordon notes, in the same article he consistently defined socialists as male.

It is the very ambivalence of the views expressed, however, that needs to be explored and understood. What was crucial in the period was that newspapers such as *Forward* provided a space for male and female writers to debate the nature of socialism and women's role within it in a way which challenged the underlying assumptions of a socialist politics that was masculine in its theory and its practice. It enabled women to express, in a hard-hitting way, a refusal to be viewed simply as an auxiliary to the 'men's party' and to demand a broader role for themselves and their concerns.

Further reading

E. C. DuBois, 'Woman suffrage and the Left: an international socialist-feminist perspective', *New Left Review*, 186 (1991).

E. Gordon, *Women and the Labour Movement in Scotland, 1850–1914* (Oxford, 1991).

K. Hunt and J. Hannam, 'Propagandising as socialist women: the case of the women's columns in British socialist newspapers, 1884–1914', in B. Taithe and T. Thornton, eds, *Propaganda: Political Rhetoric and Identity, 1300–2000* (Stroud, 1999).

J. Purvis and S. S. Holton, eds, *Votes for Women* (2000).

L. Ugolini, '"It is only justice to grant women's suffrage": ILP men and women's suffrage, 1893–1905', in C. Eustance, J. Ryan and L. Ugolini, eds, *A Suffrage Reader: Charting New Directions in British Suffrage History* (2000).

Notes

1. Mrs Phillip Snowden, *The Real Women's Party* (Reformers' Bookstall Ltd, 1920), pp. 4, 15.

2. The Independent Labour Party (ILP) was formed in 1893. Its socialism was derived from a variety of sources and it is usually characterised as non-dogmatic and pragmatic. The motive force for change was assumed to be the 'moral conviction and informed opinions of "the people"' rather than class struggle. David Howell, *British Workers and the Independent Labour Party, 1888–1906* (Manchester University Press, 1983), p. 362. The ILP was affiliated to the Labour Party but retained its own separate organisation.

3. The ideas discussed at the beginning of this chapter are developed more fully in June Hannam and Karen Hunt, 'Gendering the stories of socialism: an essay in historical criticism', in M. Walsh, ed., *Working Out Gender: Perspectives from Labour History* (Ashgate, 2000).

LIVERPOOL JOHN MOORES UNIVERSITY
LEARNING SERVICES

4. For recent examples of such socialist history texts, see Keith Laybourn, *The Rise of Socialism in Britain, c.1881–1951* (Sutton, 1997); Neville Kirk, *Labour and Society in Britain and the USA*, vol. 2 (Scolar Press, 1994).

5. ILP views towards women are explored in June Hannam, 'Women and the ILP, 1890–1914', in D. James, T. Jowitt and K. Laybourn, eds, *The Centennial History of the Independent Labour Party* (Ryburn, 1992); Laura Ugolini, 'Independent Labour Party men and women's suffrage in Britain, 1893–1914', PhD thesis, University of Greenwich, 1997.

6. For an account of the development of this alliance, see Sandra Stanley Holton, *Feminism and Democracy: Women's Suffrage and Reform Politics in Britain, 1900–1918* (Cambridge University Press, 1986).

7. Hannam and Hunt, 'Gendering the stories of socialism'.

8. *Common Cause*, 19 September 1912.

9. Carolyn Steedman, *Childhood, Culture and Class in Britain: Margaret McMillan, 1860–1931* (Virago, 1990). Criticisms were also put forward by Hannah Mitchell, a member of the ILP and the militant Women's Social and Political Union. Hannah Mitchell, *The Hard Way Up: The Autobiography of Hannah Mitchell: Suffragette and Rebel* (Faber & Faber, 1969), p. 129. The ambivalent attitudes of the ILP are discussed in Jill Liddington and Jill Norris, *One Hand Tied Behind Us: The Rise of the Women's Suffrage Movement* (Virago, 1978), and Helen Lintell, 'Lily Bell: Socialist and Feminist, 1894–1898', MA thesis, Bristol Polytechnic, 1990, Chapter 1.

10. June Hannam, *Isabella Ford, 1855–1924* (Blackwell, 1989), p. 135.

11. This is discussed more fully in Hannam and Hunt, 'Gendering the stories of socialism'.

12. For example, see Holton, *Feminism and Democracy*.

13. The policy of the Second International was to work for universal suffrage for all men and women. This was confirmed at the Stuttgart Congress of 1907.

14. This is particularly the case when the ILP is compared with the other important British socialist group, the Social Democratic Federation, which adopted an adult suffrage position. Thus, Olive Banks claims that the ILP was 'feminist from its inception' while the SDF was 'anti feminist'. O. Banks, *Faces of Feminism* (Blackwell, 1981), p. 123. See also Liddington and Norris, *One Hand Tied Behind Us*, pp. 44 and 127.

15. For example, see Liddington and Norris, *One Hand Tied Behind Us* (a view which is still being repeated in the latest textbook on the subject, Barbara Caine, *English Feminism, 1780–1980* (Oxford University Press, 1997)). See also Holton, *Feminism and Democracy*; Lesley Parker Hume, *The National Union of Women's Suffrage Societies* (Garland, 1984).

16. For an interesting discussion of the complex political identities of socialist women, see Clare Collins, 'Women and labour politics in Britain, 1893–1932', PhD thesis, London School of Economics, 1991. The tendency of historians to categorise the women's movement in terms of distinct strands is discussed in Karen Offen, 'Defining feminism: a comparative historical approach', *Signs* 14/1 (1988).

17. Fred Reid, 'Keir Hardie and the *Labour Leader*, 1893–1903', in J. Winter, ed., *The Working Class in Modern British History* (Cambridge University Press, 1983); Lawrence Thompson, *The Enthusiasts: A Biography of John and Katharine Bruce Glasier* (Gollancz, 1971), Chapter 8.

18. Deian Hopkin, 'The socialist press in Britain, 1890–1910', in G. Boyce, J. Curran and P. Wingate, eds, *Newspaper History: From the 17th Century to the Present Day* (Constable, 1978). Between 1890 and 1910 almost 800 papers, half of them socialist, were published in the interests of labour (p. 294).

19. Howell, *British Workers*, esp. Part 2; James, Jowitt and Laybourn, eds, *The Centennial History*.

20. Joan Smith, 'Taking the leadership of the labour movement: the ILP in Glasgow, 1906–1914', in Alan McKinlay and R. J. Morris, eds, *The ILP on Clydeside, 1893–1932: From Foundation to Disintegration* (Manchester University Press, 1991), p. 61.

21. Ibid.

22. Delan Hopkin, 'The newspapers of the Independent Labour Party, 1893–1906', unpublished PhD thesis, University of Aberystwyth, 1981.

23. Annot Erskine Robinson, 'The missionary I.L.P.: the women's gospel', *Labour Leader*, Supplement, 9 January 1913.

24. Teresa Billington, 'The women and their critics', *Forward*, 26 January 1907.

25. *Labour Leader*, 5 November 1909.

26. *Labour Leader*, 4 May 1906. See also 6 April 1906.

27. Tom Johnston, *The Case for Women's Suffrage and Objections Answered* (Glasgow, 1907).

28. *Forward*, 1 March 1913.

29. *Labour Leader*, 5 June 1906.

30. *Labour Leader*, 5 June 1908.

31. Christine Collette, *For Labour and For Women: The Women's Labour League, 1906–18* (Manchester University Press, 1989), p. 73.

32. *Forward*, 22 February 1913.

33. For a discussion of socialist support for the WSPU at a local level, see June Hannam, '"I had not been to London": women's suffrage – a view from the regions', in J. Purvis and S. S. Holton, eds, *Votes for Women* (UCL, 2000), pp. 233–6.

34. *Forward*, 18 May 1907.

35. *Forward*, 25 May 1907.

36. Annual Conference Report of the ILP in *Labour Leader*, 5 April 1907.

37. Steedman, *Childhood, Culture and Class*, p. 138.

38. *Labour Leader*, 5 June 1908.

39. June Balshaw, 'Suffrage, solidarity and strife: political partnerships and the women's movement, 1880–1930', unpublished PhD thesis, University of Greenwich, 1999, Chapter 3.

40. For example, see Margaret E. MacDonald, 'The case against the legal minimum wage', *Labour Leader*, 7 June 1908; Mary Macarthur, 'Socialism and the sweater', *Labour Leader*, 14 June, 21 June and 28 June 1907; Margaret McMillan, 'A London school treatment centre' and 'The school clinic and land values', *Labour Leader*, 11 December 1908 and 15 January 1909.

41. David Neville, *To Make Their Mark* (Centre for Northern Studies, University of Northumbria, 1997), pp. 15–16.

42. *Labour Leader*, 5 June 1894.

43. For example, see F. N. Harrison Bell, 'The suffrage procession', and L. E. Simm, 'Women and the vote', *Northern Democrat*, July 1908 and October 1908.

44. Hannam, *Isabella Ford*, Chapter 6.

45. Collins, 'Women and labour politics', p. 123.

46. *Labour Leader*, 23 October 1908.

47. *Forward*, 9 February 1907.

48. Thomas Johnston, 'What will happen when women get the vote. No. 111 – the woman of the future', *Forward*, 19 November 1910.

49. See, for example, the articles in the Special Suffrage Supplement, *Labour Leader*, 9 January 1913.

50. Neville, *To Make Their Mark*, Chapter 8.

51. Eleanor Gordon, *Women and the Labour Movement in Scotland, 1850–1914* (Clarendon Press, 1991), pp. 271–2.

CHAPTER NINE

Chasing shadows: issues in researching feminist social histories of women's health

CATHY LUBELSKA

Disease, disorder and destiny

By the late nineteenth century ideas about women's health, increasingly and predominantly emanating from the medical profession, had become pervasive in the definition and legitimisation of distinctive differences and divisions in gender roles within society. Historians working from feminist and other perspectives have rightly emphasised the centrality, even universality, of motherhood and reproduction as the major organising themes and preoccupation of discussions about women and health.[1] Feminist theory and research, in particular, have demonstrated how, by the turn of the century, these discussions took place within a wider physical and cultural context where the female body came to be seen as fundamentally 'disordered'.[2] Apparently separate areas of concern were connected by the central focus upon the 'disordered' female body, with motherhood, reproduction and, increasingly, sexuality as the key interconnected components of gendered representations of women's health. The dominance of these themes reflects the pervasive voices of the medical profession, and of the male professional, in general: those who produced the apparently authoritative sources upon which historians have routinely drawn during their research.

What is particularly striking within a feminist analysis of the sources on health is their representation of women as being 'pathological' in a number of ways. This framed contemporary constructions of and responses to a range of women's health issues in at least two important respects. First, where women are present in discussions of social concerns and policies they are likely to be represented as social problems. Women are most visible within the sources where there is perceived to be a failure or inadequacy, for whatever reason, in the execution of their fundamental responsibilities for reproduction, motherhood and allied issues. This is clearly manifest, for example, in the obsession with working wives as bad mothers which is present as a continuous and developing discourse from at least the 1830s until well into the twentieth century.[3] The words 'women' and 'health' appear alongside each other in analyses which reflect prevalent social constructions both of health and of gender, where women's behaviours, rather than any 'objective' assessment or concern with women's own health needs and experiences, are the focus of attention. Consequently, where 'women' and 'health' are both under discussion the focus is seldom upon women's own health needs, but, rather, upon the apparent needs of society.

Second, views about the naturalness of motherhood and domesticity for women, which had been recurrent themes in social policy for decades, became transmuted into an all-encompassing, biological determinism which potentially embraced every aspect of women's existence and, specifically, of her role within society. The gendered tenets of Social Darwinism, in particular, not only pegged women at a lower, inferior evolutionary stage than men, but also served to bolster essentialist notions of womanhood. Here women's own health and that of the whole of civilised society was seen to hinge upon the fulfilment of the female reproductive role, or women's 'biological destiny'.[4] Women who chose to reject this role could be seen as endangering both themselves and others. In 1887 Dr Withers-Moore, chairman of the British Medical Association, stated:

> I think that it is not good for the human race, considered as progressive, that women should be freed from the restraints which law and custom have imposed upon them, and should receive an education intended to prepare them for the exercise of brain power in competition with men. And I think this because I am persuaded that neither the preliminary training for such competitive work nor the subsequent practice of it in the actual strife and struggle for existence, can fail to have upon women the effect more or less (and rather more than less) of indisposing them towards, or incapacitating them from their own proper function – for performing the part, I mean which . . . nature has assigned to them in the maintenance and progressive improvement of the human race.[5]

Since antiquity motherhood had been seen to play a central role, in various ways, in determining women's health. The essentialism of late nineteenth-century scientific and medical thinking, within an evolutionary context, purported to verify women's imperfect nature and traced all ill health suffered by women to the vagaries of the reproductive function. The apparently natural female processes of menstruation, pregnancy and menopause became medicalised as health 'problems' and understood as produced by the 'tyranny of the ovaries'.[6] Possession of these organs sexually differentiated women from men and determined women's most feminine characteristics, as well as being the cause of the 'natural' pathology of the female body and condition:

> accepting, then, these views of the gigantic power and influence of the ovaries over the whole animal economy of woman, – that they are the most powerful agents in all the commotions of her system; that on them rest her intellectual standing in society, her physical perfection, and all that lends beauty to those fine and delicate contours which are constant objects of admiration, all that is great, noble and beautiful, all that is voluptuous, tender and endearing . . . her fidelity, her devotedness, her perpetual vigilance . . . all those qualities of mind and disposition which inspire respect and love . . . spring from the ovaries.[7]

The impact of such thinking has been well documented by feminists across a range of health problems and issues for women, including sexuality, sexual regulation and mental health.[8]

While women's reproductive apparatus was seen both to govern and disorder the female body as the source of women's propensity towards illness, failure to heed its dictates was seen as both a primary cause and a symptom of ill health. These two elements were completely complementary. Where women transgressed their socially acceptable roles their behaviour was seen as dysfunctional. The 'disordered' woman was seen to be so because she was 'out of place'. Thus perceived, female non-conformity came to be viewed as either product, cause or both of the 'diseased' and 'disordered' woman. The idea of the inherent pathology of women came to underlie not only an increasingly gendered and numerous range of female maladies, but also the parameters of women's 'proper' role within society. The terrain covered by contemporary discourses on women's health could, potentially, encompass all aspects of women's social roles. Crucially, they also functioned to demarcate these from men's, clearly and categorically, along the lines of an apparently biologically determined sexual division of labour. Within these parameters women's health is visible within the authoritative sources both as a social issue and as a medium through which to control and regulate women's behaviour.

Where women did break out of the domains prescribed for them it was thought that the consequences could be dire. The opponents of educational and occupational aspirations among women littered their arguments with tales of the terrible afflictions liable to affect those who sought too much 'exercise' for either their brains or their bodies. According to Arabella Kenealy, writing as late as 1920:

> Our school-girls and work-girls, in whose already impoverished, or degenerate, bodies this battle for their resources between Nature and Culture (or Industrialism) is waged – the one to make them normal, the other to make

them abnormal – are all more or less in states of disease: are chlorotic, anaemic, neurotic, dyspeptic, hysterical; or suffer from ailments special to their sex.[9]

The relationship here between physical and mental health centres attention on the deleterious effects of such intrinsically unfeminine behaviours upon the *whole* woman. The idea that women could 'unsex' themselves, for example, is a recurrent one, and also preoccupied Kenealy. Once again, the unifying theme is the primarily reproductive nature of female biology, here articulated within a Social Darwinist and eugenic frame of concern with degeneracy and possible racial deterioration.

There are obvious class differences, dependent upon the object of concern and the analysis made. Emphases on the dangers of women's mental overstimulation were almost exclusively directed at the middle classes, with concerns about physical exertion centred on the dangers of exercise and games. The focus of attention for working-class women tended to be upon the inappropriateness and unhealthiness of women in the workplace. In the latter case the motif of 'protecting' women against themselves and others is common. Concerns about the physical over-exertion of working women centred upon manual work, ranging from a focus upon hours and conditions of work to scrutiny of particular tasks and processes involved.[10] Unsurprisingly, women's work which came in for particular criticism, such as at the coal face and, later, at the pit brow in mining, was seen as unhealthy, at least in part because of its overtly masculine connotations. Angela John has shown, for example, how the focus upon the pit brow girls' apparent propensity to wear trousers, smoke clay pipes and adopt a masculine appearance was frowned upon.[11] There was also distaste for the scanty clothing sometimes worn by female chainmakers who worked in hot, humid and physically arduous conditions.[12] These and other examples of objections to particular kinds of physical toil for women serve to illustrate the unhealthiness of women in those environments where they were seen to be out of place.

Generally, the mixing of the sexes within the workplace, and the opportunities for misconduct this was considered to present, were seen to be morally, as well as physically, dangerous to women's health and to the well-being of society as a whole.[13] By the late nineteenth century, as occupational and educational opportunities and aspirations expanded for middle-class women, concern with the unwholesomeness of mixing the sexes moved beyond its primary focus on women within the manual working class. Shop work, as a 'respectable' pursuit for girls from the affluent working class or lower middle class, rested on its predominantly female and carefully cultivated image as providing a morally regulated, 'family-style' working environment.[14] Domestic service, too, benefited from its location within the homes of the respectable middle classes, where it was supposed that the employer – helpfully, though not always accurately, personified as female – would take a direct interest in the moral welfare of their employees.[15] By contrast, medicine was vocal in opposing women's entry to the profession on the grounds that women's desire to enter the occupation was unnatural.[16]

Occupations were also often gendered in terms of what were seen to be the particular susceptibilities of women to certain industrial diseases and work-related illnesses. Lead poisoning, which was a major occupational hazard for many women, was sometimes seen as particularly afflicting females, as 'phosy jaw' affected those engaged in match making.[17] It is notable that in relation to these and other apparently gendered industrial diseases, seemingly more obvious causes of illness, such as the dangerous nature of the substances used, processes engaged in or the working environment as a whole, were overlooked or masked by the focus upon sexual difference as a key determinant of illness. Concern with women's reproductive health in a workplace context tended to centre on the welfare of the child rather than the mother, or simply served as ammunition for the opponents of married women's work in general. Thus the role of the working environment as a whole in generating ill health for both women and men could be sidestepped or played down. The numerical predominance of women in some occupations did not, in itself, suggest, therefore, that women were more susceptible to illnesses associated with those occupations; it does suggest, however, that women were often disproportionately located in less eligible and more dangerous areas of work.

The social pathology of female non-conformity

What is clear is that the emphasis on women's particular susceptibilities, be they physical or moral, was disproportionately focused on the appropriateness of women in the workplace rather than upon the prevalence of demonstrable physical illness *per se*. Even where women were permitted to work, much was made of their lack of 'natural' capabilities in denying them access to skilled or supervisory work – which is evident throughout the history of cotton textiles and blatant in its application, for example, in relation to the issue of 'substitution' of female labour for male during the First World War.[18] The emphasis of protective legislation and campaigns to limit women's role in the workplace and of women's experience of employment during and after the First World War lends itself to a feminist analysis which focuses upon the conjunction of the interests of capitalism and patriarchy in restricting women's role and status within the workplace.[19]

The notion that women 'out of place' were both victims and perpetrators of illness in themselves and society went beyond the realm of the workplace and merged into larger discourses about women's place in society as a whole. Thus the closer women stayed to domesticity and the privacy of the home the 'healthier' their behaviours and their bodies were deemed to be. Conversely, the prostitute, especially the streetwalker, with her public workplace and the assumed threat she posed to the sanctity of family life, morals and health, stood at the opposite end of the spectrum as a public danger, nuisance and source of disease. The concern about women in public, another recurrent motif, reached its apogee in the late nineteenth century in an atmosphere of apparent desire to protect women as potential victims, generated, or at least justified, by salaciously sensationalised stories in the press about the 'white slave' trade, 'Jack the Ripper' and prostitution. As Judith Walkowitz has convincingly shown, all this was fuelled by the diseased image of the prostitute which had become pervasive thanks to the vociferous advocates of the Contagious Diseases Acts, despite their repeal in the 1880s.[20] The theme of women in public – and, therefore, out of place – as possessors of dangerous and unhealthy sexualities is well established by the late nineteenth century. This is encapsulated by, for example, the moral messages of the 'vice and vigilance' vigilantes so comprehensively documented by Lucy Bland, and the related concerns of the early social hygiene movement before the First World War, which continued well into the twentieth century.[21]

Whilst, at one extreme, the hardened prostitute symbolised the threat of social contamination and disease, at the other the respectable middle-class woman trying to make her way in the world away from the safety of the familial, domestic environment was seen to be particularly vulnerable to sexual transgression and its consequences. Public speaking and campaigning by women was also viewed as socially disruptive and unhealthy behaviour. Whichever class vantage point is taken, sexual regulation was viewed as intrinsic both to women's own health and to that of society as a whole. Physical location within domesticity was seen as essential to healthy sexualities, and it was assumed that even the poorest of women so placed could fulfil their social and biological roles as wives and mothers, if they were adequately educated to do so.[22] By contrast, women outside these domains were potentially either sick or sickening, or both, either by virtue of their class position as working wives or by the apparent sexual 'irregularity' of existing, as either a lesbian, a spinster, a prostitute or some other non-conformist, outside the bounds of married heterosexuality. Which women were represented as being more pathological in their behaviours than others was almost completely contingent upon contemporary perceptions of society's needs and problems at any particular moment. As has been amply documented elsewhere, discussions of motherhood, imperialism and national decline were suffused with evolutionary and eugenic thinking about the 'fitness' and numbers of appropriate breeding stock needed to combat the apparent threat of racial deterioration.[23] By the turn of the century there was growing anxiety about the decline in the middle-class birth rate, alongside the existing concern with the inadequacies of working mothers and of working-class motherhood as a whole. Family limitation or childlessness among the middle class could be seen to endanger the health of the nation, but the greatest threat was perceived to come from women who, for whatever reason, failed to marry and fulfil their 'biological destinies'. It was a stated aim within the eugenics campaign that

> The best women . . . who are increasingly to be found in the ranks of feminism and fighting the great fight for the Women's Cause shall be convinced by the unchangeable and beneficent facts of biology . . . so that instead of increasingly deserting the ranks of motherhood . . . they shall . . . furnish an ever-increasing proportion of our wives and mothers, to the greater gain of . . . the future.[24]

A feminist reading of such sources highlights the way in which women's individual behaviours entered the public domain as health issues where they were not seen to conform to society's requirements at any particular historical moment. Female non-conformity, then, became both a social problem and a suitable object of intervention. Women's health, simply put, was about what was good for the nation. The notion of non-conformity as inherently pathological perhaps reaches its apogee in representations of suffrage supporters by the opponents of votes for women. All the familiar motifs of non-conformity – and hence of pathologically unhealthy behaviours – are here. Visual representations of such women were commonly drawn with masculine features and bodies, ugly by contemporary norms of female beauty, with swarthy, even dark complexions, dressed like men and engaged in 'unfeminine' behaviours (which were strongly associated with their public and highly visible presence) and neglectful of their domestic responsibilities.[25] Here the link between sexuality and 'public women' takes a new twist, where the 'fallen' woman is replaced by the unsexed, unfeminine, frigid or lesbian woman.

It can be seen, therefore, that representations which bring together 'women' and 'health', despite their different nuances and concerns of the day, are, in fact, principally preoccupied with women's responsibilities, directly or indirectly, for the health of others and with what might be termed the social pathology of non-conformity. Where women were deemed to be behaving inappropriately or to be out of place they were seen to be bad for society as a whole. Potentially, such discourses could encompass every aspect of women's behaviours, yet, crucially, they did not attempt to reflect or represent women's own perceived health needs or experiences. In many ways they actually worked to obscure or misrepresent them.

Thus constituted within discourses on women's health, it is unsurprising that women were seen to be suitable cases for intervention in many ways. Specifically medical discourses on women's health tend to reinforce this notion through their overwhelming emphasis upon the particular susceptibilities of women both to illness (as discussed above), but also to treatment. Within the medical literature of the period there exists a gendered cornucopia of ailments to which women were considered to be especially or uniquely prone. Female patients were seen as being particularly amenable to cure or rehabilitation through drugs, surgery or punitive moral improvement. The various treatments for dangerous or unhealthy sexualities across the period included the use of cliterodectomies for the treatment of nymphomania and other perceived sexual irregularities, the use of drugs, principally opiates, and the compulsory examination, detention or 'reform' of prostitutes. The ideas of sexologists and later psychoanalytic theory reinforced the notion of female sexuality as inherently pathological and deficient.[26] The unmarried mother, especially if she was poor, was likely, especially after the passing of the 1913 Mental Defectives legislation, to find herself incarcerated in a mental health institution and diagnosed as either 'feeble minded' or 'morally frail'.[27]

In stressing the links between transgressive behaviour, mental and physical illness and the well-being of society the medico-moral politics of the period further reinforced the representation of women as pathological. Within this context different and sometimes conflicting elements within contemporary constructions of femininity rubbed alongside each other. The woman who drank, for example, was more likely to be seen as being an alcoholic, and therefore suffering from an addictive disease, than a man because the activity was seen as unfeminine, especially if done in public. It was also seen as both cause and symptom of 'disorder' within the weaker female body, which was less able to resist the indulgence of baser passions and immoral behaviours. At the same time the frailties and vulnerabilities of women were also considered to engender a passivity which ensured that they yielded to treatment more readily than did men. In 'The treatment of inebriety' (1885) Howie Muir advocated isolation and rehabilitation – 'Women rarely make an effort to escape and are easily occupied with household or fancy work' – and recommended 'a small cottage with a kind hearted, strong-willed matron, assisted by a stout nursing maid'.[28] The efficacy of some of the treatments on offer is more often assumed or asserted than scientifically verified, but could be dubious. The use of opium as a 'cure' for the disease of alcoholism apparently dealt with one addiction by creating another.

Potentially harmful or addictive drug regimes were also commonplace in the treatment of women's mental health problems, where sedation helped induce appropriately passive behaviour in female patients. In the 1890s women temperance reformers expressed concern about the significance of 'Doctors' orders' in prescribing alcohol for medicinal purposes as a cause of addiction among women.[29] The confident assertion of competence by medical science as it spread its influence ever further served to obscure individual patients' experience of incompetence, malpractice or inappropriate treatment by the profession. The medical management of childbirth is a case in point. The growth of medical influence through obstetrics sits uncomfortably alongside women's own, often graphic accounts of medically managed childbirth, where mutilation of mother or child, infant mortality and enduring illness are recurrent themes.[30] Medicine enhanced its own authority and market value by drawing upon – and in turn reinforcing – contemporary social constructions of gender within which the comprehensive pathology of women and the effectiveness of its own interventions were emphasised.

Women's health revealed and obscured

In reflecting and reinforcing prevailing ideas about women rather than the experiences of women themselves the authoritative voice of the medical profession could distort and obscure the realities of women's health and effectively proscribed alternative representations and thus understandings of women's health needs.[31] The process of professional self-aggrandisement within medicine involved the marginalisation of women's knowledge about their own health and that of others. This has been well documented by feminist historians and others across a range of areas, including the relationship between women healers and witchcraft, the expropriation of midwifery, the development of Nightingale-style nursing and objections to women's entry to the medical profession.[32]

The devaluation of women's roles and knowledge in relation to both formal and informal health care was, in many respects, the corollary of the professional advancement of men through medicine. Within this context, in particular, these developments were deeply gendered and actively drew on contemporary constructions of both femininity and masculinity as a basis and justification for maintaining a monopoly of professional power and knowledge in the hands of the male medical practitioner.[33] The figure of the man of medicine, possessed of esoteric skills and knowledge, grounded in objective scientific 'truths' and hence both objective and trustworthy, contrasted strongly with the ancillary, subordinate figure of the nurse, whose skills, caring, etc. were seen to be generic to all 'normal' women. The pejorative dismissal or subordination of women's role in the provision of health care also reinforced a heavily gendered view of the masculine basis of medical authority.

Ironically, as social policies and commentators increasingly called for women to take more responsibility for the health of the nation, especially in relation to pregnancy and childbirth, women's own health knowledge and experiences were pushed aside by the commanding voices of those who were foremost in exhorting them to greater responsibilities. Furthermore, while the medical profession increasingly focused on maternal health in the context of women's ante-natal responsibilities, they also sought simultaneously to dissuade women, often in the strongest of terms, from learning more about their bodies. The aspects of taboo surrounding the female body were reinforced by medical opinion which emphasised the need for women to remain in abject ignorance of their own anatomy and physiology as essential to the preservation of womanly innocence and 'propriety'. The preoccupation with the relationships between motherhood, reproduction and sexuality within medical discourses and practices on women's health ensured that it was precisely those organs and functions that women most needed to understand for their own well-being that were considered 'out of bounds' by medics. The unnaturalness of women in medicine was, from the outset, strongly associated with their possession of forbidden knowledge about the body, and the theme of the unsexing of women who are out of place is again evident within the heavily gendered discourses of the medical profession:

> Many of the most estimable members of our profession perceive in the medical education and destination of women a horrible and vicious attempt deliberately to unsex themselves – in the acquisition of anatomical and physiological knowledge the gratification of a prurient and morbid curiosity and thirst after forbidden information – and in the performance of routine medical and surgical duties the assumption of offices which Nature intended entirely for the sterner sex.[34]

Women's ability to manage their own health needs could be severely circumscribed or prevented by medical opinion. The central role of fertility control in enhancing women's health and the lives of their families is strongly focused both in the experiential evidence and the retrospective analyses of historians. Yet a central thread in the history of birth control and contraception is the refusal, on various moral, ethical and religious grounds, to advise patients on birth control, despite increasing evidence of the relationship between family size, poverty and ill health.[35] Given the evidence that doctors, as a profession, were more likely than others to practise family limitation, there is an obvious hypocrisy in their stance.[36] Women were, nonetheless, routinely refused assistance in relation to one of their major health needs, and medicine's voice was powerful in its opposition to intervention. Here women's knowledge and experiences were devalued in relation to health care, and their own interventions were likely to be condemned, even where they could be seen as necessitated by medicine's failure to acknowledge women's own needs. Despite its illegality under the 1861 Act the widespread use of abortion, especially within the working class, continued to be a major threat to women's health, which resulted directly from medicine's deliberate resistance to meeting what women themselves clearly perceived to be one of their major health needs.[37] Rather than empowering women to take control of their own bodies, their attempts to do so were actually pathologised through, for example, the continued endorsement of the association between birth control, loss of innocence, unseemly sexual knowledge and prostitution. According to Lucy Bland, a pamphlet written by the president of the British Gynaecological Society, 'On the diminishing birthrate', noted the damage done by contraceptives, including 'neurasthenia, loss of memory and concentration, depression, even madness, symptoms similar to those supposedly caused by "self-abuse" [masturbation]'.[38]

It is a central argument of this chapter that the medically dominated sources which purport to be about women's health actually tell us very little about this. In fact, they tell us rather more about the role of gendering, and especially of the sexual division of labour, in the advancement of the medical profession. In claiming to represent women, they also served to outlaw or silence women's own insights and concerns, especially in relation to reproduction. Within such contexts women's lived health experiences and issues became hidden, obscured or, at best, misrepresented.

The shifting frontiers, conflicts and accommodations between individualism and collectivism, *laissez-faire* and state intervention of the late nineteenth and early twentieth centuries are documented and discussed by historians with a remarkably gender-blind eye. The now voluminous work of feminist historians in the area shows clearly how as a result of their alleged 'biological destiny' women became scapegoats for problems much broader than could ever be reasonably laid at their feet at particular historical moments.[39] Infant mortality, for example, was seen to be principally caused by bad mothering rather than resulting from poor housing, poverty, contaminated foodstuffs, inadequate social services and amenities and other material factors. Here certain sections of the working class tended to emerge as being particularly pathological or unhealthy in their habits and ways of life within an individualistic explanation of society's ills. Carol Dyhouse comments that 'The ideological climate guaranteed a public disposition to account for infant deaths in terms of inadequate mothering rather than poverty and working-class mothers who were employed outside the home were seen as a specific social problem'.[40] Dyhouse goes on to say that such reasoning prevailed even where there was no statistical or evidential basis for it. By heaping so much blame and responsibility upon individual women's shoulders these perspectives served to divert attention away from other potentially more cogent environmental explanations for the nation's ills and growing calls for social justice. Pressures upon women to meet, or attempt to meet, the responsibilities and standards required of them exacerbated women's own health problems and the requirement to conceal these in order to be seen to 'cope' and avoid unwelcome criticisms or interventions.

As these kinds of analyses became disseminated and popularised within the political and professional classes they were given practical application, directly and indirectly, by increased social policy interventions in women's lives before 1914. One manifestation of this was the role of new or developing occupations and organisations, such as health visiting, social work, mother and baby clinics, and the continued prominence and proliferation of voluntary organisations, which, effectively, operated as agents of class scrutiny and of the surveillance of the behaviour of working-class women in particular.[41] The growing use of legislation, much of it deterrent, aimed to prescribe and proscribe women's behaviour in various ways. A feminist reading of such initiatives makes clear both the processes and rationale whereby the scope of women's responsibilities in relation to the apparently private sphere came to be seen as so central to the health of the nation that transgression – which included failure to comply – increasingly became the subject of concern and intervention.[42] Within a context where motherhood and national decline were prominent themes within social policy the Children's Act of 1908 has been cited as a progressive 'children's charter' which centred on improving the previously neglected needs and even rights of the child.[43] This legislation was explicit in both its assertion of maternal responsibility and its condemnation of maternal failure in ensuring child welfare. Mothers who drank, for example, were seen to pose a particular threat and to be more likely to overlie their children, neglect them or lead them into bad habits by taking them into pubs, sending them to shop for drink or giving them alcohol to quieten them.[44] Henceforth, aided by the vigilant eye of the National Society for the Prevention of Cruelty to Children (NSPCC), drinking mothers risked losing their children unless they were willing to submit to treatment in homes for inebriate women or, after 1913, mental health institutions.[45] The question of why women drank, or the effects of this on their own health, were seldom addressed. Paradoxically, the consequent growth of public scrutiny over private lives existed in tension with gendered ideologies of public/private space and separate spheres. It also resulted in matters more central to women's own health becoming, if anything, less visible as women retreated into a privacy and silence which they themselves constructed in order to hide their problems – or at least, those they were seen to create – well away from the public gaze.

Roughly speaking, in the 30 years prior to the First World War social investigations and revelations of various kinds became increasingly visible as a genre or genres within a range of sources; these include the nascent social scientific research of Charles Booth and B. S. Rowntree, the more sensationalist writings of William Booth and a number of journalists such as W. T. Stead, and some of the parliamentary papers of the period which deal with social conditions and problems.[46] Within such work there is a closer focus upon the fabric of everyday realities, people's own experiences, the quality of life and the role of social observations and surveys in providing what purported to be more objective and realistic evidence about these areas. While social historians, in particular, have tended to see such material as offering a more authentic representation of the life of working people, including women, telling the story 'as it really was', the approaches and analyses employed in much of this work are widely acknowledged to reflect class bias. Less well recognised has been the extent to which these sources are also heavily gendered and coloured by prevailing discursive preoccupations, especially about women's health and national efficiency. The class-biased categorisations of 'deserving' and 'undeserving' poor are apparent in Charles Booth's concept of the residuum – classes A and B on an eight-point scale – and Rowntree's distinction between 'primary' and 'secondary' poverty.[47] What is of particular interest to feminists is the centrality within this work of judgements about the adequacy or inadequacy with which women performed their roles as wives, mothers, carers and, crucially, household managers in determining the fitness and healthiness of particular groups within the population. Within a context where poverty was still viewed, primarily, within the confines of the apparently private domestic sphere the principal focus was upon women's behaviour and strategies of management. Booth thought that families could fall into poverty if the woman drank, but he did not emphasise men's drinking as a causal factor in this way. Rowntree's concept of 'secondary' poverty, which he considered to be self-induced, rested disproportionately on the figure of the hapless wife who lacked the skills or wit to manage within her budget. Later investigations conducted by women, such as M. Pember Reeves's study, tended to reflect more sympathetically upon the complexities and difficulties of many women's lot, especially where earnings were small or irregular or men gave little of their wages to the household budget.[48] Yet there is still a strong emphasis on women *having* to manage, whatever the odds. Even those sources such as women's autobiographies, which, perhaps, get closest to the realities of women's experience and where commitment to the improvement of women's lives is most explicit, still tend to articulate the assumption that women's domestic and caring responsibilities are inevitable and pivotal in maintaining the health and well-being of society.[49] Indeed, many of the arguments of those campaigning to reduce women's health problems stressed the central importance of women's own health and 'fitness' to the fulfilment of their patriotic obligations. Maternity reform is a case in point. Arguing from a feminist perspective in 1907 Sarah Burstall asserted that:

> Important as are bodily vigour and active strength . . . in the men of the country who may have to endure the supreme test of physical fitness in war, the vitality and passive strength – potential energy – of its women are even more important, since Nature has adorned women to be the mothers of the race.[50]

While the positive material aims and gains of such strategies are in many cases clear, they continued to reinforce the principle that women were in the 'front line' in the national pursuit of health and efficiency. The popularity of the 'endowment of motherhood' was established in many feminist circles before 1914 as a means of recognising and encouraging women's contribution to the eugenic project of reproducing strong, racial stock.[51]

The reflection and articulation of biological views about women's roles and responsibilities in support of campaigns to improve women's lot worked both to highlight and to obscure women's own health needs. The significance within positive representations of working-class women of being able to 'manage' one's domestic affairs had the corollary of carrying a high price for failure. In an atmosphere of increased public scrutiny and intervention, being *seen* to manage could become more important than the cost to women of this, in material and health terms. Women could be pressurised into compromising or ignoring their own health requirements as part of their strategy for managing limited household resources. Different kinds of domestic economies could take a considerable toll on women's health, for example, eating poorer and less food than other family members, especially the male 'breadwinner', bad working conditions and the prevalence of abortion, especially among working-class women. Where very few women were covered by insurance, formal health care was considered a luxury, and its absence was evident in the range of chronic or debilitating conditions endured by women, including poor teeth, prolapsed wombs, rheumatism, varicose veins and other treatable or preventable ailments.[52] The material inadequacies of the domestic environment affected women more than other family members, with bad housing, poor ventilation, damp, crowded or insanitary conditions all contributing to women's health problems. The endurance of tuberculosis as a major cause of premature mortality for women demonstrates the continued significance of domestic environmental factors in determining ill health.[53] The strongly domesticated image of women's role within the institutions of marriage and the family, where conformity was the hallmark of the 'good' woman, had further implications for the visibility of women's own health issues. Despite some community checks domestic violence, in particular, remained a taboo area and tended to be seen as a private matter; the view that it was man's prerogative in managing his 'property' or that women could 'deserve it' still had widespread currency.[54] Given these attitudes, unsurprisingly, a major potential cause of damage to women's health could easily, even wilfully, be overlooked.

Conclusion

This chapter has not attempted to provide comprehensive coverage of women's health experiences. It has, instead, sought to illuminate some of the key features of the apparent preoccupation with women's health issues within contemporary discourses and to appraise the adequacy of these in representing and improving women's health. Women's health issues are historically located in many different sites and the meanings of key terms such as 'health', 'illness', 'women', 'class' and 'sexuality' are blurred, yet highly specific and gendered in their application. On closer examination discussions and investigations which purport to be about 'women's health' can frequently be seen to detail quite different concerns and priorities. These, in turn, are most informative about the prevailing social preoccupations, prejudices and structures of power and knowledge that flavour and, in some respects, corrupt the historical sources. Consequently, the 'real' histories of women's health tend to remain buried or misrepresented within the discourses of the apparently authoritative sources upon which orthodox historical research has traditionally drawn and which it has, in turn, tended to perpetuate. These considerations do make historical research into women's health a matter of 'chasing shadows'. They also demonstrate the value of feminist and woman-centred analyses which form the basis both of the critique of dominant representations of women's health offered here and of alternative representations of women's health focusing upon women's actual, lived experiences.

Further reading

R. Dingwall, A. M. Rafferty and C. Webster, *An Introduction to the Social History of Nursing* (1990).

C. Dyhouse, *Feminism and the Family in England, 1880–1939* (Oxford, 1989).

B. Harrison, *'Not only the Dangerous Trades': Women's Work and Health in Britain, 1880–1914* (1996).

L. Jordanova, *Sexual Visions: Images of Gender in Science and Medicine between the Eighteenth and Twentieth centuries* (New York, 1989).

J. Lewis, *The Politics of Motherhood: Child and Maternal Welfare in England, 1900–1939* (London, 1980).

M. Llewellyn Davies, ed., *Maternity: Letters from Working Women* (first published 1915; 1978).

E. Showalter, *The Female Malady: Women, Madness and English Culture, 1830–1980* (1987).

M. Spring Rice, *Working Class Wives: Their Health and Conditions* (first published 1931; 1981).

J. M. Strange, 'Menstrual Fictions: languages of medicine and menstruation, *c.* 1850–1930', *Women's History Review*, 9/3 (2000), pp. 607–8.

A. Witz, *Professions and Patriarchy* (1992).

Notes

1. See J. Lewis, *The Politics of Motherhood: Child and Maternal Welfare in England, 1900–1939* (London, 1980).

2. B. Harrison, 'Women and health', in J. Purvis, ed., *Women's History: Britain, 1850–1945, An Introduction* (London, 1995), p. 157.

3. R. Gray, 'Medical men, industrial labour and the state in Britain, 1830–1850', *Social History* 16/1 (1991), pp. 19–43, and M. Hewitt, *Wives and Mothers in Victorian Industry: A Study of the Effects of the Employment of Married Women in Victorian Industry* (London, 1958).

4. C. Dyhouse, 'Social Darwinist ideas and the development of women's education in England, 1880–1920', *History of Education* 5/1 (1976), pp. 41–58.

5. Dr Withers-Moore, *British Medical Journal* (14 August 1886), quoted in P. Atkinson, 'Fitness, feminism and schooling', in L. Delamont and L. Duffin, eds, *The Nineteenth-Century Woman: Her Cultural and Physical World* (London, 1978), p. 126.

6.   See B. Ehrenreich and D. English, *Complaints and Disorders: The Sexual Politics of Sickness* (London, 1976).

7.   Quoted in ibid., p. 33.

8.   See E. Showalter, *The Female Malady: Women, Madness and English Culture, 1830–1980* (London, 1987), and O. Moscucci, *The Science of Women: Gynaecology and Gender in England, 1800–1929* (Cambridge, 1990).

9.   A. Kenealy, *Feminism and Sex Extinction* (London, 1920), p. 83, quoted in Atkinson, 'Fitness, feminism and schooling', p. 127.

10. N. Osterud, 'Gendered divisions and the organisation of work in the Leicester hosiery industry', in A. John, ed., *Unequal Opportunities: Women's Employment in England, 1800–1918* (Oxford, 1986), p. 50.

11. See A. John, *'By the Sweat of their Brow': Women Workers at Victorian Coalmines* (London, 1984).

12. D. Bythell, *The Sweated Trades: Outwork in Nineteenth-Century Britain* (London, 1978), Chapter 3.

13. B. Harrison, *'Not Only the Dangerous Trades': Women's Work and Health in Britain, 1880–1914* (London, 1996), pp. 142–3.

14. See L. Holcombe, *Victorian Ladies at Work: Middle-Class Working Women in England and Wales, 1850–1914* (Newton Abbot, 1973).

15. See P. Horn, *The Rise and Fall of the Victorian Servant* (Dublin, 1975).

16. W. Rivington, *The Medical Profession* (London, 1879), pp. 135–6, quoted in L. Duffin, 'The conspicuous consumptive: woman as invalid', in Delamont and Duffin, eds, *The Nineteenth-Century Woman*, pp. 47–8.

17. Harrison, *'Not Only the Dangerous Trades'*, p. 171; L. Satre, 'After the matchgirls' strike: Bryant and May in the 1890s', *Victorian Studies* 28/1 (1982).

18. B. Drake, *The Women's Trade Union Movement* (London, 1920), p. 70.

19. S. Walby, *Patriarchy at Work* (Oxford, 1986), pp. 55–7.

20. J. Walkowitz, *Prostitution and Victorian Society: Women, Class and the State* (Cambridge, 1980), Chapter 4.

21. L. Bland, *Banishing the Beast: English Feminism and Sexual Morality, 1885–1914* (London, 1995), pp. 95–123.

22. C. Manthorpe, 'Science or domestic science? The struggle to define an appropriate science education for girls in early twentieth-century England', *History of Education* 15/5 (1986), pp. 195–213.

23. A. Davin, 'Imperialism and motherhood', *History Workshop Journal* 5 (1978), pp. 10–65, and see Lewis, *The Politics of Motherhood*.

24. C. W. Saleeby, *Woman and Womanhood* (London, 1912), p. 14.

25. See L. Tickner, *The Spectacle of Women: Imagery of the Suffrage Campaign* (London, 1988).

26. See L. Bland and L. Duan, eds, *Sexology Uncensored: The Documents of Sexual Science* (Cambridge, 1998).

27. K. Jones, *A History of the Mental Health Services* (London, 1972), pp. 198–208; J. Ussher, *Women's Madness: Misogyny or Mental Illness?* (London, 1991), Chapter 5.

28. H. Muir, 'The treatment of inebriety', *Proceedings of the Society for the Study and Cure of Inebriety* 5 (1885), pp. 6–14.

29. Report on a talk by Miss Richardson, 13 October 1892, in *WINGS* with which is incorporated the *British Women's Temperance Journal* 10/119 (November 1892).

30. R. Hall, ed., *Dear Dr Stopes: Sex in the 1920s* (Penguin, 1981), pp. 194–5; M. Llewellyn Davies, ed., *Maternity: Letters from Working Women* (first published 1915; London, 1978), pp. 66–7.

31. A. Witz, *Professions and Patriarchy* (London, 1992), pp. 84–5.

32. See C. Blake, *The Charge of the Parasols: Women's Entry into the Medical Profession* (London, 1990); R. Dingwall, A. M. Rafferty and C. Webster, *An Introduction to the Social History of Nursing* (London, 1988); J. Donnison, *Midwives and Medical Men* (London, 1977); Witz, *Professions and Patriarchy*.

33. Witz, *Professions and Patriarchy*, p. 75.

34. Rivington, *The Medical Profession*, pp. 135–6.

35. Hall, *Dear Dr Stopes*, pp. 19, 23, 40, 43.

36. Ibid., Chapter 5, and see J. A. Banks, *Prosperity and Parenthood: A Study of Family Planning Among the Victorian Middle Class* (London, 1954).

37. A. McLaren, 'Women's work and the regulation of family size: the question of abortion in nineteenth-century England', *History Workshop Journal* 4 (1977), pp. 48–70; E. Roberts, *A Woman's Place: An Oral History of Working-Class Women, 1880–1940* (Oxford, 1984), pp. 98–100; E. Ross, *Love and Toil: Motherhood in Outcast London, 1870–1918* (Oxford, 1993), pp. 104–5.

38. Bland, *Banishing the Beast*, p. 200.

39. G. Boch and P. Thane, eds, *Maternity and Gender Policies: Women and the Rise of the European Welfare States* (London, 1991), p. 10.

40. C. Dyhouse, *Feminism and the Family in England, 1880–1939* (Oxford, 1989), p. 84.

41. G. Jones, *Social Hygiene in Twentieth-Century Britain* (London, 1984), p. 13.

42. C. Smart, ed., *Regulating Womanhood: Historical Essays on Marriage, Motherhood and Sexuality* (London, 1992), pp. 23–4.

43. G. Behlmer, *Child Abuse and Moral Reform in England, 1870–1908* (Stanford, Calif., 1982), p. 162.

44. P. Jennings, *The Public House in Bradford, 1770–1970* (Keele, 1995), p. 199.

45. D. Gutzke, '"The cry of the children": the Edwardian medical campaign against maternal drinking', *British Journal of Addiction* 79 (1984), pp. 71–84; *idem, Protecting the Pub: Brewers and Publicans against Temperance* (London, 1989), pp. 243–4.

46. See C. Booth, *Life and Labour of the People in London*, 17 vols (London, 1889–1903); W. Booth, *In Darkest England and the Way Out* (London, 1890); B. S. Rowntree, *Poverty: A Study of Town Life* (York, 1901); W. T. Stead, 'The maiden tribute of modern Babylon', the report of the *Pall Mall Gazette* secret commission (London, 1885), and, for example, *Report of the Royal Commission on Housing and the Working Class* P.P. (1884–5); *Report of the Inter-Departmental Committee on Physical Deterioration* P.P. (1904); *Report of the Royal Commission on the Poor Laws and the Relief of Distress* P.P. (1909).

47. Booth, *Life and Labour*, vol. 1, pp. 28–62; Rowntree, *Poverty*, pp. 295–8.

48. M. Pember Reeves, *Round About a Pound a Week* (first published 1913; London, 1988), pp. 66–74.

49. M. Llewellyn Davies, *Life as We Have Known It* (first published 1931; London, 1982), p. 36.

50. S. Burstall, *English High Schools for Girls: Their Aims, Organisation and Management* (London, 1907), p, 90, quoted in Atkinson, 'Fitness, feminism and schooling', p. 126.

51. Dyhouse, *Feminism and the Family*, p. 92.

52. See Hall, *Dear Dr Stopes*, Llewellyn Davies, *Maternity*, and, for a slightly later period, M. Spring Rice, *Working-Class Wives: Their Health and Conditions* (first published 1931; London, 1981), esp. pp. 57–63.

53. See L. Bryder, *Below the Magic Mountain: A Social History of Tuberculosis in Twentieth-Century Britain* (Oxford, 1988).

54. E. Ross, '"Fierce questions and taunts": married life in working-class London, 1870–1914', in *Feminist Studies* 8/3 (1982), pp. 575–602; N. Tomes, '"A torrent of abuse": crimes of violence between working-class men and women in London, 1840–1875', *Journal of Social History* 1/3 (1978), pp. 328–45. See also A. J. Hammerton, *Cruelty and Companionship: Conflict in Nineteenth-Century Married Life* (London, 1992).

LIVERPOOL
JOHN MOORES UNIVERSITY
AVRIL ROBARTS LRC
TITHEBARN STREET
LIVERPOOL L2 2ER
TEL. 0151 231 4022

CHAPTER TEN

Towards a feminist framework for the history of women's leisure, 1920–60

CLAIRE LANGHAMER

It is the common fate that a great part of our living should be earning a living, and, in consequence, the hours of leisure, when we are to a greater extent our own man, are the most valuable and significant hours in our lives. The man with no leisure is either a slave or a fool.[1]

In his 1929 book *After Working Hours: The Enjoyment of Leisure*, Sidney Dark utilises a specific notion of leisure, one which has frequently been employed by historians of leisure over the past three decades. At the centre of Dark's understanding of leisure is its relationship to paid work: work and leisure are perceived to be sharply differentiated, although mutually reliant, activities. Underpinning this conceptualisation is an unproblematic notion of time as subject to clear distinctions within which it is possible to experience designated 'hours of leisure'. Leisure time itself is presented as a means of attaining personal fulfilment; an arena for self-discovery and autonomy. The audience for Dark's advice concerning the use of leisure time is assumed to be male; certainly the particular construction of 'leisure' used is one rooted in a male, wage-earning experience. It seems unlikely that the experiences of adult women in the 1920s performing unpaid domestic labour and the work of childcare, perhaps in addition to paid employment, would be readily encompassed by Dark's particular representation of leisure.

This chapter takes as its focus the complex, and apparently problematic, relationship between women and the category 'leisure'. This relationship has infrequently been addressed within the historiography of leisure and is, in fact, only partially understood within the existing parameters of that field. My central concern is with the theoretical and methodological issues implicated in an attempt to access women's daily leisure experiences within a particular historical period, that of 1920–60. The chapter opens with an analysis of the theoretical assumptions that lie behind much recent leisure history. It argues that the definitions of 'leisure' hitherto employed by researchers have been rooted in a specifically male, wage-earning model, similar to that employed by Sidney Dark in 1929. Particular forms of leisure have been privileged in historical representations: in effect, 'leisure' as constructed by historians has constituted a gendered concept. I will provide evidence of the extent to which women's experiences have been misunderstood or excluded within such a model. Having explored the weaknesses in current orthodoxies, the chapter will suggest an alternative conceptual framework for the history of women's leisure which draws upon feminist scholarship in a range of disciplines. It will outline a fluid theoretical framework within which meaning and context assume central importance and will explore the methodologies most suited to a historical study of women's leisure experiences. The opportunities that the oral history interview method presents for accessing self-representations of leisure will be of particular concern. Throughout, examples will be drawn from a study of Manchester women's leisure in the period 1920–60.

Leisure and its historians

Since the 1970s, historians have conducted research into a wide range of leisure forms and pursuits including sport, music making, the pub and the seaside holiday. Yet our knowledge of the leisure experiences of women remains limited: indeed, a recent bibliographical guide to British women's history included categories on women and health and women and empire but had no category for writings on women's leisure.[2] The threadbare nature of this historiography can be explained in two ways: first as a simple matter of focus and secondly as a more complex result of the conceptual frameworks utilised by leisure historians. It is with the second of these explanations that this chapter is primarily concerned. However, I will begin by addressing the question of focus.

At a basic level, then, a privileging of certain forms, and representations, of leisure over others has led historians in the field to exclude or misunderstand women's experiences. In particular, a preoccupation with 'institutional', commercial, or organised, out-of-doors leisure 'activity' has led to a neglect of those arenas more likely to encompass women's experiences. As Clarke and Critcher write: 'Much of the day to day fabric of life has eluded historical analysis.'[3] Those texts which do examine the leisure experiences of women have tended to follow this model of leisure behaviour. For example, there are studies of women's sporting activities, women and the music hall and female youth organisations. And yet, the question 'what did leisure mean to women and how did they experience it?' has rarely been addressed directly by historians. Studies of women's leisure remain largely rooted in the 'topic' approach: the starting point for such work is a particular activity rather than the more general subject 'leisure'. Particular activities have been studied, but these were not necessarily central to the lives of many women. Representations of women's leisure experiences have been determined by the specific interests of researchers, rather than the complex everyday realities of women's lives.

Recently, however, historians have begun to recognise that an emphasis upon commercial or sporting activities at the expense of the informal realm of street and neighbourhood can produce only a partial picture of leisure experience. Indeed, work in the 1990s has successfully accessed informal and street-based leisure patterns and in so doing has begun to push research on leisure into new areas.[4] Yet, while the pursuit of the informal illuminates the stage upon which many women act, illumination is not the same as explanation. The most recent work on women's leisure succeeds in widening our understanding of the nature of 'leisure', but it largely fails to fundamentally challenge definitions of the concept. As such, wider questions concerning the relationship between women and leisure have remained unanswered.

Within this chapter, I want to argue that the misrepresentation of women's experiences within leisure history research cannot be remedied simply by extending our focus to include informal leisure. Rather, the field needs to fundamentally rethink the definitions of leisure that it employs. To put it bluntly, the existing conceptual frameworks of leisure history are not appropriate to the study of women: the definitions of leisure often employed by historians are grounded in a specifically male experience and within this model assume the male wage-earning experience to be normative. In essence, historians have implicitly assumed that leisure exists in direct opposition to paid labour and have thus conceptualised it as freely chosen reward for that labour, unambiguously structured in terms of time and space. As Bailey writes: 'modern leisure is a certain kind of time spent in a certain kind of way. The time is that which lies outside the demands of work, direct social obligations and the routine activities of personal and domestic maintenance; the use of this time, though socially determined, is characterised by a high degree of personal freedom and choice.'[5] Indeed, the chronology of leisure development, utilised by historians in the field, highlights the crucial role of industrialisation in promoting a spatial and psychological separation of work and leisure from the mid-nineteenth century onwards.[6] Such a separation is contrasted with the more integrated experiences of the pre-industrial age.[7]

Feminist theories of leisure

A feminist critique of 'common sense' notions of leisure, defined as time off from paid employment, enjoyed outside the home, is, in fact, available to the historian if she turns from the field of leisure history to that of leisure studies. Feminists working within this field have argued that a conceptualisation of leisure as fundamentally distinct from work is unhelpful to the study of women's leisure and, indeed, actually *invalidates* the experiences of women.[8] Unwaged domestic labour is often excluded from the category 'work' within this conception, and consequently the leisure experiences of those who work in the home are not represented. Indeed, Lenskyj notes an underlying assumption in leisure studies, based upon notions of 'intuitive' mothering and maternal 'fulfilment', that most of women's day is 'free' and that their labour is closer to leisure than it is to a male defined work.[9] As McIntosh notes, it is this assumption that is at the root of the opinion that women do not work and therefore neither need nor deserve leisure in the same way as men.[10] Wearing and Wearing discern a tendency for women to internalise this idea, being reluctant to put aside time for themselves or experiencing feelings of guilt if they do.[11] Feminists also argue that a conceptualisation of leisure as separate and opposite to paid work *distorts* the experiences of women. Few women experience a sharp distinction between work and leisure, and for many the two interact, often occurring simultaneously. For example, a 'work' activity such as ironing may be accompanied by the 'leisure' of listening to the radio. Other activities may be work or leisure at different times (an example would be cookery), and in other circumstances, work and leisure can be different dimensions within a single activity, the self-catering holiday being one such case.

Researchers within leisure studies argue that this blurring of work and leisure for women stems, fundamentally, from the nature of domestic labour. Both housework and childcare are forms of work with little self-sufficient shape: they are to some extent self-defined, but subject to stringent external and internalised standards. For women working in the home there is no one point when the working day ends and leisure time begins. The work is dictated by task, not time, with given tasks revolving around the actions of other family members. Consequently, 'time off' is fitted around the timetables of others. Time itself is fragmented and leisure slotted into any available space. Moreover, because the workplace also acts as the living place, chores are ever present, a constant reminder of work to be done. It is within this context, feminists argue, that the leisure experiences of women must be understood.[12]

Thus, feminist scholarship offers a fundamental challenge to definitions and representations of leisure which foreground its oppositional relationship to paid labour. Feminist researchers point to other shortcomings in the definitions of leisure used within the field of leisure studies. In particular, writers such as Liz Stanley have criticised the use of pre-determined, activity-based conceptions of leisure, arguing that such definitions actively exclude the experiences of many women, who are, therefore, absented from leisure studies research. As Stanley writes: 'By including swimming, golf, pub-going and dancing, but not knitting, drinking tea with neighbours, or simply sitting and reflecting, a whole host of assumptions and interpretations are built into research which inevitably structure and so construct its outcomes.'[13] Instead of an approach to the subject which assumes definitional certainty, Stanley suggests one in which complexity is foregrounded. Rather than approaching both 'work' and 'leisure' as given activities, she proposes that they be addressed as conceptual constructions.

While feminist researchers differ in their particular emphases, it is possible to identify a characteristic approach to women's leisure arising out of their critique of leisure studies. Within this approach, key importance is assigned to the *meaning* that women themselves give to their actions as leisure, work, or a combination of the two. However, it is acknowledged that the meanings attached to particular activities differ between individuals and over the course of the life cycle. Consequently, researchers emphasise the importance of establishing the *context* within which actions take place. For Stanley, 'leisure' should be examined within the context of everyday, lived experience. As she writes: '"Leisure" certainly does not make sense on its own; it has to be understood as part of a conjunction of interests, needs, skills, commitments and obligations in women's lives most importantly including those of "work".'[14] In consequence she argues for a rejection of abstraction in favour of an examination of women's leisure experiences 'in the round'.[15] For other researchers, the process of contextualisation demands an emphasis upon the structural constraints upon women's leisure. For example, a common constraint may be identified as 'patriarchal control', exercised in the allocation of family resources and in the male policing of 'public' places.[16] Others foreground the interaction of class and gender, noting the extent to which economic circumstance provides the central context for the leisure experiences of women.[17] Elsewhere, researchers are beginning to address the particular constraints experienced by women of colour.[18]

Thus feminist researchers point to the constraints that frame women's experiences of leisure. However, few would argue that women are inevitably trapped within these constraints. One of the most helpful lessons that the historian of leisure can draw from leisure studies concerns the consistency with which women carve out spaces for themselves to enjoy time for themselves. For example, in their study of two English pubs, Hunt and Saterlee discovered women legitimising their presence in the pubs, and participation in pub culture, by playing darts. This also allowed the women to enjoy a period of time away from the responsibilities of home and to take pleasure in the companionship of the darts team.[19] Similarly, Dixey and Talbot have shown the importance of bingo to many working-class women as a legitimate public arena for leisure, 'a home from home, an invaluable source of companionship, a refuge which offers excitement'.[20] Other studies have shown how women whose leisure is spent predominantly within the home carve out areas of their lives for relaxation and sociability, albeit against a background of fragmented time and the ambiguities of 'work' and 'leisure' in women's lives.[21]

Liz Stanley has emphasised the particular importance of a historical understanding of women's leisure, arguing that contemporary leisure experiences can be better understood in the light of historically changing ideas around 'work' and 'leisure'.[22] However, historians themselves have largely failed to engage with the analyses offered by feminists working within leisure studies and have been slow to utilise the insights into the nature of women's leisure outlined above. This omission has led to a serious misrepresentation of women's leisure experiences over time: our historical understanding of women's leisure has been limited by researchers' preoccupation with a 'male' model of leisure. In contrast, this chapter draws upon feminist research in leisure studies to suggest that historians too must approach 'leisure' and the inextricably linked category 'work' as fluid concepts, open to changing meanings and inseparable from the contextual and historical background against which they are experienced. Fundamentally, the chapter suggests that the work of feminists within leisure studies can be used as a theoretical base upon which to build a historical study of women's leisure experiences.

A feminist framework for the history of women's leisure?

I want to demonstrate how this approach to the history of women's leisure might work through a focus upon three key areas of my recent research into the leisure experiences of Manchester women in the period 1920–60. First, I will outline the way in which oral history methodology can help to illuminate the complex relationship between women and the category 'leisure'. Second, I will explore the ambiguities in defining 'leisure' within women's lives evident in a careful reading of one documentary source. Finally, I will demonstrate the importance of locating women's leisure experiences within the changing context of life-cycle stage; just one of the many contextual backgrounds against which women's experiences should be understood and represented.

Leisure and oral history

Those recent works on leisure history which do examine the experiences of women, as well as men, have placed oral testimony at their centre. As Davies writes, 'women's leisure as well as men's can be traced during interviews, providing an important balance to the male-orientated nature of many contemporary sources'.[23] Oral evidence provides the historian of the twentieth century with an additional source from which to construct a history of leisure. In particular, it enables the historian to access aspects of leisure experience not recorded in the documentary source material. For example, interviews provide a means of accessing 'hidden' areas of experience, such as the secret courtships of youth or the social visiting of adult life, and point to the opportunities and constraints which framed leisure experiences.

Informed by the lively feminist debate around the practice of oral history, however, I would argue that oral history can be even more useful than this. Rather than acting simply as a compensatory source, filling in the gaps left by incomplete documentary sources, oral history can provide an invaluable means of reconceptualising, and thus re-presenting, understandings of leisure, in the light of individual respondents' recollections and understandings of their everyday experiences. To illustrate this, I will focus upon two key areas, meaning and language, using examples drawn from a series of interviews conducted with 23 Manchester women of working-class and lower middle-class social status.

Oral history methodology of the type I am outlining here invests key importance in the way women themselves define, understand and represent their experiences; in effect, this means asking women about the meanings they attach to historical experiences. Within my own interviews, respondents were asked to explain, in their own terms, the contexts within which activities were deemed to be work, leisure, or a complex mixture of the two. Their responses showed clearly the problems inherent in defining certain activities as leisure without considering the meanings attached to these activities by individual women within the context of everyday life.

For example, the problematic nature of the family holiday as work *and* leisure for women was apparent in a number of the interviews. Both Dorothy and Joan remembered the 'apartments' system of holiday accommodation from the seaside holidays of their inter-war childhoods. As Joan explained:

204

You didn't er, full board there. If you know what that means, to us, you bought your own food er, your er landlady cooked your dinner, er, you'd buy the meat and take it to her and she'd cook that er, you had to have a cold tea, which you provided yourself. She gave you a little cupboard, put your butter and your bread in and usually it was, mice ridden or something like that, you know so very few people, unless you were wealthy er, boarded, you, you used to call it apartments you see . . . So of course you spent half your day foraging for food, for the next day, you know.

When asked who took responsibility for purchasing the food while on holiday, both women remembered it as daily work for their mothers. Under this arrangement the landlady charged for the basics which she supplied: the 'cruet'.

The holidays that Dorothy took in her post-war married life were similarly not free from work. The camping trips that her family so enjoyed gave no respite from the work of feeding and clothing her family. As she stated: 'It's hard work. Not a holiday as such.' When asked why she continued to take holidays which she did not enjoy, she replied that she did it for her family: 'You don't mind what you do for your kids really, but I was quite delighted when I didn't have to go camping.' Here, leisure activity was viewed as an arena for service and duty. In fact, Dorothy re-presented 'leisure' as work when located within the family. In contrast, Margaret noted that her holidays were a real rest for her: a time when her husband relieved her of her responsibility for the household finances, and she had money in her pocket to spend entirely on herself. As she recalled: 'That was a real holiday. And we never went camping or in caravans or anything. We went in hotels. He said they might go camping or hire a flat next door, he said, what holiday does Mrs Ramsey have? If you go in a flat you've still got to cook, wash, iron and everything. Go in a hotel you're looked after.'

Other examples of the ambiguity of leisure and work within women's lives which emerge from the interview method include the extent to which home-based activities such as needlecrafts or cookery could be a pleasurable and creative use of time or necessary, time-consuming work, depending upon the economic context. Elsewhere, the way in which so-called 'family leisure' was intimately linked to notions of duty and service was apparent as women recalled their role as facilitators of leisure for other family members.

Within the interviews, I was also concerned with the language that women themselves chose to describe their experiences. Initially, I asked women for their own understandings of the term 'leisure'. The aim here was to explore the relevance of this single word, so heavily laden with particular assumptions rooted in the male experience, to the everyday lives of women. For many of the women interviewed, 'leisure' was not a word which they would have automatically used to represent their experiences. Indeed, the term 'leisure' often conjured up very specific images related to physical exercise and other activities experienced within fixed time boundaries, from which women felt excluded. Those who did use the word often employed it to describe only particular stages of their passage through the life cycle. For example, Dorothy clearly associated 'leisure' with her youth, stating: 'Really, my leisure ended when I started my family . . . I mean my husband and I did other things erm, after we were married.' For this woman, 'leisure' represented the freedom and independence of youth. Others used the term in a way which demonstrated the complicated relationship between work and leisure in women's lives, exemplified in the words of Edith: 'Well, my, my leisure was like coming home and seeing to kids and cooking for 'em, because I, you know, I, I bake and you know. Er I enjoy it.' This ambiguity in defining leisure and work in women's lives, and the interviewees' own awareness of it, was evident again and again.

Over the course of the interviews, particular attention was paid to the alternative words women themselves chose to articulate their experiences. Consideration of these descriptive terms helped me to open up the category 'leisure' and to explore the complex and sometimes contradictory elements which constituted women's experiences within the period 1920–60. Spare time, pleasure, enjoyment, hobbies, social life and even rest constituted different aspects of the 'leisure' experienced by Manchester women. The evidence I gathered demonstrated contradictions between women over the use and meanings of particular words. However, with the exception of the less commonly used term 'hobby', these words ultimately pointed to a common experience among the women interviewed. Personal leisure time, although characterised in different ways, generally constituted a snatched experience, something 'fitted in' to everyday life. In contrast, more organised forms of leisure had to be planned for, and were often beyond the reach of adult women among whom time was both limited and fragmented.

Leisure and documentary sources

Oral testimony is particularly useful to the historian of leisure because it allows for the examination of interpretation: the historian can interrogate her sources in a very real way. The relationship between a historian and her documentary sources is somewhat different. Nonetheless, a careful reading of the documentary sources also enables the historian of leisure to deconstruct the category and explore the fluidity with which leisure meanings operate over a particular historical period. Here I want to focus particularly upon the role of newspaper evidence in helping us to access leisure experiences. Specifically, I will refer to a comprehensive study of one local newspaper, the *Manchester Evening News*, chosen because it was the city's most widely read local evening newspaper throughout the period 1920–60.[24]

This chapter has already argued that 'leisure' constitutes a historically changing concept, dependent for its meaning upon the context within which it is both perceived and experienced. Newspaper analysis affirms the need to approach leisure in this way and provides yet more evidence of its ambiguous nature within women's lives. However, care is needed when allocating historical specificity to a particular conception of leisure: the newspaper offers contrasting evidence, often simultaneously. Moreover, the historian must be alert to the tone as well as the content of newspaper reports. Sometimes there appears to be considerable divergence between what was written and what was meant, as writers employed double-edged stereotypes, archetypes of 'the local' and sex role-based humour, within their articles. In contrast to oral history, this is a source which cannot be verbally interrogated for meaning. Nor can its impact upon the audience be satisfactorily gauged. While audience reaction was articulated on the letters page of the newspaper throughout this period, this constituted a self-selected sample, made more problematic by the editorial power of veto.

Nonetheless, the local newspaper can provide the historian of women's leisure with useful evidence. The *Manchester Evening News* targeted women in two ways. First, it was concerned to attract them as an audience reading the newspaper in their leisure time, and second, it addressed their needs as consumers of leisure with an interest in the subject. Its efforts to fulfil the second of these remits provides the historian of leisure with a considerable volume of material concerning the local experience. For example, a growing interest in chess and a 'fever' for crosswords were just two of the female trends detected by the newspaper in the 1920s.[25] Perhaps more interesting, however, is the manner in which the *Manchester Evening News* sought to attract its female audience by actively participating in discussion concerning the nature of women's leisure. For example, a 'feminist' concern with the nature of housework was evident as early as 1925 when one article noted that the constant presence of work to be done within the home, combined with feelings of guilt or 'conscience', prevented the wife from taking time for herself: 'To a man it seems incredible that a woman should almost boast of her inability to sit down all day because of her household duties. "Sit thee dahn lass; sit thee dahn", he will say, but conscience, that relentless slave-driver of housewives replies, "Not till the work is done".'[26] Several *Manchester Evening News* articles also demonstrated both an awareness and a rejection of the tendency to represent housework as nearer leisure than work and advanced alternative representations of the work–leisure relationship. One woman writer felt it necessary to argue in 1930 that 'housekeeping remains a job and not a pleasant recreation'.[27] In 1955 an inclination to regard the housewife as primarily a woman of leisure was questioned by Joyce Stranger in an article entitled 'The little woman's no lady of leisure'. Referring to 'the delusion that the housewife has all the time in the world', she proceeded to catalogue her own day's work, describing housewives as 'very busy women, working to a far stricter routine than many shop and office workers'.[28] The strictness of this routine seemed to stem from its being organised around the activities of other family members.

Elsewhere, the ambiguous nature of the family holiday as leisure for women was a matter of debate for writers. In 1925, Valerie Rutland observed that for mothers, the family holiday could include elements of both work and leisure. Arguing that the 'family' holiday signified an enjoyable rest for the husband and constant joy to the children, she observed that, for the mother, it necessitated packing and unpacking, worrying and looking out for the children *as well as* a much needed rest.[29] A decade later, the problematic nature of the family holiday as leisure for women was again addressed in the article 'Include your wife in this year's holiday'.[30] Here, husbands were urged to consider their wives' enjoyment, and to ask themselves, 'Is her holiday just a continuation in other surroundings of the work and worry which is normally her lot?' Identifying the tendency of husbands to plan holidays to suit themselves, not their wives, the writer suggested 'holidays which will mean a real holiday for the womenfolk as well'. It was further suggested that this would entail a change from housework, washing-up, the preparation of meals *and* relief from the duties of childcare. This article clearly acknowledged that activities generally regarded as 'leisure' often involved real work for women and that representations of leisure as an uncomplicated experience for women simply masked this work element. Later in the period, 'Holiday Bureau' received a letter from a 'Bothered Mother' keen to take a holiday that would please all her family. Her assessment of one particular form of self-catering holiday neatly sums up the problematic nature of the family holiday for women: 'We've tried caravans, but with the shopping, cooking, bed-making etc., that's no holiday for ME.'[31]

This self-conscious debate around women's leisure demonstrates that in utilising a theoretical framework drawn from recent feminist research, the historian is not indulging in an anachronistic activity, but entering a very real debate concerning the representation of women's leisure on its own terms. In effect, the *Manchester Evening News* actually mirrors the concerns around the definitional fluidity of 'leisure' and 'work' in women's lives which, I have argued, need to inform research into women's leisure. Elsewhere, the source demonstrates definitional ambiguity itself in its coverage of areas such as shopping and sales. Generally these were regarded as leisure activities, despite their status as real work for women with families.

In the first half of this period, shopping and sales were reported as differing degrees of leisure for women by *Manchester Evening News* reporters. In 1920, sales were described as 'women's joy days',[32] and in 1925, one writer employed a clear leisure metaphor in her assertion that 'there are ladies who look forward to these sales with all the ardour with which firstnighters at the theatre look forward to the first performance of a play by a well-known dramatist'.[33] Shopping was also referred to as 'a fascinating winter sport'.[34] In wartime, however, attitudes towards shopping changed; a shift clearly evident in the *Manchester Evening News*. Under titles such as 'Now is the time to be hunting for bargains as never before!', the emphasis was on the 'good buy', not on the enjoyment of the sale as a leisure activity in itself.[35] Sensible shopping became valuable and time-consuming war work, thus providing a key example of the influence of historical context upon leisure meanings.

Leisure in the life cycle

So far, I have outlined a feminist approach to the history of leisure which draws upon research in other disciplines and have examined the ways in which particular sources can help the historian of leisure to open up the category 'leisure' as it operated within women's lives over a specific historical period. In the final part of this chapter, I will use oral history evidence to demonstrate the importance of exploring the ways in which women themselves theorise their own experiences of leisure. Specifically, I want to examine women's understandings of the changing nature of leisure, and what it represented, as they progressed through the life cycle.

Life cycle stage played a crucial role in structuring the leisure patterns of Manchester women. It both influenced individuals' expectations concerning their leisure opportunities and experiences and determined society's opinion of appropriate behaviour: in fact, it provided an organising concept for this. For the majority of the women I interviewed, 'leisure' was something associated with the particular life cycle stage of youth. Most respondents characterised the years between leaving school and marrying as a time of freedom and independence; a period with no major responsibilities and no developed sense of duty to others. In effect, youth constituted a period of legitimate leisure. As Margaret, recalling her early leisure experiences in the inter-war period, put it: 'I had nobody to bother about.'

Freedom and independence in youthful leisure were founded upon a range of factors which combined to create a notion of 'earned' leisure. These included the assumptions of contemporaries, as well as participation in paid labour, within clearly defined hours, in exchange for financial reward. Young women pursued their pleasures in a variety of ways, the cinema and dance hall being particularly popular, of course. However, young women's experiences were also framed by limitations: time and money were not always available for leisure, allocated as they were according to class and gender. Moreover, courting activity could precipitate a move away from much loved activities, acting as an introduction to an adult world where the leisure preferences of others took precedence. And yet, despite a range of obstacles which operated in different ways across the social classes and the historical period, women themselves perceived their youth to have been a period of legitimate, personal leisure. Oral testimony shows that women were, on the whole, far more likely to complain of some constraint upon their leisure in youth than they were to object to its virtual absence in their married life. In youth, women felt that they *deserved* personal leisure. Once married, the relationship between women and leisure changed markedly, and duty and service replaced freedom and independence as its overriding characteristic.

Certainly the problematic nature of 'leisure' as a category of historical analysis is acute when addressing the experiences of married women. Respondents often recalled that the years after marriage, and particularly after the birth of children, heralded fundamental changes in their relationship to leisure. For example, Mary recalled her aspirations for married life: 'You looked forward to a different sort of life, you see, looking after your own home. And we all looked forward to that.' Other women observed that marriage effected a concentration upon the home and family which consumed their spare time. When asked about the post-war period, Hannah recalled: 'You didn't really do anything very much apart from er, home and children and garden.' For many women the demands of housewifery left them with little time for leisure outside the family. As Celia noted, 'my life centred around, er, my husband . . . we didn't really bother going out. I was quite happy, you know looking after the home . . . .' Indeed, many of the women interviewed offered the view that once married they no longer needed, deserved or even wanted leisure for themselves: most observed that in adult life the choices of other family members took precedence over their own use of time.

The decline of personal leisure after marriage was not just a by-product of family life: in some cases it was perceived to be a necessary condition for it. The analysis which Dorothy gave of her leisure over the life cycle demonstrates not only the extent to which family life superseded notions of personal pleasure, but also the way in which particular 'leisure' activities ceased to be perceived as such if conducted out of a sense of duty to others. Thus she reinforces the need to ascertain the meanings which women gave to their experiences as well as the context within which they occurred. I will quote her words at length because they demonstrate the complexity of interviewees' own understandings of their experiences over the life cycle.

Dorothy was born in 1925, married in 1946 and subsequently had three daughters. In Dorothy's youth, leisure had been a high priority. Dancing, in particular, had been a much loved activity and one which she had pursued several times a week throughout her wage-earning years. When interviewed, however, Dorothy asserted that her 'leisure' ended shortly after her marriage at the age of 21. As she recalled:

> I'm awfully sorry that really my leisure ended when I started my family which was 1948. But I thought you just might be interested in, you know, before that. Is there anything else you wonder about? *Well I'm interested in the period afterwards as well. Did you feel that you would have liked more leisure after you had your children?* No, No. I was perfectly happy. No, I think, the fact that I had all this, I had quite a lot of, you know, erm, I think probably I, I from about 15 to meeting my husband at 19 erm, really that was enough for me, you know. I mean my husband and I did other things erm, after we were married and had the children erm, we didn't have many baby-sitters but erm we managed to do things with the children. And we belonged to a church and you know, all their activities, with the children. And he then belonged to a dramatics society, and got two of the children interested in that. And erm. No I did honestly feel erm that I'd had enough of, you know erm. We went to the cinema, but I, I, I did try going dancing when, we couldn't get baby-sitters, or we couldn't afford them. And erm, we had one night out a week each, and erm, he went out about 9 o'clock, for a drink, got back about 11. And he had a game of cards. And I tried going back to the Ritz and, with my sister, erm, but I didn't feel right, you know, I didn't feel right. *Why, why didn't you feel right?* Well I ended up dancing with other men when I had a husband at home, you know. I mean erm, erm, er, I went for a few weeks and erm [*pause*] It just didn't seem right. So I didn't do it you know, I mean I stopped doing it, you know.

Although she spoke at length about family holidays, church activities, visiting and other areas which in other circumstances might be defined as leisure, she did not herself describe them thus. The fact that these were activities carried out in, and for, the family did not in her experience mark them out as leisure. This woman re-presented 'leisure' as freedom and independence, specifically the freedom to dance, and this she only really experienced in her youth. After marriage, difficulties in acquiring babysitters, lack of money and the social meanings attached to her favoured activity constrained her movements. However, of most importance in determining her experiences was a fundamental change in attitude towards the pursuit of personal pleasure: once married, the personal was replaced by the family. Dorothy's testimony thus demonstrates a clear shift in perceptions of 'leisure', and what it represented within her life. Her husband's weekly visits to the pub are suggestive of a contrasting continuity in male leisure patterns.

Conclusion

Historians of leisure utilising an unproblematic definition of leisure have, largely, failed to address the changing ways in which women themselves understood the concept over the course of their lives. While important work has detailed gender inequalities in *access* to leisure opportunity, definitions of leisure have largely been taken as given.[36] And yet, the evidence presented here suggests that 'leisure' is itself a fundamentally gendered concept. Its very meaning and relationship to the category 'work' is rooted in gender difference.

This chapter has, therefore, suggested a theoretical underpinning to a field which is, at present, seriously undertheorised. The methodologies employed emerge from feminist theoretical concerns: in the absence of appropriate methodologies from within the field of leisure history, the approach has been interdisciplinary in nature, although firmly rooted in its historical evidence. I have argued that the use of oral history, in particular, provides an invaluable means of accessing perceptions, experiences and representations of leisure, allowing for the examination of interpretation and motivation as well as patterns of behaviour. However, I have also illustrated the contribution that documentary sources can make to the project of unpicking the category 'leisure' and have argued that these too have a crucial role to play in accessing the historically shifting nature of leisure within a particular historical period. It is to be hoped that in its theoretical and methodological suggestions, this chapter moves us closer towards a feminist framework for the history of women's leisure.

Further reading

The history of twentieth-century women's leisure forms a small, but growing, field of study. The most significant general text is Andrew Davies's *Leisure, Gender and Poverty: Working-Class Culture in Salford and Manchester, 1900–1939* (Buckingham, 1992), the first published work to approach twentieth-century leisure from an explicitly gendered perspective. David Fowler's *The First Teenagers: The Lifestyles of Young Wage-Earners in Interwar Britain* (1995) includes details of young women's leisure opportunities, whilst Penny Tinkler's 'Sexuality and citizenship: The state and girls' leisure provision in England, 1939–45', in *Women's History Review* 4/2 (1995), focuses upon state provision for girls during the Second World War. Other articles and books look at narrow parts of the terrain. For example, Jennifer Hargreaves's *Sporting Females: Critical Issues in the History and Sociology of Women's Sports* (1992) provides a comprehensive analysis of inter-war sporting opportunities, while Liz Oliver's '"No hard-brimmed hats or hat-pins please": Bolton women cotton-workers and the game of rounders, 1911–39', in *Oral History* (Spring 1997), provides a micro-study of one particular activity. Other texts which explore physical exercise include S. Fletcher's *Women First: The Female Tradition in English Physical Education, 1880–1980* (1984), J. George's 'Women and golf in Scotland,' in *Oral History* 25/1 (1997), and J. Matthew's '"They had such a lot of fun": The Women's League of Health and Beauty between the wars', in *History Workshop Journal* 30 (Autumn 1990). Useful texts dealing with other aspects of women's leisure experience include Valerie Hey's *Patriarchy and Pub Culture* (1986) and Melanie Tebbutt's *Women's Talk? A Social History of 'Gossip' in Working-Class Neighbourhoods, 1880–1960* (Aldershot, 1995). A comprehensive survey of feminist contributions to the leisure studies literature is provided by Betsy Wearing's *Leisure and Feminist Theory* (1998). Other key texts include R. Deem, *All Work and No Play: The Sociology of Women and Leisure* (Milton Keynes, 1986), E. Green, S. Hebron and D. Woodward, *Women's Leisure: What Leisure?* (1990), and E. Wimbush and M. Talbot, eds, *Relative Freedoms: Women and Leisure* (Milton Keynes, 1988). Finally, the development of feminist oral history work is surveyed in M. Stuart's '"You're a big girl now": subjectivities, feminism and oral history', in *Oral History* (Autumn 1994), while a collection of essays relating to oral history methodology can be found in S. Gluck and D. Patai, eds, *Women's Words: The Feminist Practise of Oral History* (1991).

Notes

I would like to thank Dave Russell and Cathy Lubelska, my PhD supervisors, for their comments on the chapters upon which this paper is based. I am also grateful to Cathy for the very helpful comments she has made as editor of this section of the book.

1. S. Dark, *After Working Hours: The Enjoyment of Leisure* (1929), p. 21.

2. J. Hannam, A. Hughes and P. Stafford, eds, *British Women's History: A Bibliographical Guide* (Manchester, 1996).

3. J. Clarke and C. Critcher, *The Devil Makes Work: Leisure in Capitalist Britain* (1985), p. 50.

4. A. Davies, *Leisure, Gender and Poverty: Working-Class Culture in Salford and Manchester, 1900–1939* (Buckingham, 1992).

5. P. Bailey, *Leisure and Class in Victorian England: Rational Recreation and the Contest for Control, 1830–1885* (1978), p. 6.

6. Ibid., p. 4.

7. R. W. Malcolmson, *Popular Recreations in English Society, 1700–1850* (Cambridge, 1973).

8. E. Wimbush and M. Talbot, eds, *Relative Freedoms: Women and Leisure* (Milton Keynes, 1988).

9. H. Lenskyj, 'Measured time: women, sport and leisure', *Leisure Studies* 6/1 (1989), p. 236.

10. S. McIntosh, 'Leisure studies and women', in A. Tomlinson, ed., *Leisure and Social Control* (Brighton, 1980), p. 105.

11. B. Wearing and S. Wearing, 'All in a day's leisure: gender and the concept of leisure', *Leisure Studies* 7/2 (1988), p. 14.

12. Wimbush and Talbot, eds, *Relative Freedoms*.

13. L. Stanley, 'The problem of women and leisure – an ideological construct and a radical feminist alternative', in Centre for Leisure Studies, ed., *Leisure in the 1980s* (Salford, 1981), p. 88.

14. L. Stanley, 'Historical sources for studying work and leisure in women's lives', in Wimbush and Talbot, eds, *Relative Freedoms*, p. 18.

15. Ibid.

16. V. Hey, *Patriarchy and Pub Culture* (1986).

17. C. Griffin, *Typical Girls? Young Women from School to the Job Market* (1985).

18. E. Green, S. Hebron and D. Woodward, *Women's Leisure: What Leisure?* (1990), pp. 70–81.

19. G. Hunt and S. Saterlee, 'Darts, drink and the pub: the culture of female drinking', *The Sociological Review* 35/3 (August 1987).

20. R. Dixey and M. Talbot, *Women, Leisure and Bingo* (Leeds, 1982), p. 170.

21. See, for example, Radway's research on romance reading: J. Radway, *Reading the Romance: Women, Patriarchy and Popular Literature* (1984), pp. 86–118.

22. Stanley, 'Historical sources', p. 19.

23. Davies, *Leisure, Gender and Poverty*, p. 6.

24. D. Griffiths, ed., *The Encyclopedia of the British Press, 1422–1992* (1992), p. 399.

25. See *Manchester Evening News* (hereafter *MEN*), Friday 23 January 1925, p. 8, Thursday 5 February 1925, p. 8, and Friday 27 February 1925, p. 8, for details of the crossword fever, and Wednesday 12 August 1925, p. 3, for news of its demise.

26. *MEN*, Friday 20 November 1925, p. 10.

27. *MEN*, Thursday 4 December 1930, p. 3.

28. *MEN*, Thursday 31 March 1955, p. 3.

29. *MEN*, Thursday 27 August 1925, p. 7.

30. *MEN*, Thursday 9 May 1935, p. 3.

31. *MEN*, Tuesday 15 February 1955, p. 2.

32. *MEN*, Wednesday 29 December 1920, p. 2.

33. *MEN*, Monday 5 January 1925, p. 4.

34. *MEN*, Thursday 30 May 1935, p. 4.

35. *MEN*, Thursday 27 June 1940, p. 2.

36. Davies, *Leisure, Gender and Poverty*, p. 171.

INDEX